ROADS AND THEIR TRAFFIC
1750-1850

The London and Bristol mail coach, near Hungerford, Berkshire

ROADS
AND THEIR TRAFFIC
1750–1850

by

JOHN COPELAND

with plates and text illustrations

DAVID & CHARLES: NEWTON ABBOT

7153   4219   3

Printed in Great Britain by
Latimer Trend & Company Limited Plymouth
for David & Charles (Publishers) Limited
South Devon House   Railway Station
Newton Abbot   Devon

To my Mother

Contents

		page
	LIST OF ILLUSTRATIONS	9
1	THE ROADS IN THE MID-EIGHTEENTH CENTURY	11
2	ROAD IMPROVEMENTS, 1750–1850	23
3	THE CARRIAGE OF GOODS	64
4	THE CARRIAGE OF PASSENGERS	85
5	THE CARRIAGE OF MAIL	109
6	TRAVELLING IN STYLE	133
7	THE FIRST GENERATION OF STEAM CARRIAGES	163
8	COMPETITION WITH THE RAILWAYS	184
	AUTHOR'S NOTES AND ACKNOWLEDGMENTS	195
	BIBLIOGRAPHY	197
	NEWSPAPERS CONSULTED	199
	INDEX	200

Illustrations

PLATES

The London and Bristol mail coach, near Hungerford,
    Berkshire   *frontispiece*

facing page

1a	*The Overset*	32
1b	Hyde Park Corner turnpike in 1794	32
2a	Toll-house at North Weald, Essex	33
2b	*The Turnpike Gate*	33
3	Plan of a toll-house and gates	48
4a	An eighteenth-century carrier's waggon	49
4b	A carrier's waggon, showing the canvas hood folded back	49
5a	A baggage waggon, 1805	80
5b	The *New Inn*, Gloucester	80
6a	*An Awkward Place in a Frost*	81
6b	*What Became of the Mail*	81
7a	*The Plymouth Fly*	96
7b	Highway robbers at work	96
8a	The original Bath mail coach	97
8b	*A Mail Coach at an Inn*	97
9a	Mail coach guard	144
9b	A mail coach forces the Cheltenham *Magnet* coach to give way	144
10a	Patent chariot, 1809	145
10b	A barouche	145
11	A selection of private carriages: barouche, brougham, landau, travelling coach, dress coach, chariot	160
12a	Post-chaise	161
12b	*The Drag*	161

facing page

13   Gurney's steam carriage, 1827   176

14a   Hancock's steam omnibus, *Enterprise*   177

14b   Dr Church's steam carriage, 1833   177

15   Cartoonists at work: (*above*) The boiler bursts; (*below*)
      Heavy Traffic in the Whitechapel Road   192

16a   The last mail coach through Newcastle, 1847   193

16b   The end of the stage coach   193

TEXT ILLUSTRATIONS

page

1   A gauge for pitting the road   30

2   Plan of a proposed turnpike road from Edensor to
     Ashford   38

3   Extract from turnpike accounts   53

4   Arrivals and departures at the Post Office, Birmingham,
     in 1837   113

5   York and Manchester mail coach time bill, 1840   124

6   A snow plough   128

CHAPTER 1

The Roads in the
Mid-eighteenth Century

> This day an inquest was taken at Ingatestone on the body of
> Richard Aimes, when it appeared that the deceased was thrown
> from his horse, a little on this side of Ingatestone, into a ditch, and
> was suffocated by mud and filth.

THIS report in *The Ipswich Journal* for 18 March 1769 is typical of
countless other instances when eighteenth-century travellers
ended up in the roads rather than on them. Complaints about their
shocking condition were frequently made, particularly during the
winter months when the highways became impassable in a sea of
mud.

In the mid-eighteenth century the roads were in a poor state in
most parts of the country. In the south, an enraged correspondent
of *The Gentleman's Magazine* for December 1757 complained about
the condition of those in Sussex. In Petworth, the writer had
passed through a street 'two hundred yards long, full of deep
holes, and a precipice on one side of the street, without so much
as a rail for twenty yards, though exposed to every drunken traveller or stranger on horseback'. A similar complaint was made by
Horace Walpole in 1749 when he commented that the county's
roads had long been notorious for their execrable condition.

Cornwall had the distinction of having hardly any roads suitable
for wheeled traffic in the mid-eighteenth century. In Gloucestershire, W. Marshall in *The Rural Economy of Gloucestershire* (1789),
described the county's roads as being 'such as one might expect to
meet with in the marshes of Holland or the mountains of Switzer-
land'; while in Herefordshire the absence of a reliable alternative
in the navigation of the Wye 'choaketh up the commodities of
corne and fruit in plentifull yeares'.

Northern England fared little better. This is shown in a Report
of a Committee of the House of Commons, dated 26 January 1740,

relating to a bill to amend the highways from Selby to Leeds, Wakefield, Halifax and other adjoining places. Manufacturers in the area reported that the roads were virtually impassable for waggons and carriages during the winter months, causing serious difficulties in the carriage of coal, corn, lime and woollens. In the more sparsely populated districts of Yorkshire, as in most other remote regions, little if any attention was given to the roads that existed.

In earlier times most goods had been carried in long strings of pack-horses, and this form of transport was still in existence in some parts of the country in the mid-eighteenth century. In Somerset, for example, pack-horses were used a good deal in the first half of that century, each horse carrying about 2½ cwt over distances ranging between 15 and 20 miles. Pack-horse traffic in Lancashire often travelled along paved tracks, known as causeys or causeways, which were sometimes placed by the side of the ordinary highways. On the Pennine moors of Lancashire and Yorkshire, these pavements were made up from slabs of millstone grit; while in the south-western parts of Lancashire pebbles or cobbles formed their basis.

Some information on pack-horses is given in a report in *The Essex Standard* for 14 October 1836:

> In 1739, not quite a century ago, two gentlemen going from Edinburgh to London state that they rode the journey on horse-back; that there was no turnpike road till they came to Grantham within 110 miles of London; that up to that point they travelled upon a narrow causeway with an unmade soft road on each side of it; that they met from time to time strings of packhorses, from thirty to forty in a gang, the mode by which the goods seem to have been transported from one part of the country to the other. The leading horse of the gang carried a bell, to give warning to travellers coming in the opposite direction; and they said that when they met these trains of horses with their packs across their backs, the causeway not affording room to pass, they were obliged to make way for them, and plunge into the side road, out of which they sometimes found it difficult to get back again upon the causeway.

Streets within towns and cities were invariably in a deplorable condition. One East Anglian newspaper in May 1741 mentioned that in the centre of London 'the sides of the carriage way were full of absolute holes where the rickety coach was often stuck as in a quagmire. Some of the leading streets even to the time of George II were almost as impassable as the avenues of a new American town. The only road to the Houses of Parliament before

1759 was through King Street and Union Street, which were in so miserable a state that faggots were thrown into the ruts on the day on which the king went to Parliament to render the passage of the coach more easy'. It was also difficult to get into London, as Lord Henry, living in Kensington, complained in 1736: 'The road between this place and London, is grown so infamously bad that we live here in the same solitude as if cast on a rock in the middle of the ocean. All Londoners tell us that between us and them is an impassable gulf of mud.'

After the Romans had departed, the English roads deteriorated, though in some places the solidity of the long, straight, raised structure of their roads retained some of its usefulness. Under the manorial system, the lord of the manor would direct roads to be made as part of the labour services due to him, but these are to be thought of rather as tracks over which there was a right of way, little being done to provide any foundation or surface for a road in the modern sense. The Church later assumed some responsibility for road repairs, but this work came to an end with the dissolution of the monasteries. The next major step was in 1555 when a new form of organisation was brought in by Parliament to deal with the roads.

Under the terms of the 'Statute For Mending of Highways', 1555 (2 & 3 Philip and Mary, c. 8), the inhabitants of each parish were to be responsible for the repair and upkeep of the roads within their parish. Every person holding land of an annual value of £50, and everybody 'keeping a draught (of horses) or plough in the Parish' had to provide at the appointed times 'one wain or cart furnished after the custom of the country, with oxen, horses, or other cattle, and all other necessaries meet to carry things convenient for that purpose, and also two able men with the same'. All householders in the parish, and every labourer, other than servants hired on a yearly basis, had to work on the road, or alternatively send 'one sufficient labourer in his stead'. The Act ruled that the teams had to be provided and the labouring performed for eight hours on four days appointed by the surveyor, a period increased to six days in 1562. Fines were imposed on all those who refused to perform this statute duty.

The Act ruled that 'the Constables and Churchwardens of every parish shall yearly, upon the Tuesday or Wednesday in Easter week, call together a number of parishioners, and shall then elect and choose two honest persons of the parish to be surveyors and orderers for one year of the works for amendment of the highways in their parish'. The main tasks of the surveyors were to keep accounts, which had to be submitted to the Justices of the Peace; survey all the roads and bridges under their jurisdiction at least three times a year, and report their condition to the Justices; ensure that there were no nuisances upon the road, all ditches were clear, and no trees were overhanging or in any way interfering with the roads; and to see that the statute duty was performed at the right time and in the right amount.

The system, unfortunately, did not work well. Many smaller parishes, some of which might have long stretches of important main roads in their area, frequently found that their resources were insufficient to keep the highways in repair. This happened to the parishioners of Widford, in Essex, who petitioned the Justices in 1716. The Justices decided that:

> Their parish is so small that there are no more than two teams therein and that the high road to London is near two miles in length in the said parish, which they are unable to repair without some help, and humbly praying assistance from the turnpike, it is ordered by this court that it be referred to the Justices of the Peace for the Chelmsford Division to examine and enquire into the matter and make a report thereof at the next Sessions.

Later on came the report:

> We whose names are hereto subscribed, Justices, persuant to the above order, have viewed the said highway and do find the matter of the complaint set forth by the said petition to be true. We do think the parish of Widford ought to be allowed fifty pounds towards the mending the said highway. SIGNED: Samuel John Guyon. E. Williamson.

Some Justices, however, were not so tolerant, for in 1765 the inhabitants of another Essex parish, Toppesfield, were threatened in the following terms:

> It is ordered by this court that a fine of £100 be set on the inhabitants of the parish of Toppesfield upon a presentment against them for not repairing their highways, but that the same be not levied until after the next General Quarter Session.

In some instances fines were nominal. The inhabitants of Thorpe in Nottinghamshire, who were 'presented by Lewis Disney, Esq (a local Justice) on his own view for not repairing Thorpe Lane leading from East Stoake to Newark within the parish of Farndon, in length ten yards and breadth sixteen feet, being miry, deep, broken, and in great decay' were only fined sixpence.

Despite the penalties, numerous people refused to perform their statute duty, as the following extract from the Malling (Kent) Petty Sessions Minutes for 4 November 1752 suggests:

A warrant was this day signed, upon the complaint of William Lee one of the surveyors of the highways for the parish of West Peckham, to distrain the several persons hereunder named for makeing default in their days labour towards repairing the highways in the said parish.

Team Defaulters

		£	s.	d.
Richard Fairman	two days		10.	0.
Thomas West	one day		5.	0.
Robert May	two days		10.	0.

Labourers Defaulters

Benjamin Streaton	two days		3.	0.
Margaret Fairman	six days		9.	0.
George Luck	three days		4.	6.
Robert Stone	one day		1.	6.
William Barton	one day		1.	6.
John George	one day		1.	6.
John Goodwin	two days		3.	0.
John Hills	six days		9.	0.
Benjamin Jarrett	four days		6.	0.

It became increasingly obvious that the system of statute labour was inadequate to deal with the repair of the roads. In an issue of *The Gentleman's Magazine* for 1763 a writer pointed out that 'more work could be done with three hired teams than five statute teams, and more with five hired labourers than twenty others'. Another writer, John Billingsley, in his *Survey of Somerset*, 1798, made the following comment:

Whenever a farmer is called forth to perform statute labour, he goes to it with reluctance and considers it a legal burden from which he derives no benefit. His servants and his horses seem to partake of the torpor of the master. The utmost exertion of the surveyor cannot rouse them, and the labour performed is scarcely half what it ought to be.

Because of these difficulties, requests were sometimes made for highway rates to be levied. An application for such a rate came from the surveyors of the parish of Newington-next-Sittingbourne on 2 April 1757:

That the highways throughout the said parish are in so bad repair that it is impossible the same can be put into good repair again by the statute duty only and especially in the manner the inhabitants of the said parish perform it, for it is observed that one hired day labourer will do more work in the highways in one day than seven or eight men who work according to the statute duty.

That your petitioners are of the opinion that an assessment on the inhabitants, owners and occupiers of lands, tenements and hereditaments within the said parish at the rate of sixpence in the pound to be made levied and collected after the manner of the poor's rate would in a year or two put the highway into such a condition that an assessment afterwards of threepence in the pound would continue the roads in a very good repair for many years. That such an assessement is generally approved of by the inhabitants of the said parish as greatly beneficial to the same and a great ease to the poorer sort of people.

Under the Act of 1662 'for enlarging and repairing of the common highways', surveyors had authority to levy a highway rate not exceeding sixpence in the pound with the sanction of the Justices of the Peace. Under an Ordinance of 1654, the assessments could be made by the Justices themselves, and the maximum rate was one shilling in the pound. A further step in the breakdown of the system of statute labour came with the General Highway Acts of 1766 and 1773, which enabled people liable to statute duty to pay in money for the upkeep of the roads rather than perform the hated labour services.

The practice of levying highway rates appears to have been adopted slowly, but even when a rate was imposed, there was still no guarantee that the roads would be kept properly repaired. A good deal depended on the efficiency of the surveyor; it seems that good ones were few and far between, and that not many performed their tasks properly. The general method of repair was to rake the road surface as smooth as possible, and then cover it with a layer of stones. Because little, if any, attention was given to drainage, the winter rains inevitably transformed this covering into a sea of mud, and further repairs then became necessary.

The surveyors were obliged by Act of Parliament to keep accounts. These sometimes show that the surveyors could barely read or write, as is illustrated by the account submitted by one at Holne (Exeter Trust) for part of 1792:

August 9:	a man to repair the road in the Chast and breakin stons on goallakecoas	2s.	4d.
September 12:	a man & hors to drawing of stons on the road to Grenan and a boay ...	1s.	11d.
			6d.
September 16:	a man and two horses to carry robel to Grenan half a day..................	1s.	3d.
	One man half a day to dig robel ...		7d.
	a man half a day to Grenan		7d.
	a boay half a day		3d.

The total disbursements covering the period Michaelmas 1792 to Michaelmas 1793 amounted to £12 4s od, while the revenue was £15 19s 9¼d.

The accounts usually give a good idea of the nature of the work that was carried out during the year. The surveyor's accounts for the Essex parish of Great Sampford, submitted in 1794, have the following entries:

		s.	d.
March 15th:	John Harrington, 4½ days in pit ...	5.	3.
	ditto two sons 3½ days ditto	1.	9.
March 22nd:	William Joyce, 6 days scraping roads	7.	o.
March 29th:	Richard Whybrow, wife, two loads stones	2.	o.
	John Harrington, stubbing and sifting 10 loads gravel	5.	o.
April 25th:	John Harrington, emptying Ware Fuller's ditch		6.
May 4th:	A wire sieve	5.	6.
May 13th:	Robert Pryn, 2 days work in the road	2.	4.
May 17th:	John James for spreading gravel ...	6.	6.
May 26th:	8 bushels lime	5.	8.
	500 bricks	10.	o.
	4 pounds white lead	2.	4.
	1½ pounds linseed oil		10½
	½ lb nails		2.
	Making a rate	1.	o.
	Journey to Sessions	5.	o.
	Isaac Goulet, cleaning drains	1.	2.
July 29th:	Gravel out Butt's pit, 67 loads @ 6d.	33.	6.
December 5th:	John Gray, repairing the bridge ...	46.	o.

All matters concerning the roads, as indeed all matters relating to the parish, were discussed at the Vestry meeting of the parishioners. Among the entries in the Vestry Minute Book for the parish of Snave in Kent, is one of 13 October 1797, when the parishioners had cause to complain about the activities of their surveyor, John Terry, 'in not obeying the order of the Vestry holden some time in May last, concerning making the road leading from Hangmantoul to Brenzett Green'. The parishioners thought 'his proceedings unjust and unreasonable; unreasonable in making the road crooked when it might be nearly made straight; unjust in not makeing it straight in the middle to give each proprietor an equal chance to inclose waste land if it is right that he should doe so'.

B

Fortunately it appears that there were some efficient surveyors: a Suffolk newspaper for May 1826 comments:

> We are glad to find that the spirit of improvement which appears so conspicuously in the turnpikes in this county, is at length manifest in the parish roads; which we think may be chiefly attributed to the fact that the most intelligent surveyors avail themselves of M'Adam's 'Remarks on the Present System of Roadmaking and Repairs' for their guide, which they purchase and charge the cost of the book to the parish account.

The Justices must bear part of the blame for the inefficiency of some surveyors, for they did little to give them guidance on their work and duties. On the other hand, the Justices appear to have exerted a good deal of control over the prevention and removal of nuisances on the highways. Numerous Quarter Sessions Order Books show that offenders were frequently being brought to justice for allowing animals to stray on the roads; not pruning hedges; allowing their trees to overhang the highway; allowing their ditches to overflow; putting refuse on the roads; and undermining the highways. At the Maidstone Quarter Sessions of April 1759, a butcher from the parish of Cranbrook was indicted 'for a nuisance in laying dung, blood and other filth in a certain part of the King's high road at Milkhouse Street in the said parish of Cranbrook'. In Nottinghamshire, a labourer decided to dig several pits in search of coal in the middle of the road, 'whereof the King's subjects during the time aforesaid could not pass, return, ride and labour with their horses, coaches, carts and carriages'. These and other court cases seem to suggest that some people had little respect for the roads during the eighteenth century.

The maintenance of bridges raised all sorts of problems, and many disputes arose in different parts of the country as to who was responsible for their upkeep and repair. The Statute of Bridges of 1531 stated that in default of any special liability, a county was responsible for the upkeep of public bridges, except in corporate towns. Parishes were only held responsible when a definite case could be made out that they had such responsibility, and this was usually very difficult to prove. In his book, *The History, Antiquities and Topography of the county of Sussex*, published in 1835, Thomas Walker Horsfield wrote:

> The bridges in this county are repaired and maintained in various ways: those called county bridges are repaired as follows:—in the eastern division, out of the general county rates, raised within the same for county purposes; in the western, by rates made on the several Rapes within which the bridges are situate. There are other

bridges (not being county bridges) repaired by the Hundreds, Parishes, Tythings or Hamlets, or by certain lands or individuals, but as the custom varies so much, it is almost impossible to ascertain the same within any degree of certainty.

So far as the county bridges were concerned, the county authorities, the Justices in Quarter Sessions could appoint bridge surveyors, and rates could be levied for repairs. From time to time, these surveyors were expected to submit reports on the state of the bridges within the county. Typical of many is one submitted in January 1809 by James Green, which showed that most of the bridges in Devon were apparently about to collapse. The following are some of the entries in the report:

Hatherleigh Bridge, Hatherleigh
. . . this bridge is built wholly of rubble masonry and so many settlements appear in it, especially on the western pier, that considerable danger is to be apprehended in the course of the winter; it is altogether in a very bad state, but the water is so high, it is impossible now to say what is best to be done with it.

Poulston Bridge in Liston
. . . the whole bridge has been much shaken, and for so public a situation and so rapid a stream the bridge is altogether inadequate, as well as extremely inconvenient from its great length and narrowness.

Austins Bridge, Staverton and Buckfastleigh
This bridge is altogether in such a deplorable state that I conceive any sum expended in repairs would be next to thrown away . . . it is even seen to shake in every considerable flood.

In the north of England, the expansion of industry often demanded bridge improvements to accommodate the increasing traffic. Edmund Holme, bridge-master, in submitting an account of the public bridges within the Hundred of Salford in 1782, mentioned that Bury bridge over the Irwell was causing great inconvenience on account of its narrow construction, 'the number of carriages of all kinds passing and re-passing having greatly increased in the space of a few years'. The same was true of Ringley bridge, on the road between Rochdale and Leigh; Holme remarking that 'the carriage for coal over it is now considerable and the confusion, and delay occasioned by the narrowness of the bridge very great'.

With a similar increase in traffic after cotton mills had been established in their area, the inhabitants of Glossop and neighbourhood appealed in 1830 for help in improving Broadbottom bridge across the Mersey, jointly maintained by the counties of

Derbyshire and Cheshire. The magistrates of Cheshire had directed their surveyor to prepare an estimate for the improvement of the bridge, but as their fellows in Derbyshire followed the all too common practice of refusing to contribute their share of the cost of improvements, the repairs were not undertaken. In the circumstances, the inhabitants petitioned the magistrates in the hope that the matter would be taken up again, especially as the lives of travellers passing over the bridge were in danger.

When faced with bridge repairs, many parishes tried to get help from the county or from turnpike trusts, or, when all else failed, denied all responsibility. The parishioners of Hulcott in Buckinghamshire during the early years of the nineteenth century asked the Aylesbury–Hockliffe turnpike trust for help in rebuilding Rowsham bridge. The parish had in the past done repairs from time to time, but eventually it was decided that the bridge was in such a poor condition that only rebuilding would put things right. Responsibility for undertaking this work was a matter of some dispute. When application was made for help to the turnpike trustees, they decided that the bridge was not their concern, for although it was situated 'on an ancient and common highway between Aylesbury and Wing', which by Act of Parliament had been made into a turnpike road, there was no provision in the Act which said that the trustees had to repair or contribute to the repairs of the bridge. Mr N. C. Tindal, the solicitor to whom the case was referred, stated that he could see 'nothing in this case which will relieve the county from the common law liability of rebuilding and keeping in repair the bridge in question . . . the slight repairs that have been done from time to time by the parish surveyor will be referred either to ignorance of the nature of their obligation, or a wish to avoid the expense and trouble of applying to the county'. This tendency to place responsibility for bridges with the county became more marked during the course of our period.

Sometimes turnpike trustees insisted upon the county repairing the bridges. The Wendover and Buckingham turnpike trust, in August 1841, instructed their clerk to write to the clerk of the Buckinghamshire Justices to call attention to 'the dangerous state of the bridge between the townships of Aylesbury Hamlet and Weedon, called Holman's Bridge'. Unless the county put the bridge in a proper state of repair, the trustees threatened 'to cause an indictment to be presented at the next Sessions'.

Whenever possible, the county tried to deny responsibility. In 1843 the New Bailey bridge between Manchester and Salford was reported by the bridge-master as being in a dangerous state, but at the annual Sessions, the court was of the opinion that the county had no liability. Nevertheless, the court decided to set up a committee of magistrates to inquire into the case, which subsequently decided that it was, after all, a county bridge, and the county was therefore faced with a bill for over £9,000 for building a new one in place of the old rickety structure.

Not infrequently during the nineteenth century, demands were made by industrialists and others for new bridges to be built to improve communications. In Herefordshire a petition was drawn up in the 1820s by the 'owners and occupiers of land and other inhabitants of the county of Hereford and Monmouth and of the undersigned occupiers of sand, coal, iron and tin works, stone quarries and lime kilns and other inhabitants of His Majesty's Forest of Dean and elsewhere in the County of Gloucester' for a bridge to be built at Kerne over the River Wye. The demand was made more urgent, so it was claimed, by the large quantities of coal, coke and lime that were transported in the district. In their petition, the interested parties complained 'that there is not at present any bridge over the River Wye between the towns of Ross and Monmouth, a distance by water of twenty miles or thereabout' —which meant that the villages on the Herefordshire side had great difficulty in getting supplies of coal, coke, lime and stone from the Gloucestershire side of the river. Some of the more intrepid carriers risked fording the river at Lydbrook, but, complained the petitioners, 'there is no public way through such ford; it is used by sufferance only and on the payment of a considerable toll to the owner of Courtfield Estate, and moreover it is extremely uncertain and dangerous'. The petitioners got their way, for on 24 May 1826 a contract amounting to £4,000 was entered into with Richard Burton for building a bridge. It was to be 22 ft 8 in in the clear between the parapet walls, and the contractor was 'to find at his own expense all stone, lime, engines, pumps, tools and all other materials and things and requisites necessary for and appertenant to the undertaking which is to be completed in a good and workmanlike manner'.

Money for bridge building could either be raised through the levy of a rate, or, as in the instance of the bridge at Kerne, by Commissioners appointed by Act of Parliament in a similar fashion to turnpike trustees, empowered to borrow money on the security of the tolls charged to travellers using the bridges. In 1788 an Act was obtained for building a bridge over the River Trent near Sawley ferry. The qualification of the trustees was fixed at £1,000 estate in land or an income of £50 a year in rent; and the required money was raised in £50 shares. Coaches were charged 2s 6d; chaises and two-wheeled vehicles 1s 6d; four-wheeled waggons 1s 6d; two-wheeled waggons 1s 0d; horses not drawing 1d; for every drove of hogs, swine, 6d per dozen; and for all cows and horned cattle 1d each. Tolls had only to be paid once in each day, and the penalty for evasion was fixed at 20s.

At the same time as these improvements were being made, turnpike trusts were building new roads and improving and repairing others in different parts of the country. As industry and trade developed during the eighteenth century, there were increasing demands for better roads, not only in the northern industrial districts, but also in the farming areas of the south. Landowners as a class were in the forefront of those petitioning for better roads, for their names can be seen on many of the petitions complaining about their inadequacy.

Where the turnpike roads passed through a parish the statute duties still had to be performed, under the direction of the trust's surveyor. Although many trusts allowed parishioners to pay in money instead of services, labour duties could be demanded right up until 1835, when the General Highway Act finally abolished the system, substituting instead representative boards of management in parishes having more than 5,000 inhabitants, with powers to nominate a paid surveyor with authority to levy highway rates and to employ hired labour. These representative boards were set up by the meeting of ratepayers in Vestry assembled, and were to be relatively free of interference from the Justices. Under the terms of the Act the parish became the administrative unit, one which subsequently proved far too small for efficient management of those roads that were not controlled by turnpike trusts.

Initially, it had been hoped that parishes would combine to form highway districts, with one surveyor to supervise the roads of the combined parishes, but this did not happen. Many parishes did not like the thought of such combined action, fearing that the district surveyor might neglect their roads for those of other parishes. Most of the thirty years after the Act was to be spent in trying, in the face of parochial opposition, to form larger administrative units.

CHAPTER 2

Road Improvements,
1750–1850

EARLY in the eighteenth century 'several Gentlemen, Merchants,
Tradesmen and other inhabitants living in and near the Road from
Liverpool to Prescott' sent a petition to Parliament in which they
complained:

> That the Road . . . is very much used in the carriage of coals (to
> Liverpool and also from Liverpool) to the towns of Wigan, Bolton,
> Rochdale, Warrington and Manchester, and to the counties of
> York, Derby and other eastern parts of the kingdom, in the car-
> riage of wool, cotton, malt, and all other merchants goods; where-
> by several parts of the said road are so very deep, and other parts
> so narrow, that coaches, waggons, and other wheel carriages
> cannot pass through the same; nor can the same be effectively
> repaired and enlarged, without some further provision be made
> for that purpose.

As a result, Parliament authorised the setting up of a turnpike
trust, giving the trustees power to raise capital for road improvements on security of the charges levied on road users as they
passed through the toll-gates.

The first effective toll-gate was set up at Wadesmill after the
Justices of the counties of Hertford, Cambridge and Huntingdon
had in 1663 been given by Parliament the right to levy tolls for
repairing sections of the Great North Road. The preamble to the
authorising Act read: '. . . whereas the ancient highway and post-
road leading from London to York and so into Scotland . . . by
reason of the great and many loads which are weekly drawn in
waggons . . . is become so ruinous and almost impassable, that the
ordinary course appointed by all former laws and statutes of this
realm is not sufficient for the effective repairing of same.' Other
gates were proposed for Caxton and Stilton, but these aroused so
much opposition that they proved to be ineffective; indeed, the

latter was never erected. Later, similar powers were given to other
Justices in various parts of the kingdom, but by the first decade
of the eighteenth century Parliament preferred to grant a Private
Act to individuals to form turnpike trusts to undertake the building and repair of roads.

One of the first steps in forming a turnpike trust was to find out
what financial backing would be forthcoming for the proposed
roads. Advertisements in the local newspapers would set out the
advantages that would follow to all sections of the community,
and investors would be invited to lend their money on security of
the tolls. The interest offered varied according to the market rates
for the time, generally between 4 and 5 per cent. Interest of 4½ per
cent was paid in 1759 on the £100 borrowed for the Ashton Road
by the trustees of the Liverpool–Prescot, St Helens, Warrington
and Ashton roads, and a similar rate was often paid by other
northern trusts. The more usual rate was 5 per cent. In 1779, for
example, the trustees of the Bromyard turnpike road paid 5 per
cent on the £450 that was borrowed, and in 1823 the £3,500
borrowed by the trustees of the Teignmouth to Dawlish road was
charged at the same rate 'upon the security of the tolls which upon
the lowest calculation will amount to £435 a year. For the convenience of the public Deeds Poll will be granted for any sums of
not less than £20'.

Details of the amounts lent to the trusts is usually given in their
minute books. The Storrington & Balls Hut turnpike trust included in its list of subscribers £1,500 from the Duke of Norfolk;
£2,000 from Lord Delazouche; and £50 each from two clergymen.
Members of the aristocracy also figured in the original list of
subscribers to the Aylesbury–Hockliffe trust:

	£
The Duke of Bedford	200
Marquess of Buckingham	300
Lord Carrington	200
Earl Temple	100
William Lowndes Esq	100
Sir George Nugent Bart	200
Thomas Hussey Esq	200
William Rickford Esq	200
Acton Chaplin Esq	200
Lord George Cavendish	100
Neale & Co	100
John Barker, the younger	100
	£2000

An entry in the minute book for 22 March 1770 of the Chester–Tarvin–Nantwich turnpike trust reads:

> Mr Kelsall for the trustees of the poor of the parish of Dodleston proposes to lend as soon as wanted at lawful interest £67. 10s od . . . Rev Mr Dickenson, his own money £100; Mr John Hignett, merchant £300.

Information about subscriptions was given in the Press, as for example the entry in *The Ipswich Journal* for 24 December 1762:

> A turnpike road is going to be made from Cambridge to Ely for which purpose the subscriptions are begun with great encouragement, one for free gifts, the other for money to be lent on the credit of the tolls to be established by Act of Parliament on the said Turnpike road. The whole expense . . . will amount to £4,000 or upwards. The Lord Bishop, gentry and clergy of Ely have subscribed above £1300, Lord Royston £500, and the late Mrs Riste by will £200 and many other sums are promised and expected.

The trustees of the Gander Lane–Sheffield–Clown turnpike road, on the other hand, apparently found it difficult to obtain sufficient capital for their projected improvements, for their minute book for 10 December 1788 records that it was decided to send the clerk to Sheffield 'to solicit further subscriptions there'.

Once the required support had been obtained or promised, an application would be made to Parliament for a Private Act. This would give details of the road to be made or repaired, the required qualifications of the trustees, and the maximum tolls that could be charged, with a list of permitted exemptions. Obtaining such an Act was an expensive matter, as is shown by the account submitted in 1833 by Messrs Bramwell Son & Fenner of 3 Paper Buildings, Temple, to the trustees of the Bishop Waltham & Winchester turnpike road. The account is divided into expenses incurred in the House of Commons and in the House of Lords:

House of Commons	£	s.	d.
Corresponding with Mr Grinner and advising on the proceedings preparatory to the application to Parliament	2.	2.	0.
Drawing state of proofs to be produced before the Committee on the petition and Bill, fair copy ...	1.	1.	0.
Perusing and settling draft notice of the application to Parliament		10.	6.
Perusing & settling draft petition for the Bill ...	1.	1.	0.
Attending at the King's printers to procure prints of modern road Acts and paid		8.	5.

House of Commons	£	s.	d.
Perusing plan & other documents & attending to deposit same at Private Bill Office	1.	1.	0.
Paid reading of petition and reference to Committee		15.	4.
Copies to Committee on petition		13.	4.
Perusing & settling draft Bill, blanking and preparing it for the press	5.	5.	0.
Drawing motion for leave to bring in the Bill & copy for members		10.	0.
Paid reading report & order for Bill	1.	3.	4.
Copy Bill to present to the House	3.	18.	6.
Drawing brief of the Bill & copy for the Speaker	1.	5.	0.
	£19.	14.	5.

	£	s.	d.
Attending Chairman of the Lords Committee with the print of the Bill and afterwards on his Counsel when he suggested several alterations in the Bill..	1.	1.	0.
Revising and altering the Bill accordingly	1.	1.	0.
Paid fees on second reading of Bill..................	28.	0.	0.
Copies to Committee on Bill		13.	4.
Filling up Print of the Bill with proposed amendments for the Chairman of the Lords Committee and attending him therewith and thereon	1.	1.	0.
Fair copy of account of trustees to accompany same...		2.	0.
Filling up print of the Bill with the amendments and attending to deposit same in the Private Bill Office persuant to the Standing Orders and fair copy list of trustees to accompany same ...		15.	0.
Filling up points of the Bill with amounts for the Commissioners & six copies lists of trustees...	2.	10.	0.
Paid Committee fees and for copy of two petitions against the Bill	15.	15.	0.
Paid ingrossing the Bill	16.	13.	6.
Assisting in examining the ingrossment and proof print of the Bill and Act	2.	0.	0.
Paid housekeeper and messengers	4.	7.	0.
Paid doorkeepers	1.	11.	6.
Paid clerks of the Private Bill Office	7.	10.	0.
Notices to them of proceedings	1.	13.	4.
	£104.	8.	1.

House of Lords	£	s.	d.
Perusing plan and other documents and attending to deposit same at the Parliament Office	1.	1.	0.
Paid depositing same..	1.	1.	0.
Paid fees on second reading of Bill...................	54.	0.	0.
Paid Deputy Black Rod and doorkeepers	5.	5.	0.
Paid clerk putting prints on table		10.	6.
Paid for order of commitment.........................	1.	1.	0.
Paid for order on petition in favour of the Bill...	1.	1.	0.
Paid swearing two witnesses		4.	0.
Paid committee fees and clerk attending Committee	4.	15.	0.
Paid for printing Bill and Act	17.	13.	0.
Mr Fenner's attendance at the Bar of the House of Lords to be sworn and at the Committee to prove depositing plan and other	2.	2.	0.
Paid small gratuities porters, parcels letters and other incidental expenses	5.	2.	0.
For soliciting the Bill through both Houses of Parliament, attending the Committees, Members and Agents while the Bill was depending	26.	5.	0.
Attending at the King's printer to procure prints of all the General Turnpike Acts and paid for same and binding	1.	4.	5.
	£225.	13.	0.

Trustees of the Leadenham Hill to Mansfield & Southwell to Oxton turnpike roads had a bill amounting to £468 3s 3d for their Act, a sum which could be even higher if there was substantial opposition to the undertaking.

An example of the opposition that could be encountered is provided by the passage of the proposed Aylesbury–Hockliffe bill in 1810. The new road was planned to pass through Leighton Buzzard, and the inhabitants of that town, fearing that they might have tolls imposed on them, hastily called a meeting. Subsequently they presented a petition to the House of Commons which read:

Sheweth: That it appears from the votes of this Honourable House that a Bill is now pending for the more effectual amending widening and repairing the road leading from Aylesbury in the county of Buckingham to Hockliffe in the county of Bedford. That several of the clauses and provisions contained in the said Bill are highly prejudicial and injurious to the rights and interests of your petitioners and the rest of the inhabitants of Leighton Buzzard and Southcott aforesaid.

Your petitioners therefore humbly pray that they may be heard by themselves, their Counsel or agents against such part of the clauses and provisions contained in the said Bill as affect their rights and interests, and that particular provisions may be made in the said Bill on their account and that they may have such relief in the premises as to this Honourable House shall seem meet.

The inhabitants of Leighton Buzzard tried at the Committee stage of the Bill to introduce a clause that no toll-gate or weighing engine should be erected nearer than two miles from the town. Eventually, after a good deal of argument and discussion, it was agreed that no toll-gate should be set up nearer to the west end of the town than the end of Surcoat Lane next to the parish of Wing, and to the east no nearer than the hamlet of Eggington; but a following measure laid the responsibility of maintaining the road from the Grand Junction canal to the market houses in Leighton Buzzard on the parishes of Linslade and Leighton Buzzard—a reasonable compromise, presumably.

In the northern industrial districts, opposition to road improvement sometimes arose because of fears that better roads would bring increased competition from other areas. The trustees of the Liverpool and Prescot road experienced such opposition when they proposed to extend the road to St Helens. People with colliery interests in and around Prescot and Wigan feared that such a road would bring intensive competition from other collieries, resulting in lower prices all round.

Similar opposition was experienced in western England. Colliery owners opposed the establishment of the Bristol trust for fear that the tolls would add to their expenses. Fortunately, some of the trusts in Somerset allowed lower rates for carts carrying coal, but in order to make sure that this valuable traffic did not escape them, the trustees often resited their gates.

When the bill had been passed and two-thirds of the capital raised, trustees would be appointed to govern the activities of the trust. Under the terms of the General Turnpike Act of 1773, which placed trusts under sessional control, a high property qualification was endorsed for the appointment of a trustee, and no publican could be elected. Each turnpike trust fixed its own qualifications within the terms of this Act. The Gloucester–Cheltenham–Tewkesbury trust followed the precise terms of the Act in demanding that their trustees:

> . . . be seized or possessed in his own right or in the rent of his wife, and be in the actual possession or receipt of the rents and profits of land, tenements or hereditaments of the clear yearly

value of £40 above reprizes or shall have the personal estate of the value of £800 or shall be heir apparent of a person possessed of an estate in lands, tenements or hereditaments of the clear yearly value of £80.

The trustees appointed paid officials to carry out the day-to-day work of the trust—a clerk, treasurer, and surveyors. The surveyors were appointed either on a full-time basis or on a part-time contract, their salaries ranging from a mere ten shillings a week to the £500 a year, including the expense of a horse and carriage, paid to the famous John Loudon Macadam in 1817 as general surveyor of the Bristol District of Roads. In his contract drawn up in December 1815, Macadam's duties included attendance at meetings of the trustees 'and to report to them everything which respects the actual state of such roads'; drawing up specifications for all contracts; and 'to make himself fully acquainted with the state of repair and the local circumstances in respect to materials, carriage and labour of each separate road, to visit each Road its whole extent as frequently as time will permit'.

Like most surveyors, he of the Exeter turnpike trust had to make periodic reports to the trustees, and these indicate that some of the roads, despite his care and attention, were still far from satisfactory. Along a section of the Bath road between St Anne's Chapel and Pin Pound, for instance, he mentioned that the road was 'in a very defective and dangerous state. In several parts there are ruts for a considerable distance, from twelve to fifteen inches deep; and in consequence of the water table not having been kept in a proper order, the water overflows many parts of the road'. On the London road from the bottom of Paris Street to the old county gallows conditions were little better, for the surveyor described them as being 'in a most wretched state; the whole of the surface is entirely broken up in parallel ruts from four to six in number, and in many places a foot deep; the road in many places is completely worn out'.

In reporting the condition of the roads the surveyors were usually charged with the task of making 'pittings' to determine the depth of the surface at various points along the road. The Exeter surveyor used the gauge illustrated overleaf, pittings being made every furlong. On the London road he recorded the average depth of the surface materials as being $1\frac{1}{4}$ in, and on the Exmouth road an average of $1\frac{3}{8}$ in. In commenting on these and other figures, the surveyor wrote in his report: 'Although the foregoing average statements show some quantity of macadamised material on each road, yet many parts of these roads are completely worn down, the foundation stone appearing much above the proper line of the surface of the road.'

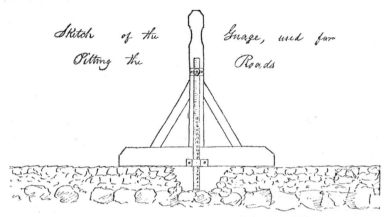

Sketch of the Pitting the *Guage, used for Roads*

FIGURE 1. Sketch of guage for pitting the road

Among the surveyors' many duties was that of keeping an eye on householders and others living along the roads to see that they did not remove soil, stones and other materials needed for repairs. From the records of various trusts, especially the Droitwich to Bromsgrove, it would appear that many people were not averse to carrying off these items for their own use. An entry in the Droitwich to Bromsgrove trust's minute book for 1766 reads:

> Ordered that the surveyor do give notice to every person intending to take soil for manure or any other purpose from the side of the road that they must not take away the same as it is in general wanted for filling up the holloways.

The trust's records also show that the highways were often used as dumping grounds for householders' rubbish. In June 1776 there is the following entry:

> That notice in writing be given to the several persons who have laid manure upon the road, committed any encroachment or caused any other nuisance thereon that the same be removed within a fortnight from such notice and that the surveyor do prosecute such persons as shall make default therein by indicting them at the next Assizes or Sessions.

Unfortunately, there is evidence to suggest that some of the surveyors were incompetent. The Droitwich to Bromsgrove trust, for instance, reprimanded their surveyor at a meeting in September 1782, when they threatened to fine him twenty shillings 'for neglecting his duty and suffering the streets in Droitwich to remain in a dangerous state from breaking up the pavement to repair the water pipes'. Other trusts had to dismiss surveyors who were found to have no knowledge whatever of building and repairing roads.

The surveyor also had to keep milestones and signposts in a good state of repair. On 15 March 1839 the surveyor of the Ross road was ordered by the trustees 'to examine all the milestones and direction posts . . . and cause the same to be fresh painted and renewed where necessary, also that he see that the names of the towns or villages are painted on some wall or board as required by the Act 3 Geo. IV c. 136, section 119'.

Opinions differed considerably about the best method of constructing and repairing roads. Macadam, who believed that the roads had to be made to accommodate the traffic, emphasised proper drainage and the use of suitable materials to make a firm foundation suitable for the heaviest vehicles. As he explained in his book *The Present System of Road Making*: 'a road ought to be considered as an artificial flooring forming a strong, smooth, and solid surface at once capable of carrying great weight and over which carriages may pass without meeting any impediment. He told the Committee on the Highways & Turnpike Roads in England & Wales in 1819 that he preferred a soft foundation to a hard one: 'I think when a road is placed upon a hard substance, such as a rock, the road wears much sooner than when placed on a soft substrata.' He said that a road should be as flat as possible 'with regard to allowing the water to run off it', for as he explained:

I have generally made roads three inches higher in the centre than I have at the sides, when they are eighteen feet wide; if the road be smooth and well made, the water will run off easily on such a slope.

Stones used in surfacing Macadam's roads had to be of an exact size. 'I always make my surveyors carry a pair of scales and a six ounce weight in their pocket,' he informed the Committee, 'and when they come to a heap of stones, they weigh one or two of the largest.' On the roads under his care, men and women were employed breaking stones, using a hammer with a 15 in handle and a 1 in face. These broken stones were then laid on the roads as evenly as possible, ideally a 6 in layer to begin with, followed by a further 6 in a few weeks later. He estimated that the expense involved in preparing and relaying a rough road to a depth of 4 in should cost not more than 1d or 2d a square yard; which meant that a 6 yd wide surface could cost in the region of £88 a mile.

Macadam repeatedly emphasised the need for efficient training of surveyors. At the same time he maintained that all trust officials should be paid an adequate salary, to prevent corruption. 'Gratuitous services', he explained, 'are ever temporary and local; they are dependent on the residence and life of the party; and have always disappointed expectation. Skill and executive labour must be adequately paid for if expected to be constantly and usefully exerted; and if so exerted, the price is no consideration when compared with the advantage to the public.'

A large number of trusts adopted Macadam's principles, for, in addition to being General Surveyor of the Roads of the Bristol District, a post which he took up in January 1816, he visited or advised trusts at Epsom, Egham, Newbury, Oxford, Chester, Winchester, Ledbury, Plymouth, Exeter, Henley, Pontefract, Tunbridge Wells, Macclesfield, Wellington, Cheshunt, Devizes, several in Sussex, Cardiff, Northampton, Newport, Bath, Preston, and many others.

In London some of the streets were surfaced on his principles— the term Macadamizing being the word used to describe the process. On 8 October 1824, *The Times* announced:

> Yesterday the workmen began to Macadamize the wide roadway from Charing Cross to Parliament Street. Temporary fencing is raised half way over the street from the Admiralty to the Horse Guards, thus preventing any interruption of this great thoroughfare. The great granite stones are broke into small pieces as soon as they are taken up, and thus, as rapidly as the way is cleared the materials are ready for the commencement of the Macadamizing system.

Towards the end of 1826, *The Times* was able to report that 'Macadamization is making rapid progress throughout the principal streets at the West end of the metropolis'.

The Committee on the Highways & Turnpike Roads in England & Wales in 1819 spoke in glowing terms of Macadam's road construction, and recommended a Government grant to him as an appreciation of his services; this was eventually made up to £2,000. Macadam's sons followed in his footsteps, and in 1822 James Nicoll Macadam was the surveyor of some thirty trusts.

Other famous road engineers of the period were John Metcalfe and Thomas Telford. Metcalfe, born at Knaresborough, Yorkshire in 1717, became blind at the age of six, but this apparent handicap did not prevent him from embarking on a memorable career. His work on road improvements began when he was commissioned to build a stretch of road for the Harrogate-Borough-

1a. *The Overset*, by Thomas Rowlandson.
1b. Hyde Park Corner turnpike in 1794.

2a. The toll-house at North Weald, Essex, now converted to a private house.
2b. *The Turnpike Gate*, by Charles Cooper Henderson.

bridge trust, and later he went on to build and repair nearly two hundred miles in the Pennine regions of Lancashire, Yorkshire, Cheshire and Derbyshire. His general system of road construction was to lay down a surface of stone and gravel over bundles of ling or heather, and to dig ditches along the sides of these convex roads to provide the necessary drainage.

Telford, born in 1757, the son of a shepherd, earned his reputation as bridge builder and road engineer. His first major work was the design of a three-arched stone bridge across the Severn at Shrewsbury, completed in 1792. He later furnished designs for some 1,200 stone or iron bridges in the Scottish Highlands and the west of England, work which was to culminate in the famous suspension bridge which he designed to connect Anglesey with the mainland as part of the Holyhead improvement scheme. In road construction his name is associated with the improvement of that from Carlisle to Glasgow, and the famous Holyhead road, the latter marking the first attempt at a national road. In 1808 the Post Office tried, unsuccessfully, to run a mail coach between Holyhead and Shrewsbury. Following this failure, it was decided to improve the communication between London and Dublin by way of Holyhead. In May 1810, Telford was authorised to survey the line of road between Holyhead and Shrewsbury, and also from Bangor to Chester, and he made his report in the following year. A Board of Parliamentary Commissioners was set up, and in 1815 a grant of £20,000 was allocated by Parliament for the improvements. Telford was appointed to oversee construction, most of it being done on contract. Along the line of road there were some twenty-three separate trusts, with which Telford had to work in making improvements. The organisation of two of them, the Whetstone and the St Albans, proved to be so incompetent that it was proposed by a House of Commons Committee in 1828 to transfer the trustees' powers to the Holyhead Road Commissioners for a period of three years. The threat was not in fact carried out, but drastic action was taken with six Welsh trusts which were merged into one, with fifteen trustees, which was controlled by Telford and the Holyhead Road Commissioners. When all the roads were completed, a surcharge of 50 per cent was added to the existing tolls, the additional revenue going to the Parliamentary Commissioners.

Like Macadam, Telford believed in keeping the roads as level as possible, his general rule being that the slope should not exceed 1 in 30. Unlike Macadam, though, he believed in having a very firm foundation. Upon a solid stone foundation he recommended

c

that broken rock should be placed as a covering, with the middle, or working part, of the road as hard as possible. The foundation was made up of stone blocks, measuring 7 in by 4 in, with stone chips wedged between them. On this a layer of stones was placed to a depth of 6 in, and then above it a further layer of small stones, or in some cases gravel. The working part of the road would be about 18 ft, with a lesser surface of 6 ft on either side suitable for lighter traffic.

The materials locally available very largely determined the type of road that could be constructed, though some trusts went to the considerable expense of importing stone from other areas. In south-eastern England, especially in the London area, Macadam pointed out that the material used was gravel 'of a very bad quality', mixed with an inseparable loam. This inevitably resulted in poor roads, made worse by the problem of drainage and the very heavy volume of traffic. In Derbyshire conditions were very much better, according to John Farey in his book, *A General View of the Agriculture of Derbyshire*. He explained that 'materials for making roads are very plentiful and good', hard limestone being readily available in most parts of the north-western districts of the county. To the south, quartz gravel was widely used to provide a good road surface, but in the eastern and northern parts, suitable materials were scarcer and more expensive.

Materials used in Lancashire varied in different parts of the county. In the north and east limestone was readily available to provide a good road, and this was used by the Bury, Blackburn and Whalley Trust from the limestone quarries of the Clitheroe district. Towards the south-west, the roads were made largely of pebbles taken from the river beds, and in some parts slag from the copper works at St Helens and Liverpool provided a first-class surface. Very heavy traffic in and around Manchester, Liverpool and Wigan required large stones, sometimes imported from the coasts of Wales and Scotland, to make a foundation substantial enough to take the weight of coal waggons and carts. These stones usually formed a pavement in the centre of the road, with gravel placed on either side.

In the west country the roads of Herefordshire were described by John Duncomb in *A General View of the Agriculture of the County of Hereford*, published in 1805. He comments:

Coarse limestone, properly broken, is the material generally used for making or repairing roads in those parts of the county where it abounds. When it does not, the roads suffer from the want of it; the north side of Herefordshire has the worst public roads; the private are universally bad, excepting those situated on sandy or gravelly soils, which naturally require but little attention or expense.

On the roads of the Bath turnpike trust the general surveyor, William Macadam, son of J. L. Macadam, explained in a report dated 4 October 1827 that he had extended the use of Black Rock stone over a considerable length of the roads. 'Of the flints,' he observed, 'so much has already been said at the Board as to leave me little to add, further than that I am, by the experience of last winter, still of opinion they are a very cheap article; and for this Trust, dependent as it is on imported materials, a very advantageous means of supply in case of any monopoly or other circumstance rendering the Black Rock beyond the reach of your funds.'

These differences in local materials were reflected in the specifications that were issued for the construction of new roads and the repair of existing ones. In March 1806, the trustees of the Leadenham Hill to Mansfield & Southwell to Oxton roads invited tenders for the construction of a new road from Farnsfield Lordship to Mansfield:

> The road to be formed forty feet wide and to be made what is called a concave or hollow road, eighteen feet of the soil or turf to be cut in the middle, of such depth as may receive the ling and gravel below specified.

The centre of the road had to be covered with ling, and then with a 6 in thickness of unscreened gravel and afterwards with 9 in of the best seasoned gravel 'that can be procured contiguous to the line of road'.

Another specification for the formation of a new road is for one built by the Wendover and Buckingham trust through Oakham and Buckslow farms in the parish of Swinbourne in the 1820s. According to its terms, the road had to be staked out 50 ft wide, the actual width being 34 ft, with 3 ft on either side for the guard fence. The screened gravel had to be laid 18 ft wide and 15 in thick on average; and the camber of the road had to be such that it rose to 24 in in the centre when completed. The contractor was to have the liberty of digging gravel 'where they can find it to the most advantage, and the trustees should pay the damage for same'.

Several estimates were submitted for building the road. Messrs James and George Soden agreed to construct it 'to be formed and finished in a workmanlike manner, at ten shillings per yard, running measure', with quicking and fencing with substantial materials at an extra 10s per pole. Mr James Bull could undertake the work for the sum of £575, finding 'sureties to any amount you may approve of and to take the money every six weeks according to the work done', while the rather illiterate Thomas and William Morris and William Alderman gave the following undertaking:

> Wee will well screen the gravill and make good stoff of it and wee will complet the gob in a workman like manner acording to the contrack and the speceycation. On condition of receiving three forths of the money as the work is done wee will undertake to do the whole as above stated at eight pound nine and six pence per chain, if wee are required to lay culverts wee will agree to take what Mr Perrin shall think a reasonable price. If bondsmen are required wee can bring forward these that will be sufficient.

The last-named gentlemen were eventually awarded the contract, which was dated 7 May 1826. They were required to work under the supervision of the trust's surveyor, and the work had to be completed by the following 30 October. Other requirements in the contract demanded that the contractors before making the road should:

> Throw up the bank and erect the guard fence . . . with good oak posts morticed and three rails, the same to be also nailed to the middle stakes so as to prevent any cattle from trespassing or doing damage on the adjoining lands during the time of forming and making the said road.

They were also required to dig a ditch 4 ft wide and throw up a bank which had to be planted with white-thorn sets. All tools, transport, stones and gravel had to be provided by the contractors, and the trustees agreed to pay for the work at £8 9s 6d a chain, and 10s per pole for fencing; three-quarters of this being paid at regular intervals, and the remainder on completion of the road, 'less two shillings for every pole of the fencing', which was to remain in the hands of the Treasurer for five years. Any damage done by the contractors in digging for gravel and carting was to be paid for by the trustees.

A stoned road was built by the Teignmouth–Dawlish turnpike trust from east Teignmouth church to the bridge at Dawlish in 1823, the road being part of a planned £12,000 scheme for improving the entrances into east Teignmouth and Dawlish 'and in almost entirely getting rid of the hills between those places', by lowering some, and building new roads round others. The road involved two sections: one from Dawlish 'to join the present road near Northcote cottage', which had to be 'twenty four feet wide including footpaths and all cuttings, and to be stoned eighteen feet wide and six inches thick in all cuttings and eight in all the embankments forming a convex of four inches with hard stones well broken of the materials found now forming the present road and in the different cuttings—to be broken to the size of a pattern to be fixed upon'. The contractors were required to set hedges, and all necessary drains across the road had to be provided within the price. The other section, from Northcote cottage to near east Teignmouth church, involved widening the road to 20 ft. An estimate for the work, submitted by Mr Hopkins, quoted the sum of £3,125 2s od. Another trust, the Rochdale & Burnley, in making a road over Deerplay Moor in 1755, specified one 7 yd wide, with a drain on either side 1 yd in width; the middle part of the road being stoned to a width of 4 yd, with small broken stones to a depth of 12 in on the crown, gradually diminishing to 6 in on either side. The road had to be covered with 6 in of good gravel on top of these stones.

A large expense that turnpike trusts had to meet was that of purchasing land. In November 1779 the Gander Lane–Sheffield–Clown trust paid between £47 5s od and £60 an acre for land, while in the early nineteenth century the trustees of the Aylesbury–Hockliffe road paid £120 an acre. In 1827, £10,000 was paid for 100 acres by the Bath turnpike trust. Compensation had also often to be paid to owners of property along the course of the intended roads, especially when buildings had to be pulled down.

With the road completed, the next task was to build toll-houses and erect gates where the tolls would be collected that travellers would have to pay if they wished to use the road. The siting of the gates was important. A report in *The Dorset County Chronicle* for 31 August 1843 stated that the trustees of the Wimborne and Piddletown road had met 'for the purpose of ordering and directing the number and situation where the toll gates, turnpikes, side-bars, chains, toll houses etc, and other conveniences thereto shall be severally erected and placed on or across on the said road and where and from what time the taking of such tolls shall commence, and take into consideration what highways, bridle roads or footpaths adjoining to the said turnpike road or communicating therewith, and the footpaths leading into or out of the same roads become useless or may for the convenience of the public be advantageously diverted'. The trust later stopped up many of the side roads and bridle paths, thereby forcing travellers to use the turnpike road. A similar course was taken by the Storrington & Balls Hut turnpike road in May 1825, when they ordered their clerk to take steps to close any roads 'he may consider to interfere with the collection of toll'.

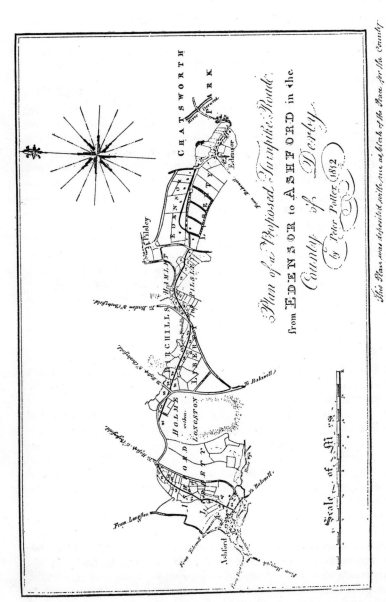

FIGURE 2. Plan of turnpike road

In 1759 the trustees of the Leadenham Hill to Mansfield & Southwell to Oxton roads decided to erect a bar 'across the said road in Easthorpe at the south corner of Chimes Close and also a bar on the side of the said road at the end of the said Close across a lane leading to the burgage of Southwell, and that toll shall be only taken, as the Act of Parliament for repairing the said road directs, at the said barriers for such carriages as shall be loaded with or carry coal, coakes or drive manure through the same, not having paid toll at any other bars now erected'.

During June 1810, the trustees of the Aylesbury–Hockliffe road invited tenders for the 'building of all or any of the toll houses, toll gates and weighing engines to be erected on the road leading from Aylesbury to Hockliffe'. Among the tenders received was one from Mr R. Gurney, dated 9 July 1810. The estimate read as follows:

An estimate for building a turnpike house near Aylesbury on the road from Aylesbury to Hockliffe with two large gates and fence (across) the road, the house to be twenty four feet long from out to out and thirteen feet wide from out to out, and seven and a half feet high from the floor to the ceiling, with a chimney at each end and a lean-to behind five feet wide. The house to be divided into two rooms to be built with nine inch brick walls and slated and with Swedish fir timber and deal hedged doors and floors, including glazing and painting three coats with best white lead, the lean-to timber built and boarded, the posts and gates to be oak and deal bars to the gates. Four posts to be eleven feet long 11 ins × 11 ins, the other posts to be nine feet long 8 ins × 8 ins. The rails to be 2½ ins × 4 ins including iron work to the gates and fastenings to ditto with nuts and screws along the top bar into the two uprights; and a single raised bar across the road leading to Broughton with posts to ditto eight feet long 7 ins × 7 ins; the rails to be 3 ins × 4½ ins oak, will amount to the sum of £160 to be completed within one month and the house two months from the present date and to be paid for as soon as completed.

Among the plans submitted for other toll-houses for this trust was the one shown in Plate 3, which is similar to that specified by Mr Gurney.

The toll-house keeper would either be appointed by the trustees, or, when the tolls were farmed out, by the contractor for the particular gate. The toll collector, or pikeman as he was usually called, was responsible for seeing that tolls were collected by day and night. At their meeting held on the 14 January 1819, the trustees of the Essex turnpike trust appointed Robert Felton 'to be collector of the several tolls and dues payable at the turnpike gate called the Bulmer gate, and the fines for overweight at the said weighing machine, with full power and authority given to him to ask demand collect and receive the same of all persons liable to pay the same, he the said Robert Felton rendering a just and true account of all such monies as he may receive at the said gate into Lewis Majendie Esq at such times as may be demanded of him (and) to continue in such appointment until the said trustees or their successors, or any seven of them shall appoint any other collector in his place'.

When a toll collector was required for the turnpike road between York and Tadcaster in 1799, the trustees advertised for a person with an undeniable character who had to find 'good sureties for his duly collecting and paying over the tolls (which are now let at £680 per annum)'. His duties were to include 'keeping distinct accounts . . . especially for his weighing carriages at the engine, according to the strict directions of the General Turnpike Acts, in order to detect and counteract the evasions which are supposed to have been practised on that head'. His annual salary was to be £50, and he could live in the toll-house rent free, it being described as 'a comfortable one'.

Most trusts farmed their tolls. These would be let to the highest bidder at a public auction, usually for one to three years. In September 1809, for example, the contractor of the Rivenhall toll-gate agreed to pay the Essex turnpike trust £700 a year for two years; £116 13s 4d being paid as an initial deposit, and the balance of £583 6s 8d in monthly instalments. All the expenses in collecting the tolls, such as the toll-gate keeper's wages, the issue of tickets, and household expenses such as coal, oil and candles, had to be met by the contractor; the trustees were responsible for the upkeep of the toll-house and gates. At the Shenfield (Essex) gate expenses averaged 26s a week for wages; 5s 3d a week in winter for coal and 2s 6d in summer; candles 11s in winter and 2s 6d in summer; and 12s a month for oil.

Usually this system worked well, though the Wendover–Buckingham trust had an unfortunate instance of an unreliable contractor. Their clerk, writing in April 1857 to a solicitor in Cirencester, reported that 'Mr James Webb Atkins has bolted and left our trustees one month's rent in arrear—we shall be obliged if you will enquire of your toll lessees, whether he or his sureties Joseph Atkins and Thomas Hurcomb are now to be found in your neighbourhood and let us know for we are issuing a writ against them and shall be glad of your assistance in getting it served'.

The level of tolls varied from trust to trust within the rates permitted by their Acts, but some idea of the charges for various types of traffic can be obtained from the tables below:

Essex Turnpike Trust, amending Act of 1815 'for repairing several roads leading from Shenfield to Harwich, and Rochford, and other places in the county of Essex, and for extending the said Act to the road from Gt. Halingbury to Hockerill in the county of Hertford.'

	s.	d.
For every coach, Berlin, landau, chariot, calash, chaise, or hearse drawn by six horses or other cattle	2.	6.
For every stage coach licensed to carry six or more inside passengers, drawn by four horses or other cattle	2.	0.
For every other stage coach, drawn by four horses or other cattle	1.	6.
For every coach, Berlin, landau, chariot, calash, chair or hearse, drawn by four horses or other cattle	1.	0.
Drawn by two horses or other cattle		9.
For every chair or chaise drawn by one horse or other beast of draught		6.
For every taxed cart drawn by one horse or other beast of draught		6.

For every waggon or other such four wheeled carriage, having the sole or bottom of the felloes of the wheels thereof of the breadth of 12 ins or upwards:

	s.	d.
Drawn by 8 horses or other beasts of draught	2.	0.
Drawn by 7 horses or other beasts of draught	1.	9.
Drawn by 6 horses or other beasts of draught	1.	6.
Drawn by 5 horses or other beasts of draught	1.	3.
Drawn by 4 horses or other beasts of draught	1.	0.

Waggons with 9 in wheels:

	s.	d.
Drawn by 8 horses or other beasts of draught	3.	0.
Drawn by 7 horses or other beasts of draught	2.	3.
Drawn by 6 horses or other beasts of draught	2.	0.
Drawn by 5 horses or other beasts of draught	1.	3.
Drawn by 4 horses or other beasts of draught	1.	0.

Waggons with 6 in wheels:

	s.	d.
Drawn by 6 horses or other beasts of draught	2.	0.
Drawn by 5 horses or other beasts of draught	1.	9.
Drawn by 4 horses or other beasts of draught	1.	6.
Drawn by 3 horses or other beasts of draught	1.	0.

Waggons with wheels less than 6 ins:

	s.	d.
Drawn by 4 horses	1.	6.
Drawn by 3 horses	1.	0.

	s.	d.
For every dray, cart, or other such two wheeled carriage, having the sole or bottom of the felloes of the wheels thereof of the breadth or guage of 9 ins and driven by five, four horses or other beasts of draught	1.	0.

	s.	d.
With three horses		9.
As above, but with 6 in wheels:		
Drawn by three horses	1.	0.
Drawn by 2 horses		9.
As above, under 6 in wheels		
Drawn by 3 horses	1.	0.
Drawn by 2 horses		9.
Drawn by 1 horse		6.

Droves of cattle, pigs, sheep, etc were charged by the score, the rates varying from 3d to 6d per score. A riding horse was charged one penny.

Turnpike road from Chesterfield to Matlock bridge. (*1823*)	s.	d.
For every horse mule or other beast drawing any coach, barouche, Berlin, landau, chariot, chaise curricle, caravan, chair, gig or other such carriage, hearse		4.
Any waggon, wain, cart, tumbril or other such like carriage having at the time of using thereof wheels of the breadth of 6 ins at the sole or bottom of the felloes thereof		4.
Ditto, less breadth than 6 ins		6.
For every horse, mule or other beast laden or unladen and not drawing		$1\frac{1}{2}$
For every drove of oxen, cows or neat cattle (calves excepted) per score..		10.
. . . calves, hogs, sheep, lambs		5.
For every carriage with the wheels of the breadth of 6 ins or upwards loaded with any millstone or millstone block or blocks or stone piece, or pieces of timber and drawn by 5 horses or other beasts of draught	2.	6.
If drawn by more than five horses or other beasts of draught for each horse or beast of draught exceeding that number...	1.	0.
For every carriage with wheels of the less breadth than 6 ins loaded as aforesaid and drawn by five horses or beasts of draught	3.	9.
And if drawn by more than 5 horses or beasts of draught for each horse or beast of draught exceeding that number the further sum of	1.	0.

From these tables it can be seen that higher rates were charged for narrow-wheeled waggons than for those having broad wheels. These differential rates followed a long and complicated series of Acts which will be discussed in the next chapter, but it is necessary to note here that Parliament limited the number of horses that could be used in each type of waggon, trustees being encouraged to put higher tolls on narrow-wheeled waggons to discourage their use. The prevailing view was that narrow wheels did a great deal of harm to the road surface, causing deep ruts that made difficulties for other road users. Clerks of turnpike trusts were usually made responsible for seeing that offenders were brought to justice, a task in which they were aided by informers who were only too pleased to reap the promised rewards in giving notice of the guilty parties. An account of these informers is given in *The Ipswich Journal* for 7 June 1766:

> It having been the custom of several persons lately to watch the number of horses on narrow wheeled waggons, yesterday morning a woman at Baddow, perceiving five in one of them, took a fore horse off and yesterday applied to a Justice in order to have it allowed as her property, agreeable to an Act of Parliament; which was accordingly done. It seems her husband had followed the practice some time ago, but he laying it aside, she said it was too lucrative to go out of the family.

Sometimes the trustees appointed a person to keep a special watch for the narrow-wheeled waggons and the number of horses, as in the case of the Northgate turnpike trust. An entry in their minute book for 12 May 1761 reads:

> Ordered that the Treasurers appoint a proper person to attend upon the road to put the laws into execution against drawing with more horses than allowed by Act of Parliament and to give the person so employed such directions and such gratuity as they shall think fit.

Despite warnings and punishments, it appears that many carriers continued to disregard the law. One newspaper report for October 1797 mentioned that 'so prevalent is the practice of drawing more horses in waggons, etc., than is allowed by Act of Parliament, and travelling also on Sundays, that the magistrates are determined to suppress it; no less than three drivers were convicted by the magistrates at the Public Office, Hatton Garden, on Sunday, in the penalty of £5 each for the above offence'.

Some turnpike trusts gave preferential rates to certain types of traffic. In the northern industrial districts, for example, lower rates were often charged for waggons carrying coal. In Lancashire such tolls were usually half those paid for other loads. No charge at all was levied on coal vehicles on the Lancaster–Richmond turnpike road, while on the Rochdale–Halifax road exemption was given to unladen carts coming from Yorkshire to collect Lancashire coal. Of a rather different nature was the encouragement given to tourist

traffic in Bath during the eighteenth century, where 'all persons
. . . who with horses, coaches, calashes and chaises, shall pass
through any or either of the said places where toll is collected, for
taking the air, or for recreation, are, if they return the same day
into the city, to have the money reimbursed them, by the collectors, which they paid upon their going out of the town'.

Nearly every turnpike trust permitted certain toll exemptions,
which were written into its Act. In that of 1791 for 'amending and
widening several pieces of Road, and opening and making several
pieces of new road therein described, so as to make a convenient
Carriage Road from Buckingham through Brackley, to join the
Daventry Turnpike Road near Banbury', the exemptions included
any carriages employed in carrying stones, gravel or other materials
for repairing the roads. Vehicles carrying 'hay, straw or corn in
the straw, not sold or disposed of, but to be laid up in the houses,
outhouses, barns, yards or backsides of the owners thereof' were
similarly exempted. Mail coaches paid no tolls, and no charges
were made for 'any horse or horses carrying or conveying any
person to or from his or her parish church, or usual place of
Divine worship, on Sundays, or attending the funeral of any person who shall die or be buried in any of the parishes wherein the
said road lies, or carrying any clergyman going to or returning
from visiting any sick person, or other his parochial care or duty'.
Officers, soldiers and their baggage also passed through the gates
without payment.

Regular users not enjoying an exemption usually preferred to
pay a periodic sum instead of daily tolls. The Gander Lane–
Sheffield–Clown trust allowed the following compositions:

2 *August 1780.*
Ordered that Mr Matthew Jarvis shall be allowed to pass on the
road with one broad wheeled waggon and eight horses and a
saddle horse once a week from Monday next ensuing for the term
of twelve months and the said Matthew Jarvis paying in the
months of December, January and February eight shillings a week,
and for the remaining nine months during the year six shillings a
week, and it is further ordered that the surveyor may contract with
any other carrier, using broad wheeled waggons on the said
road . . .
3 July 1786
Mr Samuel Staniforth, on payment of 40s a year was allowed a
composition: 'all carriages going to or returning from the coal pits
at or near Mosboro' laden with coals only or returning empty shall
pass freely at Mosboro' Bar from the first day of January next
(1787) for the term of one year . . .

The first entry shows that a higher rate was charged during the winter months to discourage traffic. Some turnpike trusts went as far as to charge 50 per cent more on all traffic between 31 October and 1 May, when there would be greater wear and tear on the roads.

A problem facing nearly every trust was that of widespread toll evasions. Some people went to the most extraordinary pains to avoid payment, choosing to bump over fields in waggons and gallop through gardens in order to circumnavigate the hated toll collectors. Among the unsuccessful defaulters of the Winchester turnpike trust was a Fareham labourer who, in January 1830, drove ten sheep across fields to avoid paying 1d, a manœuvre which cost him £5. Dislike of the tolls was sometimes expressed in a rougher manner, particularly by a man who was summoned to appear before the trustees of the Shrewsbury–Wrexham road for 'forcefully passing his team through the Bryngwilch gate without paying the tolls appointed to be paid and having otherwise abused the collector'.

Trustees of the Liverpool–Prescot, St Helens, Warrington and Ashton trust experienced considerable difficulties in 1753 when they ordered 'that the clauses against persons abusing the collector of the turnpike, or pulling down the gates, be printed, and the offenders be prosecuted'. This trouble followed the raising of tolls and the setting up of new gates.

Sometimes travellers were helped to evade the toll collectors by landowners who permitted passage through their lands. The trustees of the Leadenham Hill to Mansfield & Southwell to Oxton turnpikes were faced with this problem, as they reported at their meeting on 20 February 1796:

> The road suffers considerable injury from the numerous evasions of the toll bar, which are practised by persons sheltering themselves under the pretence of Mr G's authority.

The matter was duly reported to the magistrates. Faced with the same difficulty, the trustees of the Helston road warned the offenders at their Annual General Meeting in August 1776:

> That notice be given by our clerk to the occupiers of the several estates near the turnpike road that has private roads leading to Helston that if they permit any person to pass through such road or ground in order to avoid the tolls he or they will be prosecuted according to the Act of Parliament.

An entry in the minute book of the Yeovil turnpike trust for 4 April 1842 shows that some evasions were skilfully conducted:

Complaints having been made by the lessees of the great loss they
sustained by the beer houses which from time to time had been
opened on the Midford and Preston Roads, outside Kingstone
Gate and on the Crewkerne Road, outside Hendford Gate, at
which persons frequenting Yeovil market and others stopped with
their horses and carriages in order to avoid the tolls, it was resolved
that a special meeting of the trustees be held on Thursday the 5th
May next for the purpose of determining on the prospects of
erecting toll bars or chains beyond such houses—and the clerk was
directed to give the notices required by Act of Parliament for this
purpose.

Trustees often found it necessary to resite their toll-gates to prevent traffic escaping payment. The trustees of the Chesterfield to
Matlock bridge road for instance, had this to say on the subject at
their meeting on 22 October 1812:

And whereas a considerable quantity of ore and lead is now carried
upon this road between Darly bridge and Harewood cupola for
which no toll is paid at any of the bars upon this road, it is therefore
ordered that a toll gate or bar be forthwith erected across part of
this road where the above mentioned gate formerly stood near . . .
and that a full toll be taken for all horses and carriages for which
no ticket of payment of toll shall be produced from the Darly
bridge or Buntingford, Halepit or Walton toll gates.

The trustees who had the worst experiences were those in south
Wales during the winter of 1842–3, the period of the 'Rebecca
Riots'. A multiplication of toll-gates had brought added hardships
to small farmers, already suffering from the hardships of economic
depression, and they expressed their grievances by armed attacks
on the toll keepers and gates, causing extensive damage. Gateposts
and bars were pulled down, and in many instances toll-houses
were destroyed after the toll keepers and their families had been
forced to leave. In the counties of Pembroke and Cardigan it was
reported that not a single toll-gate was left standing after the
armed mob had completed their ravages. The mob was usually led
by a man dressed in woman's clothes; the name 'Rebecca' that was
adopted was a reference to Genesis xxiv, 60, in which the wife of
Isaac receives the promise that her seed should possess the 'gate'
of her foes. It was not until a contingent of the Metropolitan
Police was brought in to swell the ranks of the local constabulary
that order was restored.

The newspapers had a gala day in reporting these riots, all
manner of lurid details being presented. The following are typical
extracts from *The Essex Standard* quoting various other newspapers, including *The Welchman*:

February 1843: (A threatening notice) has just been received in this town (Carmarthen) threatening destruction to all turnpike-gates on a parochial road; and one by Water Street, in the old Newcastle Emlyn road is doomed for destruction . . . thirty veteran pensioners went down to St Clear's on Tuesday last and a troop of Lancers are daily expected on the spot.

February 1843: Rebecca and her Daughters: About seven years ago, a turnpike road was made below Pembroke and Carmarthen, with a view of securing a great thoroughfare by it between Ireland and London. The Liverpool & Metropolitan railway has, however, frustrated the object by leaving but 32 miles of road from Carmarthen to Hob's Point, or Milford, as a passage for the mails which seldom carry more than three passengers a day. Very little thoroughfare else exists along it, as a carrier goes but once a week between Carmarthen and Pembroke by which there is not sufficient raised to pay the interest for the capital expended, much less to keep the road in repair. The trustees have the power by Act of Parliament to put up toll bars on lanes and bye-roads, and also of throwing the expense of the main road on the parishes; and that power they have exercised, which appears to have excited the peasantry to the late and continued acts of violence. The tollage upon the road amounts to 12s 6d upon each market cart for twelve miles besides which the people have to keep the roads in repair. Rebecca has already destroyed the St Clear, Trefechan, Preadergate and Pime toll-gates. She boasts of having an auxiliary force of 500 men, true and faithful at Haverfordwest. . . .

A month later it was reported that Rebecca and her daughters were at work in Somerset. A recently erected gate at Mudgley Hill, in the parish of Wedmore, caused hardship to some of the local peasantry. 'The consequence has been', reported one newspaper, 'that very many of the poor who support themselves by selling turf for firing in the neighbourhood, have to pass through this toll-bar to fetch their turf for sale. Not being able to procure more than 1s 0d to 2s 0d by a day's sale, with their cart and horse, they felt the payment of the toll to be a sad grievance. Forthwith they banded together, destroyed both the gate and the toll house, and drove its inhabitant off with impunity.'

Charges were sometimes made at toll-gates for overweights. Under an Act of 1741, turnpike trustees were empowered, and sometimes forced by Quarter Sessions, to set up 'a crane, machine or weighing engine', and in 1751 legislation demanded that a charge of £1 per hundredweight be charged on every vehicle, drawn by six horses, carrying weights above the permitted levels. In December 1820 the weights allowed for different-sized waggons passing through the Shenfield toll-gate were given in the following table:

Size of waggon or cart wheel	tons	cwt
9 inch waggon	7	10
6 inch waggon	5	10
3 inch waggon	4	0
9 inch cart	3	15
6 inch cart	3	5
3 inch cart	2	5

Above these weights, the under-mentioned rates were charged:

Cwt		s.	d.
1 overweight			3
2	,,		6
3	,,		9
4	,,	1.	0
5	,,	1.	8
6	,,	2.	0
7	,,	2.	4
8	,,	2.	8
9	,,	4.	6
10	,,	5.	0
11	,,	5.	6
12	,,	6.	0
13	,,	13.	0
14	,,	14.	0.
15	,,	15.	0
16	,,	16.	0

£1 per cwt thereafter

To prevent a plea of ignorance about overweight charges, advertisements were put in the local newspapers, as for example, in *The Leicester Journal* for 22 March 1793:

> To carriers and others. By order of the trustees of the turnpike road from Leicester to Ashby-de-la Zouch, notice is hereby given that from and after the 24th day of March instant, all waggons, wains, and carts with the loading thereof, passing on the said road, at the weighing machine, lately erected in Frith Lane . . . will be weighed at such machine, and the tolls and penalties arising from all overweights will be entered and levied by the keeper thereof.

Carriers frequently complained about these surcharges. Pickford's, for example, apparently had cause to complain in 1818. A letter in the firm's records mentions that in November 'Whetstone Gate weigh'd the van to 2 cwt over a load, Woburn the same, Harboro' the same altho' Whetstone was the only one that demanded the money . . . (the overweight charges) are as bad as canal surcharges, they are constantly imposing on us. I beg you

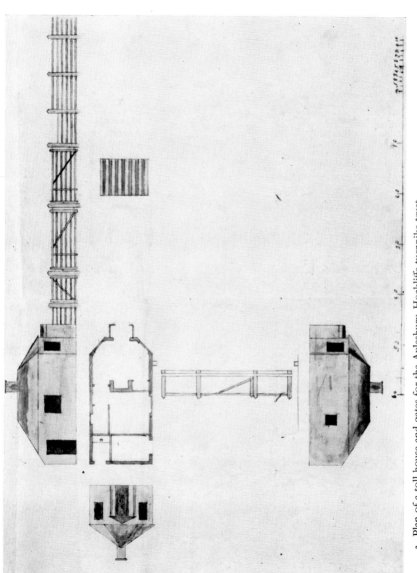

3. Plan of a toll-house and gates for the Aylesbury–Hockliffe turnpike trust.

4a. An eighteenth-century carrier's waggon, an aquatint by J. B. Pyne.
4b. A carrier's waggon, showing the canvas hood folded back.

will keep within loads whatever is the consequence and they should not forget to allow for small packages'.

The weighing machines were expensive to install and maintain and their accuracy was often in doubt. An estimate for a weighing machine for the Shenfield gate in 1826 having a cast-iron plate 13 ft by 7 ft 3 in quoted £87 complete with the brickwork. In 1822 the Gloucester–Cheltenham & Tewkesbury turnpike trust paid £100 for a machine, which was subsequently let for a year at a rental of £40. Unfortunately the machine was not a success, for the trust's minute book for 29 November 1828 records:

> At this meeting a representation was made by Mr. Thomas Turner that the produce of the tolls arising at the weighing machine on this road was not sufficient to pay the expense of keeping it and that the sum of £40 agreed to be paid by Mr. Newmard was far too much.

It was accordingly resolved that from the following January the machine should be let to the Gloucester & Cheltenham Railway company, who were asked to look after it at their own expense, and 'render an annual account of the penalties received by them in respect of such machine and pay such penalties in aid of the funds of the trust'.

The revenue from tolls that a trust could expect depended, of course, on the volume of traffic using the road. Trusts' books sometimes record the traffic passing at particular times, as in the case of the Bath trust, who made a return of the traffic passing through their various gates during the first week of April 1823. Details are given of the types of vehicle and the goods that were being carried, as well as returns for stage and other coaches:

Carriage of stone
6-in waggons	72
6-in carts	66
narrow waggons	58
narrow carts	17

Carriage of coal
6-in waggons	108
6-in carts	243
narrow waggons	96
narrow carts	435

Carriage of sundries
9-in waggons	37
6-in waggons	114
6-in carts	147
narrow waggons	128

D

narrow carts		425
light carts		665
Carriages with four wheels		
4-horse		39
2-horse		583
1-horse		55
Stage coaches		
4-horse		240
2-horse		157
Sheep, pigs	scores	73
Cattle	scores	12¾
Saddle horses		3,634
Gigs		483

Details of the volume of traffic are also given in one of the toll-books of the Broadway gate for 1779. Unfortunately there are 78 days not recorded in the year, but when allowance has been made for this, a fairly good picture of the traffic can be built up:

Broadway Toll Gate 1779	*4 horse coach*	*1 or 2 horse coach*
January (8 recorded days)	21	32
February (full month)	76	133
March (24 days)	57	117
April (full month)	57	116
May (full month)	72	150
June (full month)	67	149
July (full month)	74	164
August (24 days)	63	121
September (16 days)	42	100
October (24 days)	57	118
November (23 days)	65	102
December (18 days)	42	69
Totals for 287 days	693	1371

Expressed as daily averages, it would appear that there were three 4 horse coaches and five 1 or 2 horse coaches passing through the gate each day. Stage waggons (a 9 in waggon paid 9d toll) are detailed as follows for the same number of days:

January	15	July	48	
February	65	August	39	
March	53	September	36	
April	56	October	44	A total of 558
May	53	November	34	
June	72	December	43	

Similar information is given in a return covering the week
26 February to 4 March 1838 made at the Shenfield toll-gate:

Stage Coaches (including mail coaches)

Date	To London	From London
26 February	15	15
27 February	15	17
28 February	17	15
1 March	15	17
2 March	17	15
3 March	15	17
4 March (Sunday)	8	8

	Posting Vehicles	*Private Carriages*	*Gigs*
26 February	5	8	25
27 February	2	9	28
28 February	0	9	25
1 March	5	8	13
2 March	1	7	22
3 March	1	2	15
4 March	0	6	25

	Broad Wheeled Waggons	*Fly Waggons*	*Farmers & Tradesmens Carts*
26 February	13	5	31
27 February	8	10	31
28 February	22	12	52
1 March	13	14	34
2 March	24	21	54
3 March	10	5	35
4 March	22	4	12

	Saddle Horses	*Butchers Carts*	*Fish Vans*
26 February	33	0	0
27 February	30	0	0
28 February	26	7	1
1 March	23	0	1
2 March	11	2	2
3 March	23	0	0
4 March	0	0	1

	Sheep	*Beasts*	*Pigs*
26 February	0	1	0
27 February	109	80	100
28 February	0	27	0
1 March	0	7	0
2 March	80	40	244

	Sheep	Beasts	Pigs
3 March	1568 ⎫ 1027 ⎭	846 ⎫ 147 ⎭	o
4 March	o	o	o

A feature of the Shenfield turnpike gate is the relatively constant pattern of traffic throughout the year. This is shown in the following table in which the net receipts for three years have been expressed as quarterly totals:

Quarterly returns (from weekly figures)

Year	Jan–March	April–June	July–Sept	Oct–Dec.
	£. s. d.	£. s. d.	£. s. d.	£. s. d.
1819	488. 14. 0.	515. 10. 2.	512. 0. 0.	467. 3. 3.
1824	470. 2. 0.	463. 0. 3.	458. 9. 3.	483. 15. 9.
1830	418. 12. 6.	462. 18. 6.	416. 18. 0.	424. 18. 0.

Yearly totals

1819 = £1,983. 7. 4.
1824 = £1,875. 7. 3.
1830 = £1,723. 7. 0.

This constant volume of traffic is probably explained by the importance of the London market, which demanded goods and services at all times of the year. In less densely populated areas, there are obvious signs of seasonal variation in traffic, with peaks during the spring and summer seasons.

On the debit side of their accounts, trustees' expenses are shown in the figures of the Yeovil turnpike trust for the period 31 October 1823 to 30 October 1824 inclusive. Expenditure is given as follows:

Expenditure

To:	£. s. d.
Paid for maintenance and repair of roads between 31 October 1823 and 30 October 1824	613. 2. 9½
Repair and maintenance of houses, gates and bridges	29. 14. 4½
To paid for land purchased for widening roads	41. 10. 0.
To rent of quarries...............................	64. 3. 0.
To salaries of clerk, surveyor and treasurer	62. 0. 0.
To printing, advertising and stationery	19. 17. 2.
To interest of debt	155. 5. 0.
To incidental charges.............................	47. 18. 2½
	1033. 10. 6½

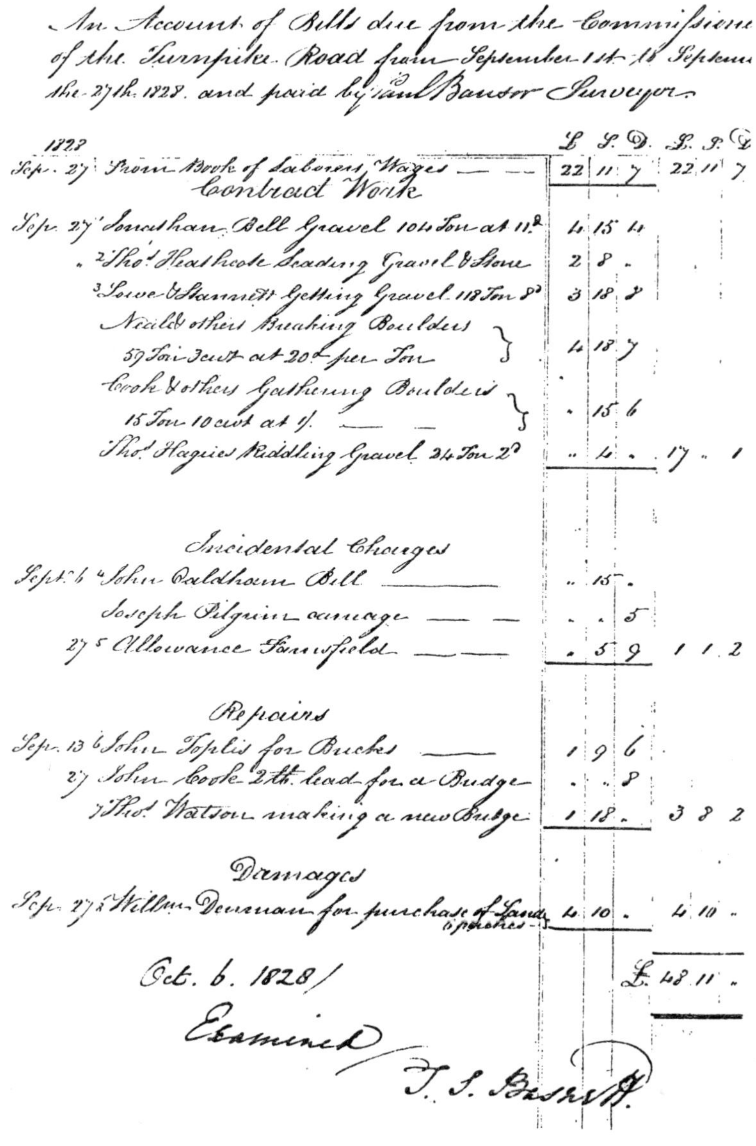

An Account of Bills due from the Commissioners
of the Turnpike Road from September 1st to September
the 27th 1828. and paid by Saml Bantoo Surveyor

1828		£	s	D	£	s	d
Sep. 27	From Book of Laborers Wages	22	11	7	22	11	7
	Contract Work						
Sep. 27	Jonathan Bell Gravel 104 Ton at 11d	4	15	4			
" 2	Thos Heathcote Leading Gravel & Stone	2	8	.			
3	Lowe & Hannett Getting Gravel 118 Ton 8d	3	18	8			
	Neald & others Breaking Boulders						
	59 Ton 3cwt at 20d per Ton	4	18	7			
	Cook & others Gathering Boulders						
	15 Ton 10 cwt at 1/	.	15	6			
	Thos Hagues Riddling Gravel 24 Ton 2d	..	4	.	17	..	1
	Incidental Charges						
Sept. 6	John Caldham Bill	..	15	.			
	Joseph Pilgrim carriage	.	.	5			
27	Allowance Farnsfield	.	5	9	1	1	2
	Repairs						
Sep. 13	John Toplis for Bricks	1	9	6			
27	John Cook 2th lead for a Bridge	.	.	8			
7	Thos Watson making a new Bridge	1	18	.	3	8	2
	Damages						
Sep. 27	Willm Denman for purchase of Land 6 perches	4	10	.	4	10	.
Oct. 6. 1828					£	48	11	.

Examined
J. S. Barrot

FIGURE 3.   Extract from accounts of Notts turnpike

As can be seen from this account, the biggest single item was of course the repair of the roads. In a report of the House of Commons in 1819 it was mentioned that the repair of the roads around London cost in the region of £470 per mile each year. But an issue of *The Times* for 1825 reported: 'Some remarkable facts appear on an examination of the Reports made to the House of Commons respecting the expense of Turnpike Roads. In Surrey, the most expensive county in the Kingdom, the expense of repairing the roads exceeds £149 per mile . . . in Sussex the expense is only £70 per mile; in Bucks £60; in Berks £47; in Hants £33; in Westmoreland £21 and in Gloucestershire £35.' On the other hand, it seems that some trusts adopted very primitive forms of repair. Not infrequently the ruts were filled up with stones, with little attempt at drainage. At other times the roads would be scraped to obtain a more even surface, and piles of mud would be left by the sides, with the result that the road level gradually sank, which, when combined with inadequate drainage, eventually made matters worse.

In undertaking repairs, a trust could either use their own labourers, or issue contracts. At different periods in its history the Exeter turnpike trust adopted both courses. Initially the trust used its own labour, and an entry in the minute book for 1753 recommends that 'John Firth be employed one day a week during the whole winter season at fifteen pence per day in order to keep the roads in repair'. The trust provided all the tools, and these, according to an inventory taken in the same year, included one hour-glass, five wedges, two rakes, twenty-one picks, three bars, eight wheelbarrows, one handbarrow and one spade. In later years the trust decided to issue a contract for the repair of the roads, based on a five and a half year period. The contract for 1816 demanded 'good durable stone, broken before laid down, at the pit or quarry where taken, so as not to exceed 2½ ins'. All loose stones and dirt, rubbish or other obstructions on the road had to be removed from time to time, and all wheel ruts had to be levelled 'and pits to be broken and widened before filled with fresh materials, and at the end of the time the road to be left in good repair to the satisfaction of the surveyor duly certified to the trustees'. Other stipulations in the contract demanded that all springs had to be drained off, all drains kept clear, and new ones made where necessary. Any damage done by the contractors in obtaining road materials from private grounds had to be paid for by them, and they had to pay a fair price for any materials that the trustees had already prepared for the roads. If the contractor failed to carry out these conditions, he had to forfeit 'five shillings for every day the same shall be afterwards neglected'.

In Derbyshire, John Farey in his book *A General View of the Agriculture of Derbyshire* quotes the contracts for the repair of the turnpike road from Chesterfield to Tideswell which, in 1808, was divided into eighteen sections, each 1½ to 4 miles in length. Particular quarries were named against each section, and details were given of the statute duty due for each. The contract demanded the use of the best-quality stones which had to be broken at the quarries and afterwards taken to the sides of the roads in single and equal loads. The quantity of stone had to be ascertained by the trust's surveyor 'who is to count the number of loads laid down, and to measure any one of them with two or four peck measure'. He also had to examine every load with a 2½ in ring gauge, and a deduction of ¼d was to be made for every stone which would not pass through it.

This system of contracting was not always successful, for many complaints are recorded in trustees' minute books about the failure of contractors to comply with the regulations, many having apparently no idea how to undertake the required repairs. In April 1817, for instance, the Exeter trustees, at a meeting of the General Road Committee, 'ordered that the surveyors do immediately communicate to the different contractors the absolute necessity of their collecting together very considerable quantities of materials for the future repair of the roads, and also to inform them that if a great deal of labour is not performed and much substantial repair done on all the roads before the next instalment becomes due the trustees will be recommended to withhold the payment of the said instalments'. The trustees of the Northgate turnpike roads, when appointing William Haviland in 1779 to keep the road from Horseferry bridge to the top of Birdlip and Crickley hills in 'good and sufficient repair' for the sum of £120, took the precaution of inserting a clause in the contract which demanded that he should leave 'as much stone upon the road at the expiration of the year for the use of the said road as was upon the road when he first undertook the repair'.

Some trusts also issued contracts for the supply of road materials. The Ross turnpike trust, for instance, signed a contract with Mr John Harris of Lydbrook in September 1838 for the supply of 400 tons of stone 'more or less at 10d per square yard at the quarry to be used on the road from Kerne Bridge to Bishops Wood'. A few years later, though, the same trust had trouble with one of their quarry contractors, for in January 1843 they decided at a meeting:

The surveyor having complained that the contractors Messrs Harris & Harrison did not supply the depots at Wilton, Glewstone and Kerne Bridge with limestone agreeably to his order under their contract—the clerk is directed to write them notice that if 1000 tons of limestone from their quarry at Lydbrook be not delivered at Wilton, 1000 tons at Kerne Bridge and 300 tons at Glewstone, by the 30th March next, the penalties of the contract will be enforced.

In undertaking their road repairs the turnpike trusts could call upon statute labour. Each year the parish surveyors would be called upon by the trusts to supply a list of the names of the people liable for this duty, giving the full annual value of their property, the rate of composition if any, the total amount liable in money, and the number of days duty work. The duties had to be performed according to the instructions of the trusts' surveyors, and at times that he appointed, the only exception being that labouring parishioners were not expected to perform their labour dues during harvest times.

As might be expected, this work was grudgingly performed, the appointed days often being regarded as holidays. In many instances orders had to be made to enforce the performance of the work. The surveyor of the Aylesbury–Hockliffe trust was ordered in January 1812 to write to the parish surveyor of Eggington instructing him to supply the list of people liable to statute duty, an order which was made all the more necessary as the road through the parish was described as being 'scarcely passable'. At a meeting of the trustees of the Bury to Thetford road in September 1805, the clerk was ordered 'to give notice to the surveyors of the several parishes if they did not immediately after harvest season complete the repairs of the road the parishes should be indicted'.

In some parts of the country the trusts gave financial grants to the parishes to help them to repair their sections of road. The Aylesbury–Hockliffe trust followed this practice, for in a letter dated 11 November 1815, it was explained to the parish surveyors that the trust would 'allow most money to that parish which had laid out most and had got its road in the best state of repair. As probably the same rule will be observed in a future division of the tolls, it will be much to the interest of your place to keep the road in the best possible state of repair, and I hope that you will accordingly give due attention to this letter'. Apparently not all parishes managed to qualify for the grant, as the surveyors of Hulcott and Bierton were told: 'Your road was in so very bad a state that the trustees would not at their last meeting order any part of the tolls to be paid to your parish.' Some parishes along the road of the Marehill–Southwater turnpike trust were even more troublesome, for in April of 1837 the trustees resolved not to lay out any more money on the roads within those parishes which had refused to perform statute labour, and the offending parishes were ordered to return all the materials that had been placed for their benefit along the roadsides.

There were stringent regulations governing the use of turnpike roads, made under the Acts 3 Geo IV c. 126 and 4 Geo IV c. 35. No buildings were to be erected within a distance of 30 ft from the centre of the road; any person causing damage to the surface faced a fine of 40s; and no iron bar, basket or any other object was permitted to project more than 30 in from the side of any horse. Any blacksmith having premises fronting the road had to have shutters fixed on the windows to prevent any light from shining on the road; and 'if any person shall make any fire or fires, commonly called bon-fires or shall set fire to or let off any squib, rocket, or other firework, within eighty feet of the centre of such road, or bait any bull, or play at football, cricket, or other game' he would be fined 40s. Cattle straying on the road were to be impounded by the surveyor, and not returned until a payment of 2s per animal plus keep had been made by the owners. No person was allowed to drive any cart or waggon if he or she was under thirteen years of age, and the name and place of abode of the owner of all such vehicles had to be placed on the sides.

In their work of improvement the trusts paid a good deal of attention to straightening and improving the course of their roads, as well as reducing slopes in very hilly areas. Sometimes these two improvements went hand in hand, as when the Yeovil trust signed an agreement with George Miller and William Pope 'to cut down and lower a certain hill called East Cross Hill in the parish of Haselbury Plucknett in the said county (in the line of the said turnpike road) and to raise the road at the foot of the said hill, on each side, so that the ascent between the bridge called Philps's bridge and the gate leading to Mr Henry Draper's house, shall not, at any point, exceed two inches in a yard—the cutting to be forty feet wide at the surface, gradually declining, so that the bottom of the said road, at the deepest cutting, shall be twenty two feet wide. The said George Miller and William Pope also agree to divert and alter the line of the said road over the adjoining waste . . . and to new form and stone the whole of such road in a substantial and workmanlike manner, the road to be made twenty two feet wide throughout and to be stoned one foot deep in the centre, gradually declining to nine inches at the sides—and the stones not to exceed in admeasurement two inches and a quarter either way'. An example of a road improvement in Derbyshire is shown in the plan shown in Fig 2.

Turnpike trusts were often faced with building and repairing bridges. The Maidstone–Tonbridge trust built a bridge at Hadlow Bourne in 1765 at a cost of £96, and in July 1791, the trustees of the Leadenham Hill to Mansfield & Southwell to Oxton roads:

> Ordered that a bridge be erected and built over the riverlet or dike called Bullivant Dike in the parish of Southwell for the passing of carriages, the estimate of which is given at £21 or thereabouts, and that two-thirds of the expense be paid out of the tolls arising upon the road, provided his grace the Archbishop of York as Lord of the Manor of Southwell (who is liable to the repairs of the present old bridge) pay the other third part of the said expense, and that such new bridge be repaired in future in the same proportions.

There is also evidence that some trusts gave grants to the county surveyors for the repair of bridges, even though the turnpike trusts had no direct responsibility for them.

Other road improvements of the period were undertaken in towns by corporations and Improvement Commissioners. An Act of 1786 gave the Corporation of Liverpool powers to widen the streets within the city. 'At that time,' wrote Thomas Baines in his *History of the Commerce and Town of Liverpool* (1852), 'there was not one wide or well constructed street in Liverpool . . . under the ample powers by this Act the Corporation set to work vigorously . . . the sum expended under the powers of the Act was £150,000.' At Bury, the Improvement Act of 1846 placed roads formerly under the control of turnpike trusts in the hands of the Commissioners, and henceforth the trustees were not permitted to collect any tolls upon the town sections of the road from Prestwich to Bury.

In Kent the work of the Sandwich Pavement Commissioners included street repairs, drainage, the control of nuisances, collection of refuse, and lighting the streets. A list of street repairs not exceeding £40 were listed in July 1831 as follows:

Moat Sole: The public pavement in front of Mr Gent's and Mr Baker's cottages to be relaid and flat stone to be placed to each of the cottage doors.

New Street: The pitchers at the entrance of Mr Drayson's garden to be removed and replaced with curb and flat pavement.

Chain:	The carriage road in front of Mr Burvil's to be repaired.
Fishers Street:	The carriage road to be repaired.
Strand Street:	The carriage road in front of Mr Spelt's to be repaired.
Hogs Corner:	The carriage road to be repaired.
Quay Lane:	The drain at the lower part of the lane to be an under drain with six inch earthen pipes.
Jail Street:	The foot pavement by the smith's forge to be relaid.
Kings Street:	The carriage road in sundry places to be relaid.
Delph Street:	The pavement at the watering Delph to be repaired and the carriage road in sundry places.
Church Street:	The carriage road to be repaired.

In October 1831 the Commissioners entered into a contract with Mr George Rigden for lighting the streets. Under it, Rigden undertook 'to supply the necessary quantity of oil and labour for the lighting of ninety lamps at the rate of fourteen shillings for each lamp. The lamps to be lighted each evening at sun-set, and to continue burning untill three o'clock in the morning, omitting four nights before and the night of the full moon'.

At Ipswich in Suffolk, the Commissioners for lighting and paving the town had to decide in 1830 between macadamising or repairing the street leading from the Falcon Inn, in St Nicholas, to Stoke bridge. 'From the report of the committee appointed to make enquiry and ascertain the comparative expenses,' reported *The Suffolk Chronicle* for 17 April, 'it appeared that to macadamize the proposed line of street would cost £202, and to repair it only £112. The report also stated, that the annual expense of keeping in repair the streets which are macadamized exceeds that of the paved streets by 15–20 per cent, according to favourable or unfavourable circumstances.' After a good deal of discussion the Commissioners eventually decided on macadamising.

On occasions the turnpike trusts assisted Town Commissioners in repairing the roads in or near towns. In August 1840, the Improvement Commissioners of Exeter sought the Exeter turnpike trust's help in making 'the new line of road from the city gaol to join the New North road near the end of Pound Lane'. In asking for a contribution towards the £2,300 cost, the Commissioners hoped that the trustees would 'consider the intended new road so important an improvement to the district of turnpike roads under their charge as to induce them to look upon the work as a joint undertaking'. They agreed.

In 1833 the trustees of the Yeovil turnpike road agreed to contribute £400 to assist the Commissioners of the Yeovil Improvement Act 'in the widening of Middle Street in the town of Yeovil being the great western thoroughfare and the Mail Coach road from London to Devonport and which intersects the line of the Yeovil turnpike'. The improvement involved taking down 'the projecting houses in Middle Street belonging to Mr. Upton, Mr. Barnicott and others and Ew. Daniell's shop and warehouse for the purpose of widening the road'.

It is interesting to note that the parking of vehicles did not go unnoticed by Town Commissioners. An announcement in *The Brighton Herald* for 19 February 1842, inserted by the clerk of the Commissioners for the town, warned residents and visitors 'that if any carriage shall be suffered to stand in any of the streets for a longer period than shall be necessary for taking up or setting down any persons riding therein, the person driving such carriage is liable to a penalty of £5'—an impressive fine, even by modern standards!

As a result of the improvement made between 1750 and 1850, there is no doubt that the roads generally were in a very much better state at the end of the period. The trusts were, however, often criticised. Many surveyors, lacking previous experience and not backed up by knowledge on the part of the trustees, had little idea of how to go about improving their roads. Others, competent enough, were not allowed enough money to keep them satisfactorily repaired. Many trusts, finding themselves pressed for money, allowed their surveyors a given amount of money per mile of road, without providing, for instance, for additional repairs necessary after a bad winter; others limited the number of labourers who could be employed. Such policies often led to deterioration.

Many trusts got into financial difficulties, having borrowed money without any real idea of the income that they were likely to receive. The outcome was that numerous trusts found that they were unable even to pay interest on the borrowed capital. This happened to the trustees of the Gander Lane–Sheffield–Clown road, for at a meeting in December 1788 they resolved:

That it is the opinion of the trustees present that it will be proper at the next meeting to take into consideration the propriety of reducing the rate of interest payable to the several subscribers in respect of their subscription money, it appearing that the amount of tolls arising at the several bars is not likely to be sufficient at present to pay interest after the rate of £5 per cent per annum.

After looking at the sorry state of the trust's funds in February 1817, the General Road Committee of the Exeter turnpike trust made the following recommendation:

> . . . in the opinion of this Committee the Commissioners of the Exeter turnpike roads cannot consistently with the principle and spirit of the late Act undertake any proposal for new roads or alterations in the line of roads however desirable in themselves, beyond the maintaining in perfect repair the present roads until the Treasurer reports that the debt of the Trust is materially reduced.

Yet another example is provided by the Elton and Blackburn Trust, established in 1810. The loans raised by the trust between 1810–16 amounted to £14,830, and during the next twenty years the figure rose to £22,545. In 1859 this amount was still outstanding, in addition to £12,635 owed in unpaid interest.

Dishonesty was another difficulty. *The Edinburgh Review* in October 1819 commented on the manner in which some trusts abused their powers: 'They may suffer their road to become a perfect ruin; they may embezzle funds and commit every sort of malpractice, and yet go on levying tolls, keeping possession of the road and defying all complaints.' Parliament was probably partly to blame for this state of affairs, in not having arranged for stricter control on the activities of the trusts. These financial difficulties were further aggravated by the abolition of statute labour in 1835, estimated by Macadam to have cost the turnpike trusts in England and Wales about £200,000, and the introduction of railways, a factor which will be examined in the final chapter.

Macadam considered that the greatest evil of the turnpike system was 'the number of trusts, their small extent, and their limited means and powers'. He thought amalgamation the only way to overcome these difficulties, and when he became surveyor general of the Metropolis turnpike roads he recommended that the trusts around London should be consolidated under a single Board of Commissioners. This, he maintained, would have the advantage of reducing expenses and making greater funds available for road repairs. In 1826 such a consolidation was carried out on fourteen roads north of the Thames: it resulted in fewer toll-gates, and central administration by a Board of Commissioners who appointed an able engineer in place of many former sinecures. In the Second Report of the Lords Committee on Turnpike Returns, 1833, praise was given to this consolidation, and it was recommended that similar amalgamations should take place wherever possible. Unfortunately, the good work done in north London was not repeated elsewhere, except in three instances in Wales and Scotland.

The fact that there was no national scheme for the development of the roads was another criticism of the turnpike system. More often than not neighbouring trusts regarded each other as rivals, and lack of co-operation brought considerable difficulties. Each trust, covering only a limited section of road, was usually more concerned with its own activities than with any policy to provide a national network of roads. There were, however, exceptions to this isolationist viewpoint. In January 1829, for example, the trustees of the Yeovil road co-operated with those of the Crew-kerne trust in forming a new line of road from Haselbury to Crewkerne 'in order to avoid the narrow and hilly road upon the existing line'. With their limited funds, the Yeovil trust agreed to 'advance £1,000 in furtherance of the object in view, and to take upon themselves, as part of the Yeovil district, the future management and repair of so much of the new line, from the proposed deviation at or near Hasselbury Cross, as can be completed for that sum, the trustees of the Crewkerne district taking up the line at the point to which that expenditure will carry the Yeovil trust (which is to be considered as the future boundary of the two districts) and continuing the remainder of the line at their own expence and bearing all incidental charges'.

It has to be remembered that turnpikes formed only about 20 per cent of the total road mileage: in 1838 it was estimated that there were 104,770 miles of public roads, 22,000 miles being turn-pikes, involving 1,116 trusts, 7,796 toll-gates and bars, and 20,000 collectors in addition to the 3,555 treasurers, clerks and surveyors who annually collected £1,458,000. Many out of the way rural areas were completely untouched by turnpikes, and very little attempt was made to improve their roads during the period, despite the requirements of farmers who needed to supply large quantities of food to the expanding towns. Alderman J. J. Mechi of Tiptree Hall in Essex, noted for his farming improvements, complained in 1850 that 'it is impossible not to be struck with the present gross mismanagement of our cross-country roads'. He pointed out that surveyors had apparently forgotten that signposts were meant to guide the wandering stranger. 'Next,' he went on to explain, 'one sees the roads concave instead of convex, having high shoulders covered with grass and which effectively retain the water in the road, much to its injury . . . Depend upon it, these neglects touch the farmers' pockets, for in roads, as in other matters, a stitch in time saves nine; many an old waggon and cart would crack on for years, but for the jogs, jounces and staunces of our mismanaged cross-roads, the wheel-wright's best friends.'

Many other complaints were being made in the mid-nineteenth century about the condition of the roads. A letter in *The Suffolk Chronicle* for 23 December 1848 complained bitterly about the state of those in Haughley:

> Any man desirous of trying his patience or the strength of his shoe leather, or of ascertaining the quantity of soil which he can carry home with him, after half an hour's walk, has nothing to do but stroll through a few of the highways (the fewer the better) of Haughley, and he may be sure of exhausting the first, of testing the second, and of bearing home with him . . . sufficient manure for a cabbage garden.

Nevertheless, although much still remained to be done, the turn-pike trusts undoubtedly helped to provide long stretches of reasonable roads, and it was largely through their efforts that the coaching companies were able to offer improved time schedules.

CHAPTER 3

The Carriage of Goods

A LONDON carrier's advertisement of the eighteenth century, offering to carry goods to Chester and forward them to all parts of North Wales, read as follows:

> CHESTER ORIGINAL FLYING WAGGON, in five days to the Blossom's Inn, Chester, sets out every Saturday in the afternoon, at six o'clock, and arrives at Chester early every Friday morning.

This 'flying waggon' service, seldom averaging a speed of more than two or three miles per hour, was nevertheless an improvement on pack-horse days, for it was reckoned that one waggon could do the work of five pack-horses.

The stage waggons, or wains as they were sometimes called, appeared on the road in the sixteenth century, and during the following centuries their numbers showed a considerable increase. These early waggons were clumsy, cumbersome vehicles (see Plate 4), pulled by a team of four, six or even eight horses, and driven by the waggoner riding or walking alongside them. A canvas hood kept the goods dry, as well as the passengers who were carried from time to time, those poorer people who could not afford the fares of the stage or mail coaches.

As the number of waggons rose, Parliament became increasingly concerned about the damage they were doing to the roads. The prevailing view was that the narrow-rimmed wheels some waggons had broke up the road surface, undoing much of the good work the turnpike trusts had done. According to one eighteenth-century report, narrow-rimmed wheels were 'found to render all prevailing laws for improving the roads ineffectual; some had already become impassable, and all were growing every day worse, notwithstanding the perpetual expense of levelling and repair'.

In 1753, therefore, came an Act for 'the Amendment and Preservation of the Public Highways and Turnpike Roads of the Kingdom and for the more Effectual Execution of the Laws Re-

lating thereto'. Its main purpose was to find 'a speedy remedy to
prevent the roads of the kingdom being ruined by the excessive
weights and burdens loaded in and carried on wheeled transport
with the small breadth and dimensions of the fellies of the wheels
of such waggons and other carriages respectively'. It was laid
down that waggon wheels should not be less than 9 in wide from
side to side; a penalty of £5 or the confiscation of one of the horses
and bridles being imposed on offending owners. Modifications
were made to the Act in 1755, when it was ruled that waggons
with 9 in wheels would be exempt from toll for a period of three
years. Those with 6 in wheels were restricted to six horses, and
6 in wheeled carts to four horses, and were entitled to reduced
tolls. To compensate for any loss of revenue, turnpike trustees
were permitted to charge higher tolls for waggons with narrow
wheels. Further changes were made in the Turnpike Act of 1773,
and as late as 1822 the subject was still the concern of Parliament,
for an Act of that year decreed that waggons or carts having
wheels of less breadth than 3 in were to be banned from all turnpike roads. This Act was, however, repealed in the following year
because of a great outcry from farmers. Throughout all this complicated legislation the general principle remained, that owners of
broad-wheeled waggons were to be charged lower tolls than users
of narrow-rimmed vehicles. The various Acts also restricted the
number of horses that could be used in different-sized waggons,
the idea being to limit the carrying of excessive loads.

As might be expected, these restrictions brought numerous
complaints from the carriers, who complained that the legislation
would involve them in additional expense, as well as leading to
all manner of delays. In August 1754, *The Gentleman's Magazine*
mentioned the unhappy plight of the modified Yorkshire waggon
which 'on Saturday last, July 27th, was more than an hour in
turning in the gate of the White Bear Inn, in Basinghall Street, and
at last received considerable damage'. A few years later, a petition
was submitted to the House of Commons from the High Sheriff
and Grand Jury of the Worcester assizes, in which they made the
following plea:

. . . your petitioners perceiving by the printed notes of this
Honourable House that a Bill is ordered into Parliament for pre-
serving and amending the turnpike roads by enforcing the use of
broad wheel waggons, beg leave humbly to represent that broad
wheels, with the excessive weights they are permitted to carry,
have on experience been found very destructive to the turnpike
roads in general of this county, and in a great measure unpracti-

E

cable to the by-roads, and the small number of horses allowed by narrow wheeled carriages very inconvenient and distressing to your petitioners and their tenants in the carrying on of their farming business.

There were many instances of evasion and disregard for these laws. Ingenious wheelwrights managed to circumvent the legislation by placing narrow outer bands around the wheels, so that only a small section of the broad wheel came into contact with the road surface, thereby making the passage easier. In other cases carriers tried to fool the toll-gate keepers by unhooking some of the horses before they arrived at the gates, though they were usually detected in these malpractices.

In the carrying trade, a distinction must be made between the long-distance carrier and the short-distance operator who served a town and its immediate neighbourhood. The firm of Pickford's, which can trace its history back to 1649 when pack-horses, each carrying up to 700 lb in panniers, were used in the north-western counties, provides a good example of the long-distance carrier. During the second half of the eighteenth century, Mat Pickford advertised in *Prescott's Manchester Journal* that his flying waggon would perform the journey from Manchester to London in four and a half days.

During the first half of the nineteenth century Pickford's were running a waggon service between Manchester and Sheffield, a quoted distance of 41 miles, and records kept by the British Railways Board in London give a clear picture of the expenses that were incurred. The accounts covering the year 1835 give details of the various stations and the expenses associated with each. At Sheffield the weekly wages of the horsekeepers amounted to 46s, and the rent for a stable and two lofts was quoted at £40 per annum. Contracts were made with a blacksmith for shoeing the horses, fourteen in all, at the rate of 2s 9d per horse per month for nine months, and 4s 6d per horse for each of the remaining months.

The first stop on the way from Sheffield was Castleton, some 16 miles away, for reaching which eight hours was allowed. Here the weekly wages amounted to 35s for the two horsekeepers and a lad; and the yearly rent to £18 12s od, a sum which included straw. The next stop, Bullock Smithy, was 16 miles away, where two horsekeepers between them received 32s a week; while the rent for the year came to £11. At Manchester the records state that 'each waggoner has charge of his own horses'. Four waggoners were employed for the journeys between Sheffield and

Castleton; another four between Castleton and Bullock Smithy; and two between Bullock Smithy and Manchester, all being hired at 25s a week. The waggons themselves were hired from J. Laycock of Sheffield, who charged 3d per double mile.

The run between Sheffield and Manchester involved passing through a number of turnpike gates, and the charges for these were given on 29 September 1835 as:

Hunter's Bar	4d per horse each time of passing			
Stoney Ridge	4d	,,	,,	,,
,, Bridge	4d	,,	,,	,,
Booth's Bar	2d	,,	,,	,,
Flatt do.	4d	,,	,,	,,
Slack Hall	4d	,,	,,	,,

Say 22s. 0 per day or £6. 12s. 0d per week

Whaley Bridge for waggon		£1. 11s 6d
Stockport Moor	1s 9d	
Heaton Norris	10½d	
Rushton	10½d	4 horses each time of
Longsight	10½d	passing £2. 12s 6d.

Toll for one waggon per week = £10. 16s 0d

× 2

£21. 12. 0

or £1,123. 4s. 0d per annum

When all the expenses for the year were totalled, the following figures were arrived at:

	£.	s.	d.
Waggoners' wages ...	650.	0.	0.
Horsekeepers	293.	16.	0.
Mileage of waggons	319.	16.	0.
Rent	69.	12.	0.
Tolls	1123.	4.	0.

The number of horses used were given as:

4 teams of 7 horses each to and from Sheffield and Castleton	28
4 teams of 7 horses to and from Castleton and Bullock Smithy	28
2 teams of 4 horses to and from Bullock Smithy and Manchester	8
Castleton hill	2
Total	66

N.B. 6 horses are at work, the 7th at rest.

On the revenue side of their accounts the carriers were re-stricted as to the amount that they could charge. Carriage rates were fixed by the Justices of the Peace at Quarter Sessions, as a consequence of recommendations made by a Committee set up by the House of Commons in October 1691 to consider the former laws 'for Enlarging and Amending of Highways'. This system of rate-fixing continued until about 1827, each county deciding on its own rates without reference to adjoining or other counties. The rates fixed were the maximum that could be charged, but it would appear that competition between carriers, as well as from canals, exerted a greater influence on the level of charges than the fixed rates.

The Act of 1692 directed that the fixing of carriers' rates had become necessary because 'diverse waggoners and other carriers by combination amongst themselves have raised the prices of carriage in goods in many places to excessive rates to the great injury of trade'. However, despite the apparent urgency to limit the charges, many counties were slow to adopt the Act. Rates were fixed at the Quarter Sessions for Somerset in the spring of 1756, when the following statement was made:

> This court taking notice of the great imposition made by carriers of goods in this county doth in order to rectify the same direct the price for carrying thereof;—for the carriage of every hundred weight of goods brought by any carrier or waggoner from the City of London or Westminster to the city of Bath or town of Frome, five shillings, and for every twenty miles beyond Bath or Frome one shilling more. From London or Westminster to the town of Wincanton, six shillings, ditto one shilling more. From London or Westminster to Milborne, five shillings and sixpence, ditto, one shilling more.

Staffordshire made its first assessment in 1781, and two years later the Justices for Leicestershire decided on the following rates:

From London—	*for every cwt*	
To the Borough of Leicester	5s 0d and no more	
To Market Harborough	4s 0d	,,
To Lutterworth	4s 0d	,,
To Mountsorrel	5s 0d	,,
To Loughborough	5s 0d	,,
To Hinckley	4s 6d	,,
To Ashby-de-la-Zouch	5s 6d	,,
Market Bosworth	5s 0d	,,
Melton Mowbray	5s 0d	,,

These rates were fixed for the period between 25 March and 29

September. During the winter an extra 6d would be allowed on all rates. The same was true in Derbyshire, where the magistrates, in fixing the rates in 1808, permitted higher rates to be charged between Michaelmas and Lady Day.

Carriers sometimes applied to the magistrates for a review of rates; in January 1800 the magistrates in the West Riding of Yorkshire had many applications from carriers in the area asking for higher rates to be allowed. They decided 'to make a further advance upon land carriage, on account of the very high price of hay and corn, and it being our opinion that an advance is reasonable and proper, do hereby signify our approbation and consent to an advance of three halfpence per stone on land carriage from the date hereof until the next General Quarter Sessions of the Peace'.

Local newspapers sometimes gave details of the actual prices that were charged by the carriers, as in the instance of *The Ipswich Journal* for 22 April 1758, in which an advertisement appeared from carriers operating a service between London and Yarmouth. The prices were:

Grocery goods of all kinds @ 8s od per ton.
Weighable linens @ 12s od per ton
Hops @ 3s od per bag.
Cheese 10s od per ton.
Allum and copperas 4s od per hhd.
Spirits 5s od per pipe, or 10s od per ton.
Puncheon of rum and all other puncheons 4s od
Barrels of porter 1s 6d and all other porter casks in proportion.
All kinds of salters goods 10s od per ton.
Wool of all sorts 8s od per ton, except young fustick
Barrels of Orchell 8d per barrel.
Aquasortis @ 2s 6d a bottle.
Chests of oranges and lemons and sacks of nuts 1s od each.
Earthenware 4s od per hhd.
Square crates 2s od and crates 1s 6d each.
Trusses of woollen drapery according to their sizes
Bales and butts of leather 1s od per cwt.

In his book, *General View of the Agriculture of Derbyshire* (1817), John Farey mentioned that the average price of carrying ore in 1808 appeared to be 1s per ton per mile. On a yearly contract basis the carriage of coal in the Chesterfield area was 4s 9d per ton, the pits being 3¼ miles distant, the draught nearly all uphill and a toll of 4½d per horse in summer and 6¾d in winter, each time of passing, laden or unladen, was payable by the carter.

Two different carriers gave notice in *The York Courant* for 31

October 1808 of their intention to raise prices. Anthony Welsh, who ran the York, Leeds and Manchester daily waggon, advised 'the merchants and the public in general that owing to the high prices of horse provender etc., he is obliged to advance the rates of carriage to and from York to Leeds to threepence per stone, and to and from York to Manchester to eightpence per stone, which will take place on the 1st of November next'. The other carrier, John Hartly, who ran similar services, raised his prices to the same level, because of 'the long continued high price of horse keeping and the increased price of toll bars, etc'. Robert Russell, who ran services from Exeter to London, had to make a similar advance in his charges in 1799: 'the increased Price of Horse Provender compels me to make a small advance in the Present Rate of Carriage, from the 1st of November next, from Exeter to Plymouth and Tavistock, 4d per cwt. From Exeter to Falmouth and all towns my waggons pass through in Cornwall—also from London to Andover, Blandford, Dorchester, Bridport, Charmouth, Axminster, Honiton and Exeter, 1s. 0d. per cwt. And the like from these places to London. This advance will not repay one-eighth the increased price of hay and corn'.

The Pickford records also give an indication of the rates of carriage that were charged, as some of the selections listed below show (c 1830):

Radford to Liverpool   *Per ton*

Flour sacks or casks, grain in bags, meal, nails, vinegar or such like. Goods not very bulky or hazardous...	24s	0d
Ashes, hardware, seeds	27s	0d
Bark in bags, yarn	29s	0d
Empties	30s	0d
Cheese, long wt., cotton, hops, leather, paper, wine, wool..	31s	0d
Furniture, gentlemens' goods	55s	0d.

Radford from London

Cast iron pipes, goods heavy, molasses, sugar, soap, tallow, vinegar and such like goods not very bulky or hazardous, marble.....................................	50s	0d
Empties	55s	0d
Drapery, drugs, hops, leather, in trusses, seeds, spirits, stationery, tea, wine	60s	0d.
Gentlemens' goods..	80s	0d
Glass plate, hats	130s	0d
Gunpowder	160s	0d

Radford from Manchester
Bones loose, tobacco leaf 23s   0d
Ale, bones in hhds,* copperas, empty bottles for
   soda or blacking, flour sacks or casks, grain in
   bags, grease, hides wet, log wood in bags, manga-
   nese, nails, plaster, prepared pitch, porter, tallow,
   tar, vinegar 24s   0d

* Hogsheads.

Not infrequently carriers conveyed baggage and equipment for
the army, when the Justices fixed rates. At the Ipswich Quarter
Sessions held in January 1812, the Justices 'having regard to the
present price of hay and oats, do fix the following additional rates
or allowances to persons providing waggons for the conveyance
of His Majesty's forces, in day marches, or for their arms, or
accoutrements, to be paid by the officer or officers demanding the
same, viz: 4d per mile for every waggon with five horses or any
wain with six oxen, or four oxen and two horses, and 3d per mile
for every cart with four horses or carrying not less than 15 cwt,
and 2d per mile for every cart with less than four horses and not
carrying 15cwt'.

The loads that the waggons carried determined the amount of
money that a carrier could earn. Loads carried by a Hereford
carrier are detailed in a freight book at the Hereford City library.
The book, which gives the goods carried in waggons and by
barges, is entitled: 'Freight of Goods from Liverpool to Bristol by
Liverpool & Bristol Company smacks regular traders,' and is
catalogued by the Library: 'Carrier's account book for freight in
barges and wagons travelling to and from Hereford.' The book
covers the years 1826–7, and by the end of the period five barges
were operated by the company, and fewer waggons were being
used. Barges carried about 12 tons, while the loading of the waggons was given, as the following selections from the entries show,
as:

May 20, 1826.
By William Preece's waggon to Hereford:

	Cwts	Qrs	Lbs
1 barrel of oil	5	0	21
1 barrel of whiting	22	1	14
1 barrel of whiting	14	0	14
1 sheet of lead	9	1	21
1 sheet of lead	7	1	5
1 bottle of oil	6	0	0
	64	1	19

29 June 1826
By Joseph Griffith's waggon to Hereford:

	Cwts	Qrs	Lbs
1 large chest			
1 safe			
1 square table	13	0	26
1 secretary's bookcase			
with two beds and sundries enclosed			
2 packages and 1 coyle	3	3	0
22 cheese	3	3	7
2 bottles oil	5	1	0
1 bottle tar	6	2	7
1 hogshead sugar	15	1	16
	48	0	0

4 September 1826
By William Preece's waggon to Hereford

	cwts	Qrs	lbs
7 iron arms	1	3	7
2 barrels	7	2	14
1 bottle	2	1	21
1 box	1	0	14
2 pumps	1	1	21
1 pipe tallow	10	0	0
4 stooks oats	7	2	0
1 bottle whiting	8	1	0
1 bottle whiting	12	0	14
3 stooks oats	5	2	14
	57	3	21

Other items carried in the waggons ranged from hat boxes, starch, bacon, pitch, dyes, baskets of stones, sugar, molasses, glue, spades, glass, vinegar, wood and numerous types of cases. Apparently the usual charge was 1s per cwt, for a load carried in Norman's cart to Hereford on 24 May 1826, weighing 19 cwt 1 qr 1 lb was charged 19s; the load including various bottles, sheets of lead, a bag of dye, chests of soap, and two baskets of stones.

The returns for the Shenfield turnpike gate, made out in the late 1830s, of traffic passing through the gate also give an indication of waggon loadings:

Broad wheel waggons passing through the Shenfield toll-gate, 26 February 1838 (a Monday):

No.	No. of horses pulling	Whence and where going	How laden	Weight (tons)
1	4	Chelmsford to London	Flour	
1	5	Coggeshall to London	Boiler	5
1	5	Chelmsford to London	Wool etc	
1	4	Felsted to London	Flour	2¼
1	7	Broomfield to London	Flour	5
1	4	Cressing to London	Flour	2
1	3	Springfield to London	Flour	1½
1	5	Brockdish to London	General goods	2
1	3	Springfield to London	Flour	1½
1	7	Halesworth to London (+ 4 wheel carriage behind)	General goods	4
1	7	Woodbridge to London	General goods	4
1	3	Clare to London	General goods	4
1	5	Bury to London	General goods	4

All these entries indicate that the traffic was essentially one way—from various towns in Essex and Suffolk to London. On the following Sunday, however, the traffic was mainly in the other direction:

Broad-wheeled waggons going through gate on 4 March 1838

No.	No. horses	Whence and where going	How laden	Weight (tons)
1	6	London to Colchester	General goods	4
1	7	London to Bury	General goods	4
1	6	London to Colchester	General goods	4
1	5	London to Witham	General goods	3
1	6	London to Hadleigh	General goods	4
1	6	London to Clare	General goods	4
1	8	London to Eye	General goods	4
1	5	London to Hadleigh	General goods	4
1	6	London to Brockdish	General goods	5
1	8	London to Halesworth	General goods	6
1	6	London to Cavendish	General goods	5
1	8	London to Halesworth	General goods	4
1	8	London to Halstead	General goods	5
1	6	London to Colchester	General goods	3
1	6	London to Witham	General goods	3½
1	6	London to Norwich and Bury	General goods	5
1	6	London to Braintree	General goods	4
1	4	London to Colchester	General goods	4
1	7	London to Bury	General goods	5
1	5	London to Bury	General goods	3

No.	No. horses	Whence and where going	How laden	Weight (tons)
1	6	London to Norwich and Bury	General goods	4½
1	6	Norwich and Bury to London	General goods	6

The Shenfield records also show that there was a good deal of competition among the carriers in East Anglia. In the return for 26 February 1825 several are listed from each town. Colchester, for example, had the firm of Blyth, as well as Smith, while Chelmsford had the firms of Davey, Johns, and Whipps, all of whom served the London market. Ipswich carriers passed through both towns, and this would add a further element of competition.

In the northern industrial districts, an indication of the number of carriers is given in *The Manchester Guide*, a brief historical description of the towns of Manchester and Salford, printed and sold by Joseph Aston in 1804. In Manchester, according to this, there were 120 land carriers, conveying goods to all parts of the kingdom. The guide also mentions that there were more horse waggons and carts used in Lancashire than in any other part of the country. Twenty years later, Pigot & Dean's Directory of Manchester listed 94 carriers in the city, most of them being one-man businesses based at inns.

Few records survive of the short-distance carriers, the men who ran services between towns and their immediate neighbourhood. At the Record Office at Kendal, however, there are the day books of Walter Berry, who operated services in and around Kendal, as well as carrying items to and from Arnside. Some of his entries are given below:

October 24, 1838

		s	d
To			
15 barrels of flour to Kendal and 5 to Milnthorpe from board *Windermere**		11.	8.
To			
1 barrel of herring to Kendal and 5 to Milnthorpe from ditto		1.	o
to			
5 bags and 10 of sugar from board *Windermere* (22. 1. 6 @ 4½d)		8.	o.
John Ireland, Kendal			
To			
2 casks of wine from board *Windermere*, 82 gallons @ 1d		6.	10.

* This probably refers to craft at Arnside.

1 cask of cream tartar from board ditto ....   2.   11.
1 cask of tin from board ditto ....   1.   5.
11 bags of wool from board ditto, 19. 2. 14 @ 5d   8.   1.
   Robert Dixon, Kendal
To   s   d
1 bag of pepper from board *Windermere* ....   3.
2 hhds of sugar from board ditto, 32. 2. 16 ......   12.   3.
   (other items follow)
23 August 1847
Mrs Lough, Milnthorpe
To 3 carts of furniture to the railway station ...   10.   0.
Messrs Taylor & Briggs, Milnthorpe
To 15 bundles of sack and 3 bundles of wool
   sheets ....   2.   1.
Robert Fryers, Milnthorpe
To 40 fire bricks, 618 & 70 common bricks @ 10d   7.   6.
John Wilson, Kendal
To 2 casks of spirits from Kendal to Arnside ...   2.   6.
August 24, 1847
Robert Brocklebank
To 10 carts of stones carting from Haverbrick
   Bank to Milnthorpe ....   10.   0.
August 25, 1847
Mr George Clegg, Leeds.
To 247 bags of wool @ 11s 6d per 16½ lbs ...... £8.   12.   0.

The carriers' services were slow, however well organised, seldom exceeding a speed of 4 mph with their broad-wheeled, heavy,
canvas-topped waggons. Some idea of the times taken for various
journeys is given in the following table showing services to
London from different parts of the country:

Date	Name of carrier	To London from:	Time
1793	William Nash	Lutterworth	Every Saturday morning early and will arrive at the Windmill Inn, St John's Street, London, 10 o'clock on Tuesday morning
1787	Royle	Mansfield–Worksop–Nottingham–Leicester	Sets out from the warehouse in Mansfield every Monday & Friday morning and arrives at Ox Inn, London, every Wednesday & Saturday morning at 6 o'clock
1786	W. Wheatley	Swan Inn, Maidstone	Leaves: Every Monday morning at 7 o'clock to

Date	Name of carrier	To London from:	Time
			White Hart Inn in the Borough, arrives 6 o'clock every Tuesday morning
1789	Thomas Sherratt	Birmingham	Time taken = 50 hours, loads every Saturday night and Wednesday at 2 p.m.
1803	Snells, Slyfield & Co.	Paul St, Exeter	Time taken for journey 4 days

Notices of the sale of carriers' businesses sometimes give details of the extent of their operations. In a sale notice in *The Leicester Journal* for 6 September 1793, Robert Clarke of Leicester explained that he had carried on 'the extensive business of a carrier between Sheffield and London with great success', but had decided to retire from business. His stock in trade included fourteen 9 in wheeled waggons, and two with narrow wheels, together with 136 'capital seasoned horses all in full work, with what appertains to the business of a carrier'. The purchaser was given the assurance that he would 'be accommodated with capital warehouses and stabling belonging to Mr Clarke both at Sheffield and Leicester, and all other concerns upon the road, now used by Mr Clarke, and may likewise be accommodated with any reasonable part of the purchase money, upon a fair security'.

In the same newspaper a few months later, there was another opportunity to enter the carrying business when two waggons, formerly in the possession of John Walker of Loughborough, were offered for sale. One was a 6 in wheeled waggon, complete with six able horses and harness complete, and the other a narrow-wheeled waggon with five horses and gearing complete, both having been in 'full employ' running from Cavendish bridge to Leicester and Loughborough wharf to Leicester respectively.

In *The York Courant* for 2 January 1750, Mr Zachariah Murthwaite's business in Darlington was advertised for sale. The stock comprised 'two new covered stage waggons, and also twelve good waggon horses, with all manner of trappings, gears or harness . . . used in the carriage of goods between Newcastle-upon-Tyne and the city of York'. The advertisement added the following note: 'Whoever buys the said waggons and horses may immediately enter upon a good accustomed carriage, between the places above and will meet with encouragement.'

This 'encouragement' is mentioned in many of the sale notices; the would-be purchasers invariably being told that they were entering upon a lucrative business, as in the instance of the advertisement relating to the sale of Thomas Stevens's business as Colchester to London carrier. In an announcement in *The Ipswich Journal* for 15 March 1766, the public were told that he had 'got a very good fortune, besides bringing up and educating a large family in a handsome mansion: so, with care and industry, there is a manifest prospect for any other person, so qualified, not only to get a maintenance, but a good deal of money'.

In similar vein in the same newspaper was the announcement of the sale of Hazel's Old Established waggon, conveying goods from London to Chelmsford, Braintree, Sudbury, Bury St Edmunds, Ixworth, Stanton, Palgrave, Diss, Scole, Harleston and Beccles. 'The above concern needs no comment,' read the advertisement, 'but assuredly offers such an opportunity as is scarcely to be met with, replete with every convenience and in full trade.'

In many parts of the country the carriers came up against canal competition, and in the early stages of the development of waterways the road carriers feared, quite understandably, that they would lose a large part of their trade. The canal promoters, for their part, always tried to show that they could carry goods at much lower prices. Some idea of the comparable charges is given by an entry in *The Leicester Journal* for 14 December 1792 which read:

Ashby-de-la-Zouch intended canal. Costs of tonnage and freight of a waggon load of coals from Ashby Woulds of 50 cwt to be delivered at the intended wharfs at the under-mentioned places, at the rate of 2d per ton mile.

	miles by canal	Cost by canal		Cost by land	
		s.	d.	s.	d.
Donisthorpe	1½		7½	3	6
Measham	4¾	1	11¾	5	6
Snarestone	8	3	4	9	0
Shackestone	11	4	7	12	0
Carlton Brook	13½	5	7½	14	0
Wilsbro' Lane					
below Market Bosworth	14¼	5	11½	16	0
Cordley Furze					
in Sutton Cheney Field	17	7	1	18	0
Dadlington	20	8	4	20	0
Stoke Goldney	21	8	9	21	0
Road nr Higham	23	9	7	22	0
Turnpike Rd.					
between Hinckley					

	miles by canal	Cost by canal		Cost by land	
& Atherstone	24½	10	2½	24	0
St. Road	25½	10	7½	25	0
Burton Hastings	27	11	3	26	0
Coventry canal nr. Griff	30½	12	8½	31	6

The promoters of the proposed canal from Burton-upon-Trent to Fradley Heath pointed out in October 1792:

The public will derive great advantage, particularly in the article of lime, for by the intended navigation, it will be conveyed at least five shillings a waggon load cheaper than it is at present and will also be communicated to many places which cannot now have the benefit of it by reason of the great expense attending the land carriage thereof.

This claim was primarily intended for the farmers, but similar appeals were made to manufacturers, as the following extract from a letter written from Welshpool in October 1792 suggests:

The intended navigation from Berriew through this part, to join the Shropshire navigation from the Severn to the Mersey, is expected to answer nearly equal to any navigation in the kingdom. The extensive manufacturers in the flannel and Welsh woollen cloth carried on in this county will be much benefited by the reduction in the price of carriage which has been very high for some years past. Montgomeryshire, being a very rich and fertile county, will be still more productive by the reduction in the carriage of lime for manure; and coal (now a very dear article) will be reduced by one third, if not half in price, by this intended navigation.

A further argument in this series of advertisements in the pages of *The Leicester Journal* was that navigable canals would have the advantage of 'lessening the price of provisions by diminishing the number of horses; on a moderate calculation, every horse requires as much land to support him as, if properly cultivated, would maintain a man, his wife, and three children. The horses belonging to one waggon on the western road have been computed to consume the produce of more than two thousand acres of land'. Canal proprietors also suggested that carriage by canal was less likely to be affected by adverse weather conditions, and that the goods enjoyed a smoother passage by water.

Although at first the road carriers thought that their trade would disappear, they soon found, in fact, that they were able to co-operate with the canals, by taking goods to and from collection points along their lines. Pickford's were soon actively engaged in this link-up between canals and roads, for in addition to running their own canal boats they also made arrangements for road waggons to collect and distribute goods at selected loading points. In *The Birmingham Commercial Herald* for 21 April 1806 the firm advertised their 'fly boats' to the merchants, farmers and manufacturers of Birmingham and its vicinity. The boats loaded at the wharf at Love Lane, Aston Road, Birmingham, every day, Sunday excepted, and goods were conveyed in four days to the firm's wharf at Paddington, whence they were forwarded by road. Gradually the firm built up this system of distribution from canal centres, and their wharf at the City Basin, one of the largest on the Regent's Canal, became the main carrier's yard in London.

In other areas the road carriers had to compete with sea-borne traffic. Throughout the eighteenth century the sea was without doubt the most important means of transport, but the carriers by road were often able to provide feeder services to and from the ports.

As a class the waggoners lacked the dignity and skill that was usually associated with the stage and mail coach drivers. The quality of some of the waggon drivers cannot be commended, particularly their habit of descending hills without taking proper safeguards to prevent their cumbersome vehicles from rolling out of control. The waggoner of one of the Stanfield waggons came to grief in July 1761 when his vehicle ran out of control going down a hill, and similar incidents in other parts of the country induced turnpike trustees, worried by locked wheels damaging their roads, to issue instructions enforcing the use of skid-pans, or slippers, for the wheels. On the road governed by the Northgate district, an entry in the minute book for 14 March 1833 reads:

> It was at this meeting ordered and directed that in all cases where any waggon or cart shall descend the hills on this road called Birdlip Hill and Critchley Hill or either of them with either of the wheels locked, a skid-pan or slipper shall be used or placed at the bottom of such wheel during the whole time of it being so locked in such manner as to prevent the said road from being destroyed or injured by the locking of such wheel.

Another misdemeanour often committed by the waggoners was that of riding on the shafts, and possibly falling asleep on this uncomfortable perch. In the local newspapers there are many accounts of accidents arising from this cause, some of them fatal. The driver of Garrad's Ipswich waggon, for example, was killed near Chelmsford one Sunday night in October 1801. The local newspaper reported that 'the accident arose from the too prevalent and dangerous custom of riding upon the shafts, from which he slipped off, having, it is supposed, fallen asleep. The wheels passed over his thighs, which were crushed in a shocking manner'.

Furious driving, even within the slow limits possible for the heavy waggons, was a further fault of not a few of the waggoners. In drawing attention to this evil practice, *The Essex & Suffolk Times* had this to say in September 1838:

> We have seen them (heavily laden stage waggons, drawn by four and sometimes by five horses passing through the High Street of Chelmsford) in the middle of the street, and in the dusk of the evening, proceeding at the rate of six or even seven miles an hour, to the imminent danger of passengers in the street. We know that a heavy stage waggon, drawn by four horses, two abreast, is not so much at the immediate command of the driver as any other vehicle, and consequently more liable to mischief. A short time ago a driver of one of these stage waggons appeared before the magistrates charged with furious driving, and was heavily fined. Were a few more to be fined for this offence, which is nightly occurring, we think it would be the means of putting a stop to such dangerous practice.

Waggoners were not averse to taking rather liberal quantities of liquor at the frequent stopping places along the route, and not surprisingly this habit brought instances of drunken driving. On the road near Seabridge, some two miles from Newcastle, a publican and his wife and child encountered a tipsy waggoner in April 1816, who forced their chaise into a ditch, where it overturned, dislocating the publican's shoulder, breaking his wife's arm in two places, and killing the child. In January 1840, *The Essex Standard* reported that the driver of a waggon from Tattingstone, returning through Manningtree, was sitting on the shafts in a state of intoxication when, 'by some means (he) fell off, and the wheels passing over his body, he was seriously hurt and now lies in a dangerous state'. Hard drinking was almost a symbol of a waggoner, even though the law did all it could through severe penalties to see that the passion for drink was checked.

Waggoners were sometimes accused of carelessness in looking after the goods entrusted to them. In March 1780 *The Gentleman's Magazine* had an account of the Stamford waggon catching fire owing to the carelessness of the driver who had left a lantern unguarded, which subsequently ignited the cargo. 'Nothing escaped but a barrel of porter,' reported the magazine, 'and the bottom and one wheel of the waggon. The passengers and wag-

5a. A baggage waggon, 1809, by J. A. Atkinson.
5b. The *New Inn*, Gloucester.

6a. *An Awkward Place in a Frost*, by C. B. Newhouse.
6b. *What Became of the Mail*, by H. Alken.

goner were much scorched in attempting to throw off the loading, which, on account of the approaching fair, was of considerable value, and the damage is estimated at above £1,000.' A similar accident befell a Manchester waggon in January 1787, when the vehicle caught fire 'by the waggoner hanging his lantern carelessly at the side of the waggon, which caught the straw and burnt with great fury'. The damage amounted to about £800, and it was reckoned that the 'whole load must have been burnt, if they had not run the waggon into the river at St Albans'.

The waggoners, however, could not be blamed for all the many accidents that occurred. Some of the cargoes that they carried were extremely dangerous, particularly gunpowder. This was clearly illustrated during 1776, when a waggon, on passing through Brick Hill, Northamptonshire, 'was set on fire by the friction of the axle-tree, and three barrels of gunpowder among the loading took fire, by which the goods were blown up in the air, and totally destroyed, to the amount of one thousand pounds'. A few years later the same thing happened to a waggon loaded with gunpowder as it entered the village of Talk-on-the-Hill, Staffordshire. One dramatic account of the mishap mentioned that the explosion 'shook the whole village and scattered the limbs of the horses and driver to a great distance; one horse, with the driver, was forced through the wall of a house, which fell upon the inhabitants, some of whom were bruised in a shocking manner. The whole village is little better than a heap of ruins'.

Another explosion happened on the waggon belonging to Betts and Bury of Ipswich. On returning from London one August day in 1819, the top of the waggon was discovered to be on fire, and the flames soon spread to the gunpowder being carried. 'The whole load was blown up,' reported the local newspaper, 'and scarcely an article of any description saved.' The same fate befell Hearne's Stowmarket waggon in August 1815, when it was reported that 'the road for a considerable space, and the neighbouring fields, were covered with various property, half consumed, or otherwise destroyed, consisting of soldiers' accoutrements, wool, hops, a quantity of books, chests of tea, etc. and the remains of the waggon'.

In most cases the carriers were held responsible for the loss of any goods that they were carrying. At the Shrewsbury Assizes held in August 1812, Beck & Co, wine merchants of the town, brought an action against Evans & Co, carriers, for £140, being the value of a quantity of brandy lost from a puncheon in its conveyance from London in the carrier's waggon. During the hearing, it was proved that the cask had leaked upon the road, to which the driver apparently paid no attention. The jury subsequently awarded the wine merchants £70 in damages. With goods above the value of £5 the carriers invariably made the stipulation that they were not to be held responsible for any loss or damage unless an extra premium was paid on the goods, and entered accordingly. This defence, though, did not always meet with the approval of juries. In a case heard in August 1817, when a firm of carriers maintained that they were not responsible in view of the £5 clause, a jury awarded damages amounting to £29 10s od against them.

Losses also arose as a result of thefts from the waggons. Normally the highwaymen preferred the richer cargoes carried on the stage coaches, but some of the lesser members of the light-fingered gentry were not above relieving the carriers of part of their loads. Nearly always the thieves took the opportunity to remove the cargo while the waggoners were making their traditional stops at inns, the waggons usually being left unattended. Palmer's waggon from Bury to Norwich suffered in this manner one day in February 1812, when a truss of drapery goods, half a firkin of butter and a box of confectionery were discreetly removed whilst the waggoner was refreshing himself at *The Greyhound* in Hopton. Some years later, in the spring of 1838, *The Essex & Suffolk Times* reported that 'during the last few days, no fewer than four waggons have been robbed between Ilford and London'. Among the victims was the waggon of Mr Pease of Rayleigh in Essex, from which a large box of linen was stolen. One of the other people who suffered was Colonel Watson who had put four cases on Mr Ind's waggon, all of them, valued at nearly £500, being stolen, but fortunately the culprits were later discovered with a cart on which the stolen goods were being transported.

In December 1800 the driver of Garrad's Colchester waggon was attacked by an armed man 'in a white dress, something like a frock or a shirt'. The robber thrust his pistol at the waggoner's head 'but happily it only flashed in the pan'! 'A violent scuffle ensued'—a favourite phrase of the newspapers at that time—and on hearing the noise, another waggoner hurried to the scene with a horse pistol loaded with slugs. The villain ran off, and the rescuer 'fired at him, and from his pistol being deeply loaded, he has every reason to suppose great part of the contents took effect'. The local newspaper in reporting the incident, mentioned several other robberies on the London road, and stated that 'waggons will hereafter go well guarded during the winter season'.

The waggoners themselves sometimes operated on the wrong side of the law, especially when they carried poached game into the big towns. In January 1820, a notice was inserted in *The Ipswich Journal* warning the carriers of their guilt:

> *Caution:* It having been strongly suspected that a great many stolen fowls, and other stolen property have lately been taken up at different places on the London road, and conveyed by stage coaches and stage waggons, thus giving encouragement to a set of nightly robbers, who have lately been very active, by furnishing a ready opportunity of removing the fruits of their depredations, beyond the power of detection; the drivers of such waggons are desired to be extremely cautious as to what hampers or other parcels, they may take up on the road, and especially in the night; and to refuse such as shall be tendered in a clandestine manner, or by suspicious characters. All drivers will be aware that they are responsible to the law, should they presume knowingly to convey away stolen property.

This caution presumably followed upon court cases such as the one before Sir Charles Blois earlier the previous year, when a Halesworth carrier was fined £100 'for having in his possession twenty hares, not qualified, on the 14th February'. Some carriers obviously took the hint, for in an advertisement in *The Ipswich Journal* for 28 August 1819 one carrier had this to say:

> Wm. Smith, the London carrier, begs leave to inform his friends and the public in general, that all parcels of game sent in his waggon, are requested to be properly directed and legally qualified, or he cannot receive them.

One significant development in the carrying trade during the early years of the nineteenth century was the introduction of light, well-sprung vans which were able to travel faster than the old cumbersome waggons. Pickford's started using these vans in 1814–15, the journey from Manchester to London taking thirty-six hours, and the charge being 23s 4d per hundredweight. Unfortunately the firm had a serious accident with one of these vans in November 1818, when a driver, no doubt impressed by the speed of his vehicle, attempted to race the mail coach through St Albans. A letter from Charles Inman addressed to M. Pickford & Co, London, tells the story:

> You have doubtless before this time heard of the accident (which) happened to the van in St Albans, and I think it right to inform you what I have heard and think needfull on the occasion. Your horsekeeper was racing the mail at full gallop down St Alban's hill with six horses. The van is knocked to pieces—Collier's arm

and collar bone broken. This loss will fall on us and the repairs of the van and Collier's half wages as has been customary when guards have been injured in our service will not be less than £100, a pretty sum to suffer from the horsekeeper's folly. I am sorry he escap'd unhurt and must hope that you will take the severest measures possible against him. If you can impress him, I hope you will do it. It will be needfull to send someone down to St Albans to make what you can of the van. There are only missing 213 oysters. I fully calculate on this affair's very materially injuring the character of the conveyance, for people will cease to encourage us if our servants act thus.

This fear proved to be unfounded. The firm continued to extend the use of vans to other routes, and they were all reported as loading well. The vans proved easy to operate, and were soon to replace the familiar large, canvas-hooded waggons that had rumbled their slow passage along the roads.

CHAPTER 4

The Carriage of Passengers

THE first stage coach probably operated in England in the 1630s, but because of the deplorable state of the roads the heavy, cumbersome vehicles were not a success, being restricted to running during the summer months. One Lancashire parson, writing in 1657 after a journey in one of them, commented: 'This travell hath soe indisposed mee, yt I am resolved never to ride up agayne in ye Coatche.' Apparently a good many people shared the reverend gentleman's opinion of the new-fangled vehicles, for five years later there were only a small number of coaches running in England. An entry in *The Essex Standard* for 3 December 1831, commenting on the sensation aroused by the first coaches in this country, said that 'a coach was a strange monster in those days, and the sight of it put both horses and man into amazement; some said it was a great crab-shell, brought out of China; and some imagined it to be one of the Pagan temples in which the cannibals adored the devil'. As roads were improved, however, it became possible for coachbuilders to improve the design of coaches, making them better sprung and lighter in construction, thereby enabling higher speeds to be attained in relative comfort. From about 1780 onwards, more and more came on to the roads, and the period 1820–36 can be regarded as 'the golden age of coaching'.

In the seventeenth century a stage-coach journey between London and York took five days to perform, but in 1706 a time of four days was maintained. In 1658, when the first stage coach ran in Devon, the journey from Exeter to London took four days. Just over a hundred years later these times had been halved, the Exeter to London run being advertised to take only two days. By 1784 this service had been improved to 32 hours, while an even higher speed was attained in the year 1832 when the coaches completed the distance in 17½ hours, at an average speed of 10 mph. *The Highflyer* coach was advertised in 1790 as setting out from York every morning at 5 o'clock, to arrive at The White Horse,

Fetter Lane, the next day at noon, a time of 31 hours. In eastern England, *The Ipswich Journal* for 26 May 1827 reported that 'in the memory of some still living . . . the Ipswich post coach was two days on its way to London; now there are several stage coaches performing the journey every day in seven or eight hours'.

The size of the coaching concerns varied considerably. At one end of the scale was the big business of Chaplin & Co, operating from several taverns in London and owning between 1,300 and 1,500 horses and 64 coaches in 1834, bringing in, with the income from various hotels, about £500,000 a year, and the firms of Horne of the *Golden Cross* inn, Charing Cross, and Sherman of the *Bull and Mouth*, St Martins-le-Grand, who in the 1840s each had about 700 horses. At the other end of the scale was the small innkeeper who took a share in a coach, agreeing to provide the horses for his 'ground' in return for a share in the profits. Under this arrangement the coach would either be purchased, or alternatively hired from a coachbuilder who would charge between 2½d and 3d per double mile of operation. Usually, when taking a share in the coach, the innkeeper would make an announcement in the local press. R. Wright, for example, of the *Four Swans* inn in Bishopgate Street, in 'thanking his Suffolk friends and the public in general', told them that he had taken a share in the London & Ipswich Original Blue coaches in December 1819, and assured them that 'nothing shall be wanting on his part to provide comfortable and expeditious travelling'.

Numerous expenses were involved in operating the stage coaches, particularly the faster ones in which the horses had to be changed more frequently. These included the hiring charges for the coach; wages for stable boys; the wages of the coachman, who would expect to receive at least 18s a week, plus his keep; turnpike tolls; and the duty that had to be paid to the government. This duty, the subject of so many complaints, was based on the number of passengers for which the coach was licensed. The Stamp Act of 1804 fixed the rate for a coach licensed to carry four inside passengers (children in the lap excepted) at 5s for the licence and a duty of 2d per mile; for a coach licensed to carry six inside passengers, 6s and 2½d respectively; for eight, 7s and 3½d per mile; for ten, 8s and 4d per mile and if over ten passengers, 9s and 5d per mile. Details of the loading of the coach had to be printed on the doors, but the coachmasters were permitted to take out a licence for a smaller number of passengers during the winter months, when loadings were likely to be less.

There was also a restriction on the number of outside passengers carried, but it seems that coachmasters often disregarded it. At Hatton Garden, J. Booth, driver of the Exeter coach, was fined £40 in October 1814 'for carrying more outside passengers than is allowed by law'. Mr Keale, owner and driver of the Crouch End and Hornsey stage, was fined £20 for the same offence, while G. Gayton, owner and driver of the Edmonton stage, was also fined £20. Many of the offenders were brought to justice by informers who took their share of the fines imposed. Not, however, that informers were always successful. In April 1799, one common informer apparently became rather too keen in his vigil, for he was found guilty of perjury, having deposed 'that there were more outside passengers on a stage coach (going from the Bull & Mouth Inn) than is allowed by Act of Parliament. A clergyman and another gentleman came voluntarily forward to invalidate the information of the prisoner, which went substantially against him, and he was, after a long hearing, committed to prison'.

Another expense that coachmasters had to meet was the turnpike tolls. As might be expected, there were frequent complaints that these tolls were too high, and appeals to have them lowered. A typical claim was put forward by the proprietors of the *The Old Accommodation* coach in a letter dated 1 July 1820, written from Southwell, Nottinghamshire. In presenting their dutiful thanks for the allowance of 9d per day which had already been allowed as a reduction of the toll for the coach, they went on to ask for a reduction of a further 3d per day. 'It will then leave two shillings per day or £36 per year,' they pointed out, 'which is a very heavy toll upon our coach through a single gate.' The letter added:

> We beg to add our sole object in asking the above is owing to the badness of the times as also a great competition on the road, there being two coaches, one called *The Hope* and the other *The Wonder*. We have no connection with either from Newark to Nottingham, at the same time, and two from Nottingham to Newark at the same time, all going down the Foss Road thereby endangering the existence of the Old coach on your road—hoping you will be pleased to take the same into your kind consideration.
> (SIGNED) BOWER SMITH & GARDNER

Sometimes the problem of whether tolls had to be paid each time of passing through a gate came up. A coach-proprietor at Newark addressed a letter on this subject to the clerk of the trustees of the Leadenham Hill to Mansfield & Southwell to Oxton trust:

> We beg to assure you that should we be obliged to pay you for each time we pass through your gate the coaches through Southwell are paying so very bad and for some time have been losing

concerns to the proprietors that we shall be the necessity of running them with only a pair of horses rather than have our expenses increased. I hope the trustees of the road will consider to let the coaches remain as they are particularly as it is only so very lately that they have raised their tolls.

One of the Worcestershire trusts, in answering the criticism that their tolls for stage coaches were too high, replied in 1836 that the toll for a four-horse coach was between £6 8s od and £9 12s od per month, whereas the rate charged by adjoining trusts varied from £10 16s od to £14 8s od per month.

The costs of buying and keeping horses varied enormously, and it is difficult to give definite figures. An entry in *The Lincolnshire Chronicle & General Advertiser* for 11 January 1833, quoting an account from the *Quarterly Review*, stated that the average price for a horse for a fast coach was in the region of £23. This rather low figure was given on account of the very poor horses that were often used in stage coaches, even blind horses being worked on some of the better-surfaced roads. The average working life of a coach horse was reckoned at four years on a fast coach, and seven years on a slow one. The general practice in running a service was to have one horse in four always at rest.

For a crack coach, the horses would cost much more. Even when the coaching proprietors disposed of such horses they still fetched a high price, as was shown by an auction sale at Brighton in March 1826. Thirty horses, formerly employed in running *The Monarch*, were put up for sale, and according to a report in *The Brighton Gazette*, all fetched high prices. A brown gelding was sold for 95 guineas; a piebald for 76 guineas, and a chestnut for 70 guineas. The average price was £37 2s 8d.

Another indication of the value of horses is given in a newspaper report of 14 June 1817: 'a few days ago Mr Webb, a coach proprietor, of Lichfield, lost two valuable horses, worth 100 guineas almost at the same instant, both being killed by loose stones in the road'.

In giving evidence to the Committee on the Highways & Turnpike Roads in England & Wales in 1819, William Horne of the *Golden Cross* inn, Charing Cross, London, who provided horses for both stage and mail coaches, explained that he bought 150 horses a year 'to keep the stock in order', his stock at that time amounting to 400 horses. He considered that the stock wore out fully in three years. Another London contractor—William Waterhouse—told the same Committee that he could purchase horses for £15 'at a distance from London, equal to those that we are obliged to give £30 a piece for, on the average, for the work near town'. He also explained that the average amount that he had to pay in turnpike tolls for a four-horse coach was 3½d per mile, the charges having doubled within fifteen years, though he maintained that the roads had not been improved in the same proportion. The number of horses that he had to use on a particular run depended very much on the state of the roads. On the London to Birmingham road he required twelve horses to perform the same number of miles as eight horses on the better-surfaced Birmingham and Holyhead road. All the coachmasters interviewed by the Committee complained of the poor state of the roads around London, a factor which involved them in additional expense, as more horses were required to work the coaches. The usual arrangement was for a horse to be changed at each stage, this being a distance between ten and fifteen miles.

On the revenue side of their accounts the coachmasters were limited by several factors. In the first place, the number of passengers that could be carried on a coach was restricted by its licence. Secondly, there was the problem of light loads, for the coachmasters could not always be sure of filling the coach, even in densely populated areas. On an advertised service the coach had to run whatever the load, which caused many a headache to the operators. Some interesting details about loadings are given in the returns made at the Shenfield toll-gate in 1838. On 26 February, for instance, the under-mentioned coaches were listed:

To London Name of coach	No of passengers Inside	Outside
Chelmsford	4	4
Braintree	2	11
Chelmsford	4	9
Coggeshall	4	4
Burnham & Maldon	1	1
Wellington, Colchester	4	11
Sudbury	3	4
Ipswich Blue	4	11
Bury	4	9
Shannon, Ipswich	3	1
Chelmsford	4	4
Phenomena, Norwich	1	6
Colchester	2	6
Times, Norwich	2	2
Yarmouth	2	7
	44	90

From London Name of coach	No of passengers Inside	Outside
Yarmouth Star	0	5
Phenomena, Norwich	3	11
Shannon, Ipswich	1	2
Wellington, Colchester	3	2
Bury	3	9
Chelmsford .... 12am.	3	7
Ipswich Blue	3	11
Sudbury New	0	8
Colchester	3	10
Coggeshall	2	3
Chelmsford	2	1
Chelmsford	3	9
Braintree	2	4
Telegraph	3	9
Royal Mail	2	2
	33	93

These figures show the poor loading of many coaches. This is
even more clearly illustrated if a single coach is selected from the
returns:

Norwich Phenomena Coach: (Norwich and London) Date	No. of journeys and passengers passing through the Shenfield turnpike gate, 26 February–4 March, 1838, inclusive Inside passengers Outside passengers	
Monday, 26 February		
To London	1	6
From London	3	11
Tuesday, 27 February		
To London	2	7
From London	2	3
Wednesday, 28 February		
To London	2	5
From London	0	10
Thursday, 1 March		
To London	3	10
From London	3	3
Friday, 2 March		
To London	0	8
From London	4	9
Saturday, 3 March		
To London	3	7
From London	3	10

Sunday, 4 March

To London	3	6
From London	3	11

The returns also show a good deal of competition, as the figures for coaches passing through the gate for 26 February 1825 indicate (selected towns only):

No. of coaches	Name of coach/town	Times	No. of Days
1	Chelmsford	Up 8 am, down 5 pm	6
1	Chelmsford	Up 4 pm, down 10 am	7
1	Eclipse, Colchester	Up 11 am, down 4 pm next evening	6
2	New, Colchester	1 down 5 pm; 1 up 5 pm	7
2	New, Colchester Original	1 down 5 pm, 1 up 5 pm	7
1	Times, Colchester	Up 12 morning, down 4 pm next evening	6
2	Blue's, Ipswich	1 down 10 am, 1 up 3 pm	7
2	Shannon's, Ipswich	1 down 10 am, 1 up 4 pm	7
2	Day Coach, Norwich	1 down 8 am, 1 up 6 pm	7
2	Phenomena, Norwich	1 down 9 am, 1 up 5 pm	7
2	Times, Norwich	1 down 8 am, 1 up 5 pm	7
2	Mail, Norwich	1 each day, 5 am up, down 10 pm	7
2	Times, Harwich	1 down 1 am, 1 up 5 pm	6
2	Wellington, Harwich	1 down 11 am, 1 up 1 next morning	7
2	Star, Yarmouth	1 down 8 am, 1 up 6 pm	7
1	Telegraph, Yarmouth	Up 5 am, down 9 pm	7

Competition expressed itself in two forms: price and time schedules. Price competition became increasingly severe during the nineteenth century as more and more coaches were put into service. In July 1836, for example, one local newspaper reported:

> Such is the competition between the proprietors of coaches running between Huddersfield and Manchester that they have issued the following announcement—'Outside, what you please, inside, ditto.'

An example of price cutting in East Anglia in 1834 is provided by two groups of coaching concerns: Bird, Sherman & Co, and Haxwell, Hogarth, Nelson, Chaplin & Co. The struggle began when the latter concern reduced their fares between London and the east coast. Following this reduction, Bird, Sherman & Co made the following announcement in the local Press:

> Stimulated by exertion by a determined opposition, the proprietors of the Magnet coach are prepared to meet the crisis with the weight of superior forces, and the support of a more extensive connection. They are grateful for past favours, and will continue to deserve them by one firm undeviating line of conduct. Passengers will receive the most marked attention and accommodation. Parcels will be delivered with the most determined promptitude, and the coach timed with the utmost punctuality.

As a result of this competition, the fare between London and Ipswich, which had originally been 16s inside and 8s outside, was reduced by 2s for the inside passengers.

Another example of price competition was the battle fought between the coachmasters operating from the inns, *The Angel* and *The Bull and Mouth*, during May 1801. The coachmaster from *The Bull and Mouth* had advertised services to the north of England at prices well below those charged by *The Angel*, and this brought the following announcement in the pages of *The York Courant*:

> The proprietors of the *True Briton* coach, impressed with a lively sense of the liberal support of a discerning public, feel themselves called upon, by an advertisement from The Bull and Mouth to address the public at large: the reasons there held up, for offering to accommodate the public at such inadequate terms, are too gross to deceive the most ignorant in the knowledge of horse-keeping, and are intended only to injure the fair tradesman. The proprietors of *The True Briton* coach, therefore flatter themselves with a continuance of support from the public at the moderate price of £3. 3s 0d from London to Leeds., and other distances in a similar proportion; and hereby pledge themselves to continue their conveyances in a style of expedition and care, equal to the best connection of the kind in the kingdom. Those who travel in *The True Briton* may depend on being treated with the best attention, and genteel coaches, without being subject to the inconveniences of a carriage, made for the purpose of carrying twelve insides, which is a scheme to make up by numbers for low prices, and an imposition on the unwary, by those opponents who have not courage to contest the business at a price that will satisfy both traveller and coachmaster.
> Performed by J. Robinson, London
>   J. Hicks, Leeds.
> *Old King's Arms, Leeds, 29 May 1801*

Examples of fares charged to different parts of the country are given in the table below. They have been taken from newspaper advertisements of the coaching companies:

Date	Route	Inside £.	s.	d.	Outside £.	s.	d.
					Fares		
1790	Highflyer, London–York	2.	10.	0.	1.	5.	0.
	Short stages 3½d per mile (outside half price)						
1790	Mail Coach, London to York	3.	3.	0.	1.	11	6
1781	London to Exeter	1	18	0			
	(Inside only—post coach)						
1781	London to Exeter	2	2	0			
	(Post coach in 36 hours)						
	Short stage passengers 3d per mile						
1794	London to Leicester	1	8	0		14.	0.
1796	London to Ipswich	1.	1.	0.		10.	6.
	(Mail coach)						
1796	Norwich Telegraph, London to Norwich	1.	6.	0.		16.	0.
1800	True Briton, Nottingham to London	2.	2.	0.	1.	5.	0.
1804	The Volunteer (post coach) Ipswich to London	1.	6.	0.		15.	0.
1815	Ipswich to London		15.	0.		10.	0.
1819	Shannon Post Coach, Ipswich to London	1.	1.	0.		10.	0.
1819	Times Post Coach, London to Colchester		16.	0.		8.	0.

A number of books quote fares as being 4d to 5d per mile inside and between 2d and 3d per mile outside on a fast coach, with somewhat cheaper fares on the slower coaches, but there was such a great variation, as the above table shows if the figures are worked out on a mileage basis, that it is difficult to give any reliable national figures.

Racing was another form of competition, each coach trying to put on a faster service than its competitors. An example of what could happen when coaches raced one another was the overturning of the Winslow coach near the Kilburn turnpike gate in October 1817. The injured coachman had to be carried away in a hackney coach; three of the passengers were severely injured; another had his thigh broken; and another broke his arm. Reporting the accident, *The Morning Post* wrote: 'It is much lamented that a stop is not put to coach racing, as there is now an opposition on the Aylesbury road, and the coachmen from town are in the habit of going to Aylesbury, a distance of forty miles, in five hours, stoppages included; indeed, sometimes they have gone in four hours, which is at the rate of ten miles per hour, one coach racing against the other.'

In the same year, *The Leeds Mercury* had a similar account of an accident which resulted from these racing matches. Referring to 'another of those alarming accidents to which stage coach passengers are so much exposed', the newspaper gave the following account of the mishap:

> It appears that about six o'clock in the morning . . . both the coaches from Leeds to York entered the town at the full gallop; and the True Briton, in attempting to pass the other coach, ran over a basket of dung which stood in its way, and was overturned. At the time when the incident happened, the coach had six inside and four outside passengers; but though the position of all the passengers was perilous in the extreme, only one lady received any material hurt. The lady, who was one of the inside passengers, finding that the coach was likely to upset, seized hold of the door, and the coach falling upon her hand, either crushed off all her fingers, or bruised them so terribly, as to render amputation necessary.

The newspaper reports spared no details in describing the plight of the unwilling participants in these racing matches. Typical is the account of an accident involving two Greenwich coaches in April 1815. In the course of a race from Westminster bridge, the passengers became so alarmed that some of them on the leading coach endeavoured to jump out. One of these jumpers escaped with only a few bruises, but a less fortunate fellow traveller who made a desperate leap from the top of the coach 'fell on his face against the gravel with such force that his nose was flattened; his forehead was cut in a most dreadful manner, as were also his hands and knees'.

There were also cases of coaches racing one another in Liverpool and Manchester. A local newspaper in 1814 complained that: 'the competition between coaches that pass between the two towns has of late become so great, that, in order to secure a preference, the most violent efforts are made by each of them to perform the journey in the least possible time, and a furious contest is therefore continuously carried on. The danger to which the lives of the passengers are constantly exposed by this alarming practice is too obvious to require proof. The history of the last twelve months, if accurately stated would present a list of wounds, bruises and fractures sufficient to deter any passenger from venturing his life in one of these "flying machines".'

Parliament legislated to prevent racing, but it seems that the threatened penalties did not do a great deal to deter the coachmen. Nevertheless, there were convictions, as in the prosecution of one of the coachmen of a Hammersmith coach in October 1816 at Bow Street. According to the evidence of one of the passengers, the driver attempted to race the Brentford coach whilst on the road between Brentford chapel and the turnpike gate. The ladies in the coach apparently became 'extremely alarmed, expecting the coach to be overturned every minute from the careless manner in which it appeared to be driven'. For his misconduct the driver was fined 50s with costs.

Magistrates in different parts of the country kept a sharp lookout for these racing contests. In November 1815 a newspaper report mentioned that the Kent magistrates were 'exerting themselves to bring to punishment all drivers of stage coaches within their jurisdiction, who shall be found furiously driving, or shall carry more passengers than allowed by law'. Fines of about £10 were imposed. In some parts of the country it seems that there were 'on-the-spot' fines, as the following accounts indicate:

Chelmsford Gazette, 16 October 1828
The drivers of two new Colchester coaches were on Friday last fined £3. 7s od each, including costs for furiously driving. At the time they were observed by a worthy magistrate who for the general good of the public, enforced the penalties. The coachmen were going at the extraordinary rate of from fourteen to fifteen miles an hour.

Ipswich Journal, 15 November 1817
(Account of three coaches racing between Manchester and Liverpool)
. . . there were ladies of great respectability in the middle of the coach, who were under the most painful apprehension of being exposed to this sort of danger all the way to Liverpool. Happily their fears terminated at Warrington, for it happened that a worthy magistrate saw the whole affair and he convicted the coachman of The Defiance, on his own view, in the penal sum of £10 which was paid in Liverpool.

A factor that encouraged racing was the same setting-out time for opposing coaches. On the Leeds to Birmingham route, two coaches, *The Telegraph* and *The Pilot*, both left Leeds at six o'clock in the morning, with the inevitable result that there was a dramatic race along the road. 'Both coaches have cleared the distance between Leeds and Barnsley (19 miles) in an hour,' read one report. 'They arrived at Wakefield on Monday morning from Leeds (9 miles) in twenty five minutes. The cattle were dreadfully distressed. One minute and four seconds only were occupied in changing horses, and both vehicles went off at a rattling speed, the Telegraph leading the way.' The proprietors of the *Old Blue Coach* from London to Saxmundham announced in 1830 that 'at the recommendation of their friends, they have altered the time of leaving London from 7 to a quarter before 9 o'clock in the morning. By this alteration, which prevents the simultaneous starting of the coaches in opposing interests on the same road, all temptation to racing is removed'.

A great deal depended on the skill and reliability of the coachman in ensuring a safe journey. Usually a coachman could expect, on average, to travel about fifty miles a day, certainly a gruelling experience which demanded men of tough physique, able to withstand being exposed to all weathers. For his labours he received a weekly wage from the coach proprietors, in addition to the customary tips from passengers. All fares not exceeding 2s often went to the coachman as one of the perquisites of the job, shared with the guard. On a good run these 'shorts' as they were known, could add a considerable amount to the earnings of both men.

As might be expected, the stage coachmen shared the waggoners' liking for drink, and many charges of drunken driving were made against them. In October 1819, for example, the proprietors of the *Umpire* coach from London to Liverpool were sued for damages by a passenger who was 'thrown from the roof of that coach in June 1817 when it was upset between Northampton and Welford by the coachman, who was drunk, driving the coach up a bank'. Damages of £300 were awarded.

Most long journeys were divided into three 'grounds': the high or upper ground which was the section nearest home; the middle ground; and the lower ground which marked the last stage of the route. It was on the middle ground that the coachman's skill was most necessary, for it was on this section, away from large towns, that the poorer horses were used. The worst horses were referred to as 'Bo-kickers' and it was not unusual for a coachman to be confronted with 'three bolters and a blind 'un'. Throughout the journey the coachman had to keep the horses in step to prevent the coach from overturning, and with such an unfortunate set, this was no easy task. Going downhill was always tricky in a vehicle without brakes, and cornering had many hazards. Passengers on board Hern's Hemel Hempstead coach experienced them in July 1818 when the coach overturned after taking the bend too quickly at Hunton bridge. There were seventeen outside passengers, two of whom were killed and several

7a. *The Plymouth Fly*, by Thomas Rowlandson.

7b. Highway robbers at work, from an eighteenth-century lithograph.

8a. The original Bath mail coach.

8b. *A Mail Coach at an Inn*, by Charles Cooper Henderson. The inn is probably the *Bull & Mouth*, St Martin's-le-Grand, London.

others injured. A team of horses usually worked 'both sides of the road', that is, operated one stage during the morning, and the return stage later in the same day, thereby working 'two sweats', as the term was.

Even with the best of coachmen, passengers were subjected to all manner of perils. Not infrequently the horses became unmanageable, and on other occasions a stumble, especially when the road surface was bad, could result in a serious accident. This is shown by the unhappy fate of the Lancaster & Liverpool coach in the summer of 1802. One of the rear offside horses 'gave a stumble', and in trying to check its fall, one of the front horses 'flew on the pavement', causing the coach to run over a large stone which 'immediately overturned' the coach. All nine outside passengers were thrown some 14 ft into the river, but they apparently emerged from the water without any serious injury. Another account of difficult horses is given in *The Macclesfield Courier* in October 1839, when the coachman of the *Paul Pry* coach experienced trouble:

> As it (the coach) was passing the gate the near horse took fright at a man who was passing by, and turned so suddenly as to run the wheels into the side drain of the road, in spite of all the efforts of the coachman, who was a very steady man, and who has long been in the employ of Messrs Gilbert, the proprietors of the coach.

As a result of the accident, a man was crushed against a wall, and was rushed to hospital in a very dangerous state. William Horne explained to the Committee on the Highways & Turnpike Roads in England & Wales (1819) that he 'had accidents, and they have sometimes been attributed to the horses shying, and plunging the coach on one side, so as to cause it to overturn, from the great roundness of the road'.

Other accidents resulted from defective or worn parts of the coach. Wheels were the great weakness. In June 1805 one of the wheels of a Southampton coach fell off, two passengers being injured as the coach overturned. A rather more unusual incident happened on the road between Shifnal and Wolverhampton one winter's day in 1845. The coach concerned, *The Salopian* from Shrewsbury, was:

> Proceeding at its usual pace, when the guard, who was seated on top of the luggage, speaking to the driver, heard a sudden crash, and on turning his head round he beheld, to his utter astonishment and dismay, about thirty yards distant, the hind seat of the coach in the middle of the road, with four of the passengers on the ground. One passenger (Mr Ward of Croxton, near Shrewsbury)

G

was taken up insensible, and the other individuals were more or less bruised.

Weather conditions made life difficult for coachman and passengers: wind, rain, snow and ice caused all manner of accidents and delays. On a lonely, exposed section of road in the spring of 1830, the Lincoln and Louth *Accommodation* coach, when turning a corner, was caught by a violent gust of wind which blew it completely over, killing the coachman. Three years earlier *The Enterprise* coach from Wisbech and Kings Lynn to London came to grief during a winter fog. On nearing the Stretham Ferry bridge, neither coachman or guard could discern the road, the result being that the coach went into the side and upset. Snow and ice were perhaps the biggest hazards, bringing danger and discomfort, especially to the outside passengers. When the Bath coach arrived in Chippenham one day in March 1812, having travelled through a night of bitterly cold winds, the town folk were 'surprised at seeing three outside passengers lying in a state of apparent insensibility, but their surprise was converted into horror when they perceived, on a nearer approach, that vitality had been actually extinct in two of them for some time, the bodies being perfectly cold'.

From time to time travel hints were given to such exposed passengers upon how to avoid suffering from the effects of an English winter. In January 1837, for example, *The Aylesbury News* offered the following advice to outside passengers:

> To attain the maximum comfort which the circumstances admit, they should drink a tankard of good ale cold from the tap, and rub their hands, ears and faces with snow immediately before they start. This will produce a more lasting and agreeable glow than any other artificial means is capable of producing.

Unlike the mail coaches, which always prided themselves that the mail would be delivered on time whatever the conditions, the stage coaches often stopped running during the worst weather. Even so, there were times when they were caught out, marooned in deep drifts of snow, unable to move. On 3 January 1795 *The Ipswich Journal* carried a report that 'travelling in general has been very much obstructed by the late fall of snow, and the thaw that followed; most of the stage coaches, as well mails as others, were much impeded, and frequently met with accidents from the horses not being able to keep their feet. On the North Road many fell, and the consequence was that the harness, reins and poles were broken, and some of the coaches overturned'.

When the snow came to an end, there remained the very serious problem of floods. After the heavy snowfalls of January 1799, coach drivers and guards often had to drag their horses through the water. 'At Widford Bridge, the horses refused to go through the water,' read one Essex newspaper account, 'and the vast quantities of ice which had collected so impeded their progress, that the coachman and guard were obliged to lead them through the water at the risk of their lives, being up to their waists in water.' In 1822 conditions were a great deal worse in many parts of the country, with areas flooded to a considerable depth. Reports spoke of horses being drowned, never to be seen again, and bridges and banks being knocked down by the fury of the flood waters. 'On Wednesday the turnpike road near Spalding was overflowed by the river Welland,' reported one eye-witness in January, 'a tunnel having blown up. The whole country was in great alarm, and numbers of men were employed in what is provincially known as "cradging"—strengthening banks with hurdles, stakes, etc.'

Hold-ups of a very different nature occurred when highwaymen raided a coach. During the eighteenth and early nineteenth centuries these outlaws were a real menace to travellers, not only to the lonely horseman, but also to the crowded and usually unguarded stage coaches. Legend has surrounded these robbers with all kinds of glory and romance, but there was nothing particularly romantic about being thumped on the head by armed thugs who laid in wait on lonely stretches of road. Many of these criminals were brought to justice, often suffering the penalty of death for their sins. A father and son, executed at Lancaster on 29 September 1827, were reported to have fallen upon their victims with large clubs which they used in a manner 'too shocking to describe'. Some highwaymen organised themselves into gangs, there being no shortage of willing and able recruits for their ranks. One gang which 'infested the Essex road' during the 1780s were so successful that they were able to rent a house and adjoining land at Romford, where they spent the time farming by day and robbing by night along the nearby roads. In this way they spent many fruitful years, and it was not until one of their earlier victims, happening to pass the house, recognised one of the gang, that the enterprise came to an abrupt end. When the police raided the house they found '106 pick-lock keys, besides arms and other suspicious instruments'.

Although the stage-coach proprietors could not be held responsible for the attacks and deprivations of highwaymen, they were nevertheless accountable for the safety of the passengers, and in some instances the baggage that they carried. With baggage, the proprietors normally demanded that all goods over £5 in value had to be entered and an extra premium paid. So far as passenger safety was concerned, there were countless legal battles in which injured parties sought redress. At the Salisbury summer Assizes of 1813, John Gooden claimed damages against the proprietors of *The Auxiliary* coach, which overturned shortly after leaving *The Red Lion* inn at Salisbury, causing him considerable injury. The proprietors of the coach, appreciating their liability, paid for medical aid and agreed to pay the cost of any other expenses that might be incurred as a result of the accident. Nevertheless, the jury decided that compensation should also be paid, and £600, decided by an outside referee, was awarded. A similar court case, concerning a leg fractured in a coach mishap, ended in damages of £150 being awarded at York Assizes in August 1815 against the proprietors of *The Trafalgar* coach.

There were, however, times when stage-coach travel could be a pleasant experience, and the improved schedules of the 1820s and 1830s, associated with better roads and attempts to link up services, heralded the golden age of coaching. A good idea of the services that were available is provided by the list of coaches leaving Nelson's General Coach and Waggon Office at the Bull Inn, Aldgate Street, London, in 1822:

MANCHESTER   Independent New Post Coach
in twenty four hours, lighted and guarded throughout.
Linked up with coaches going to Warrington, Liverpool and all parts of Cumberland and Scotland.
NORWICH   Phenomena Post Coach
in fourteen hours.
The coach linked up with coaches going to Wells, Holkham, Holt and Cromer.
BATH & BRISTOL   Express Coach
in eighteen hours.
Coach linked up with coaches going to Plymouth, Exeter, Bridgwater, Taunton, as well as to parts of Ireland and Wales.
BIRMINGHAM   New Post Coach, The Sovereign
in fourteen hours.
Linked up with coaches going to Shrewsbury, Chester and Holyhead.
IPSWICH   Shannon Post Coach
in nine hours.
YARMOUTH   The Star Post Coach
in fifteen hours.
YOXFORD   Post Coach
in twelve hours.

COLCHESTER The Times Post Coach
in six hours, also Colchester and Witham Post Coach.
SOUTHAMPTON The Independent Safe Coach
in ten hours.
Linked up with coaches going to Channel Islands; Isle of Wight;
also with branch coaches going to Lymington and Lyndhurst and
all parts of the New Forest.
SOUTHEND Telegraph Coach
SOUTHEND Despatch coach
'by far the most comfortable conveyance for families.'
BLACKMORE Post coach
WRITTLE & ONGAR Telegraph coach
BURNHAM Telegraph coach
HASTINGS The Independent New Post coach in eight hours.
CAMBRIDGE The Safety coach, New post coach, in six hours.
BISHOPS STORTFORD Telegraph Coach.

The *Huntingdon Gazette* of 15 May 1830 reported that 'a person
has 1,500 opportunities of leaving London in the course of twenty-
four hours by stage coaches including the repeated trips of the
coaches which ply the short distances. It is understood that about
300 coaches pass through Hyde Park Corner Turnpike daily. There
are about forty Brighton coaches. There are eighty-four coaches
belonging to Birmingham of which 40 are daily; to Chester 19 of
which 16 are daily; to Manchester 70 of which 54 are daily. In the
year 1770 there belonged only two stage coaches to Manchester,
one to London and one to Liverpool and they went only twice a
week; now twenty coaches pass backwards and forwards daily
between these two places. There are 60 coaches belonging to
Liverpool of which 56 are daily; to Preston 12; to York 18 of
which 10 are daily; to Hull 12; to Newcastle 6; to Glasgow 13; to
Edinburgh 39 and to Inverness 3'. An item in *The Essex Standard*
for 1 June 1838 mentioned that 'from the list of licensed coaches,
published by authority by the Commissioners, it appears that
1,476 coaches leave London daily, exclusive of short stages'.

This mention of 'short stages' referred to the coaches that
operated for short distances, running from the centre of a large
town to the outlying districts. In London, for example, there were
hourly services from inns in the City and the West End to various
suburbs and villages. By 1825 it was estimated by the City Police
Committee that 418 vehicles were making 1,190 journeys from the
City. In their book *A History of London Transport*, T. C. Barker
and Michael Robbins say that at one time there were probably 600
short-stage coaches, running 1,800 daily journeys from the City
and the West End. Fares on these coaches were high, 1s 6d to

2s being charged for the single fare to the City or West End from Paddington, Peckham or Clapham for the inside passengers, and 6d less for those outside. Four or six passengers were carried inside, the number outside being limited to seven if the coach was drawn by two or three horses, and twelve if four horses were employed. Some passengers would book in advance for their journey, usually at inns which served as booking offices, but passengers were also picked up on the road, providing they were beyond the boundaries of the seventeenth-century Bills of Mortality, 'the stones'. In *A History of London Transport*, the authors quote the diary of Monsieur L. Simond (*Journal of a Tour and Residence in Great Britain during the years 1810 and 1811*), in which he described a journey in a short-stage coach between Richmond and London at the beginning of 1810. He said that the coach was:

> crammed inside and hérissé outside with passengers, of all sexes, ages, and conditions. We stopped more than twenty times on the road—the debates about the fare of way-passengers—the settling themselves—the getting up, and the getting down, and the damsels shewing their legs in the operation and tearing and muddying their petticoats—complaining and swearing—took an immense time. I never saw anything so ill-managed. In about two hours we reached Hyde Park corner . . .

Despite the Frenchman's criticism, these short-distance stage coaches performed a valuable function in carrying large numbers of passengers to and from the centre of London and other large towns, for they could offer a very flexible, door-to-door service.

Townsmen and villagers not served directly by a coach service could always try to persuade some proprietor to start a service, as did the inhabitants living between Ross and Hay. *The Hereford Journal* for 10 November 1841 announced that a meeting was to be held for starting one. The report said that the main obstacle to the service's introduction was the poor condition of part of the road between Llanavon and Hardwick which 'owing to the gross neglect of the present surveyors has fallen into a most shameful state: we have no doubt, however, that after the meeting measures will be taken to enforce a thorough reparation of it'. After the meeting had taken place, a Mr Cooper produced on behalf of a coach proprietor a statement of the probable expenses and earnings of a day coach running along the intended route from Hay to Ross, down one day and up the next in the winter months, and daily each way during the summer (Sunday excepted). From this statement it appeared that there was likely to be a loss to the proprietor for the first twenty-two weeks of the service, amount-

ing to £70, but after this period there would be a sufficient return
to justify the running of the coach. On the understanding that a
public subscription would be raised to cover him for these initial
losses, the coach proprietor said that he was prepared to operate
the service. Accordingly, the people attending the meeting agreed
to raise the money, for an announcement in *The Hereford Journal*
for 8 December 1841 gave the following details:

> *Leave Ross:* every Monday, Wednesday and Friday immediately
> after the arrival of the Paul Pry from London, through Dew-
> church, Thruxton, Kingstone, Peterchurch and Dorstone, arriving
> at Hay at 7 o'clock.
> *Leave Hay:* every Tuesday, Thursday and Saturday at 8 a.m.,
> arriving at Ross in time for the Paul Pry which reaches London at
> 8 p.m.
> The coach was to be known as *The Prince of Wales.*
> *Fares:*
> Hay to Ross   Outside   6s   od
>   Inside   10s   od
> Hay to London   Outside   32s   od
>   Inside   50s   od

In advertising the service, the proprietor said that *The Prince of
Wales* having been established 'upon a wealthy basis and chiefly
with a view to open a direct line of communication to South Wales
thro' a new and beautiful line of country, venture to anticipate
permanency and public patronage'.

So grateful were the local gentry and tradesmen that they gave
a large party in honour of the coach proprietor at the local inn 'in
order that they might testify their approbation of his enterprising
conduct in establishing the present commodious and economical
conveyance between Hay, Ross and London'. The service was
regarded as saving the tradesmen of the town of Hay considerable
sums of money, because they were now able to avoid the former
circuitous and expensive route through Hereford.

Coaching, as might be expected, had its own language. An
empty coach was a 'mad woman'; asking passengers for money
was called 'kicking' them; a passenger not on the bill, 'a shoulder
stick', a 'bit of fish', or 'a short one'; a passenger who gave only
a small tip, 'a scaly one', and one who gave no tip at all, 'tipping
the double'; a glass of neat spirits, a flash of lightning, a drop of
short, or don't-stop-to-mix-it; greatcoats were referred to as 'benjamins' or upper benjamins, while a well-dressed woman was 'a
pretty bit of muslin'. Language used to describe the horses included 'a miller' for a horse given to kicking. Galloping horses

was known as 'springing them'; and driving near to anything 'feather-edging it'. The coach was usually referred to as the drag; reins as ribbons; horses as cattle; a whip as a tool; a bad coachman as 'a spoon' or 'lame hand'; a kind-hearted master, a trump, and one always on the look-out, a tormentor.

Within the towns, sedan chairs and hackney carriages provided short-distance transport. Strict regulations governed the operators of these conveyances, whose numbers were severely limited. At Exeter, for example, a 16-page booklet, dated February 1822, set out the rules and regulations relating to the use of sedan chairs in the city. Among the principal provisions were that chairs had to be withdrawn from service on becoming decayed, soiled or otherwise unfit for service; that they had to be well made, 5 ft 3 in in height and 'of the breadth of two feet in the clear', with decent lining and a black interior; and that each chair had to show the licence number in 2-in white numerals. The chairmen were similarly regulated. They had to conduct themselves properly, were not permitted to cause obstructions at any time, and when carrying passengers at night had to have 'a clean decent lanthorn, with a proper candle lighted and burning therein'. A waiting charge of 3d for each 15 minutes was permitted.

The great advantage of sedan chairs was that they provided a very personal and flexible means of transport over short distances and were particularly suitable for use along narrow, crowded streets. After these had been improved, however, the use of chairs became restricted to the carriage of invalids. By 1821 there was only one stand in London—in St James.

In each town there were similar restrictions on the use of hackney carriages. Most early hackney coaches were private carriages that had been discarded by their owners, usually on account of age. In London, a lighter form of hackney coach, the chariot, was brought on to the streets in 1814, carrying two inside passengers and one on the box outside. A later development, in 1823, was the introduction of the one horse, open-fronted cabriolet which carried two passengers at rather lower fares. Until 1831 there was a monopoly in the hackney coach trade, because the number of licences issued had been restricted from the seventeenth century onwards. This monopoly brought severe criticism, with charges that there was bribery in the actual granting of licences. In January 1832 the monopoly came to an end, and in the following year 800 new licences were granted to more than 600 proprietors. The result was that most of the old, rickety hackney coaches that had formerly been used were driven off the streets.

In Bristol the fares and condition of hackney carriages were regulated by the city council. Details of the fares that could be charged were given in a booklet published in 1826 by J. Chilcott. Among those recorded were:

From: the stand in Wine Street to—
The White Hart at the end of Lime Kiln Lane 1s 0d
The Common Pound, Durdham Down 2s 6d.
From: The stand in the Old Market—
beyond Gloucester Row to Rownham Ferry 3s 0d
beyond that to Hotwell House 3s 6d.

Among the rules governing fares was the requirement that 'when more than three persons shall be carried inside a chariot or more than four inside a coach, the owner or driver to be entitled to one quarter more than his regular fare for each extra person, except one child in the lap, which the fare may take without extra charge'. Another rule concerned 'an airing once round Durdham Down from any stand in the city, and setting down in the city', in which circumstances 'the driver may always charge six shillings, unless the fare will come to more by time, and then he shall have his option'. For distances greater than the specified ten miles radius from the city covered by the normal regulations, extra mileage could be charged at 1s for each mile and 6d for each half mile 'beyond the farthest specified in the list of fares on the respective roads'. Extra fares were permitted to be charged at the following time rates: for one hour, 2s; for any time not exceeding 15 minutes from the end of the first hour, 6d. Fares for any carriage employed after midnight could be charged at double rates. All time rates were calculated on the understanding that the driver would travel at a speed of not less than 4 mph.

The number of hackney coaches at Exeter was not to exceed thirty, in addition to ten chariots, all of which were to be licensed by the owner on 25 January of each year. Every carriage plying for hire had 'to hang upon a level, and shall be decent, clean, strong and warm, with glass windows on each side and in front thereof; the coaches to be large enough to carry four persons inside and a servant outside; the chariots three persons inside and a servant outside; and the horses to every such carriage shall be able and sufficient for their work, free from any infectious disease and not under the size of fourteen hands'. On the panel of each door and on the back of the carriage, the letters C.B., the number of the carriage and the owner's name had to be painted in gilded letters, edged with black on a dark background.

Between 9 am and 11 pm the hackney coachmen at Exeter, when not actually conveying a fare, had to remain at one of the stands appointed for the purpose. The regulations also stipulated that the coachman had to drive at a speed no faster than a trot, and under no circumstances were they permitted to loiter. Furthermore, 'the owner or owners of every carriage shall provide a check string, to be placed in a convenient part of the same, which the driver shall hold in the hand during the time of his driving any fare, so that the same may be used for the accommodation of the said fare, in default of which to forfeit twenty shillings'. In the event of dispute between driver and passengers concerning the distance covered, the dispute was to be referred to two Justices of the city, who would have the ground measured.

In Birmingham, the hackney coach fares were advertised in *The Birmingham Chronicle* for 2 October 1823 as:

Coaches drawn by two horses			*Drawn by one horse*		
Within 1 mile	1s	0d	Within 1 mile	1s	0d
1–1½ miles	2s	0d	1–1½ miles	1s	6d
1½–2 miles	2s	6d	1½–2 miles	2s	0d
2–3 miles	3s	6d	2–3 miles	2s	6d
3–4 miles	5s	0d	3–4 miles	3s	6d

In addition to these fares, hackney coachmen are entitled to the sum of sixpence for every space of fifteen minutes over and above the first fifteen minutes they are kept waiting.

In spite of all the rules and regulations, it appears that there were frequent disputes and troubles connected with the hackney coaches. The cabmen were often accused of trying to defraud the public, and in 1815 Parliament brought in legislation to check misconduct and to regulate the hackney coachmen's language. Any driver found guilty of trying to cheat or swear at any passenger was liable to a fine of £10, and two month's imprisonment if unable to pay the fine. Another complaint levelled at the coach owners was that they used poor, often diseased horses, particularly for night work. A correspondent to *The Essex & Suffolk Times* for 4 August 1838 said that many of the London horses suffered from a severe glandular disorder:

It is a notorious fact that a great proportion of the night hackney coach and cab horses are affected with this dreadful disorder, and many of them are in such a state of disease that it is impossible to bring them out until it is dark, when their appearance cannot be observed, and by this means valuable horses, with which they may probably come in contact at the different places of amusement, or

other places where these vehicles generally station themselves, run
the risk, nay, they are almost certain to be contaminated by them,
and the dreadful disease is thus spread in the most frightful manner.

The writer went on to point out that certain horse dealers, known
as 'copers', speculated in the sale of diseased horses, and every day
at Smithfield 'captains', as the affected horses were called, were
offered for sale.

Another nocturnal mischief was that of demanding excessive
late fares. One London hackney coachman was fined 20s in September 1813 for refusing to take a passenger who was not prepared
to pay an excessive fare. In his defence the cabman argued that his
horses had been out for fifteen hours, but this excuse was not
accepted by the court, which endorsed the rule that a coachman
was not permitted to refuse to carry. During the hearing the court
was told that 'it was the common practice with the coachmen to
refuse to take any one, unless they could get the sum they demanded, and that coaches frequently drove off empty rather than
take persons unless at double the regular fare'.

Another form of conveyance came on to the streets of London
in the 1790s—the omnibus. In July 1829 services were put on by
George Shillibeer (1797–1866). Omnibuses first operated in 1662
in France where they carried eight passengers, but this enterprise
was unsuccessful. Shillibeer had a business in Paris, and during
1819 was engaged by Jacques Laffitte to work on an omnibus
design. Later, Shillibeer came to London after selling his business,
and decided to put two of his vehicles, named *The Shillibeer* and
The Omnibus, on the road. Each was drawn by three horses abreast,
and the service operated between Paddington and the Bank, four
times a day, at 1s a time. The vehicles, usually called Shillibeers,
were painted green, with yellow wheels and red curtains.

Unfortunately, Shillibeer had considerable trouble in working
the vehicles. They were constantly being opposed by stage coachmen, and the conductors employed apparently pocketed a high
percentage of the fares for their own use. Shillibeer tried to discourage these dishonest practices by putting on inspectors, but
this did not completely solve the problem. Eventually, in 1834,
when his partnership with William Morton was dissolved he gave
up the idea of running omnibuses, and after fleeing abroad from
his creditors; serving a term in the Fleet prison on his return; and
serving a further term in the Fleet for smuggling brandy, he
retired to the more peaceful realm of an undertaker's business.

His system lived on, however. In Liverpool an announcement
of 1846 in *The Liverpool Courier* reported that a model of an omni-

bus had been made for the Economic Conveyance Company in Liverpool who hoped to run services:

> The body of the carriage is divided into three compartments, having three separate entrances. The centre carriage is lower than the end ones, and is intended for passengers paying twopence per mile. The compartments in front and behind are raised somewhat higher, for the purpose of placing the wheels under the body, so that the ladies' dresses will not be soiled by entering or leaving the vehicle. But the most ingenious part of the invention lies in the wheels. There are eight, four under the front carriage and four under the hinder one, the whole of which are connected by bars from the axles which give a uniform motion to the whole, no wheel being capable of moving without giving a corresponding motion to the other seven. Two horses will generally be used, but when the line of the route is hilly, three horses will be attached abreast, as in Paris. Each station in town will be a mile, and should the passenger wish to ride further, other omnibuses will run in conjunction, so that the traveller can proceed in other conveyances either in the same line or at a tangent, as his business requires.

By the mid 1830s the hey-day of coaching was coming to an end, as railways spread quickly across the country. Once the pride of the road, they were soon to be forgotten by an age obsessed with the wonders of steam.

CHAPTER 5

The Carriage of Mail

ON Monday, 2 August 1784, a coach carrying a guard sitting by the coachman, four passengers and mail left Bristol at 4 pm bound for London. This journey, brought about by the untiring energies of John Palmer, marked the inauguration of mail coach services that were to be established throughout the country during the late eighteenth and early nineteenth centuries. The specially designed coaches, with their red wheels and undercarriage, maroon bodies and black side panels, were to offer a service that was to become the pride and joy of the nation. Townsmen and villagers would eagerly await the arrival of the mail coach, for the coachman and guard would bring with them the latest news. The coaches, however, would not stay long, for after a quick change of horses they would set off again in order to keep the strict schedules on which they prided themselves.

During the second half of the eighteenth century it became increasingly clear to nearly everybody except the officials at the Post Office that there was a need to replace the slow and antiquated system of having unarmed post-boys to deliver the mail. Sometimes it would never reach its destination, highwaymen having relieved the unwilling letter-carriers of their heavy loads. At other times there were all manner of delays, despite the fact that the post-boys were threatened with one month's hard labour in the local house of correction if they were found loitering on the road. Their time schedules imposed under the Act of 1765 insisted on a rate of six miles per hour but this speed was seldom, if ever, maintained. A good deal had been done by Ralph Allen, who became responsible for the by- and cross-road letters in 1720, to improve services to the larger towns by establishing daily horse mails, but much more was needed.

John Palmer, a theatre manager at Bath, was among the many who suffered from the appalling delays. With the system of post-boys, the Bath to London mail took nearly two days to deliver, though the stage coach managed to do the same journey in seventeen hours. Palmer thought that the mail should be carried in coaches with an armed guard, which would both quicken and protect the mail. 'The post at present', he explained, 'instead of being the swiftest is almost the slowest conveyance in the country; and though, from the great improvement of the roads, other carriages have proportionately mended their speed, the Post is as slow as ever.' Under Palmer's proposed scheme the guard would be appointed by the Post Office, while the contractors who agreed to horse the mail coach on various stages of its journey would be responsible for appointing the coachman. Revenue from the carriage of parcels and passengers would go to the contractors, who would also receive a fixed mileage payment from the Post Office. For their part the contractors would provide all the necessary horses, and pay a mileage charge for the hire of the coaches.

Unfortunately, Palmer encountered a good deal of opposition from the postal authorities, who considered that the service that they were already offering was as good as possible. Officials united in this opposition, including the Postmasters-General and the Secretary, backed up by several surveyors, among them Nathan Draper, Resident Surveyor of the Inland Office. The surveyors pointed out that no coach could hope to maintain the speed of eight or nine miles an hour that Palmer envisaged, and that the proposed change would upset the careful balance of schedules that had been established over the years.

On the other hand, the Prime Minister, William Pitt, was prepared to give Palmer's scheme a trial run, and authorised the 'Mail Diligence' on the Bristol route. The trial was to be conducted at Palmer's own expense, and was scheduled to start on Monday, 2 August 1784, with five innkeepers providing the horses for 3d per mile. Palmer maintained that he would beat the time of seventeen hours for the same run put up by the stage coaches, and succeeded in his claim. The coach reached London, on time, at 8 am the next morning, having taken sixteen hours. A return journey was then made to Bristol, leaving London at 8 pm, and arriving at Bristol at noon the following day.

An announcement in *The Bristol Journal* for 2 October 1784 gave further details of the service:

> Mail Diligence commenced Monday August 2nd. The proprietors of the above carriage, having agreed to convey the mail to and from London and Bristol in sixteen hours, with a guard for its protection, respectfully inform the public, that it is constructed so as to accommodate four inside passengers in the most convenient

manner, that it will set off every night at eight o'clock, from the Swan-with-two-Necks, Lad lane, London, and arrive at the Three Tuns Inn, Bath, before ten the next morning, and at the Rummer-Tavern, near the Exchange, Bristol, at twelve. Will set off from the said tavern at Bristol, at four o'clock every afternoon, and arrive at London at eight o'clock the next morning. The price to and from Bristol, Bath and London £1. 8s od. for each passenger. No outsides allowed.

Both the Guards and the coachmen (who will be likewise armed) have given ample security for their conduct to the proprietors, so that those ladies and gentlemen who may please to honour them with their encouragement may depend on every respect and attention.

With the success of the venture established, permission was given in 1785 for services with mail coaches to be extended to other routes. East Anglia saw the coaches for the first time in the spring; extensions to Leeds, Manchester, Liverpool and Nottingham followed in the summer, and to the west country in the autumn. Following years brought further extensions, and by 1791 the mail coach routes were listed as follows:

	miles		*miles*
Dover (to London)	74	Shrewsbury (to London)	165½
Portsmouth	72	Holyhead	179½
Poole	119	Liverpool	207½
Exeter by Sarum	179	Carlisle	309
Exeter by Bath	195	Leeds	198½
Bristol	125	Edinburgh	395½
Worcester	118	Norwich by Ipswich	115
Birmingham & Coventry	21	Norwich by Newmarket	112
Glasgow & Ferrybridge	227½	Wisbech	97
Carlisle & Dumfries	40	Southampton &	
		Lymington	18
Glasgow & Paisley	14	Bristol & Birmingham	88
Glasgow & Tyne	36	Bristol & Hibbistrie	151
York to Hull	40	Ipswich & Yarmouth	53

Per day one way 3,448 miles
Per day both ways 6,896 miles
Miles per year 2,517,040
Miles the mail coaches have travelled since they started 17,619,280

Another statement of the services is given in *The Ipswich Journal* for 27 July 1799:

The coach . . . leaves Falmouth on Monday morning at 4 o'clock, and reaches Inverness on Monday following at 8 o'clock. The distance is thus calculated: Falmouth to Exeter 98 miles; Exeter to

General Post Office, London 176; London to Edinbrugh, via Berwick and Leith 396; Edinburgh to Aberdeen, via Perth and Dundee 132; Aberdeen to Inverness 123; total 925 miles. Rest one night at Exeter of seven hours, one day in London of fourteen, a morning at Edinburgh of three; total rest 24 hours. Exclusive of the time allowed for breakfasts, dinners, suppers and stops to do post office duty and to change horses; so that the time actually spent on the road during the entire distance of 925 miles, does not exceed 130 hours.

Kent's *Original London Directory* for 1815 listed the mail coaches leaving the city at that time. The coaches 'set out every evening at half past seven, except auxiliary mails which set out at 6 o'clock: Birmingham (auxiliary), Bristol (2), Brighton, Chichester (auxiliary), Dover, Edinburgh, Exeter, Glasgow, Gloucester, Hamborough & Gottenburgh (via Harwich), Harwich (auxiliary), Holyhead, Leeds & Nottingham, Lincoln, Barton & Hull, Liverpool, Manchester, Norwich, Norwich & Ipswich, Plymouth & Exeter, Portsmouth & Gosport, Shrewsbury & Birmingham, Worcester & Ludlow, Wisbech & Cambridge (auxiliary), Yarmouth (auxiliary), Stroud (auxiliary) and Southampton. The Directory also gave details of the Principal Cross and Branch Mail Coaches, which were listed as:

York to Liverpool	Bristol to Birmingham
Birmingham to Manchester	Exeter to Falmouth
Carlisle to Port-Patrick	Canterbury to Margate
Sheffield to Doncaster	Manchester to Carlisle
Portsmouth to Chichester	Dorchester to Weymouth.

The Worcester Journal for 8 September 1836 also gives details of the extent of the services:

In England there are 55 four horse and 49 two horse mails. In the four horse mails the rate of travelling varies from 8–10 miles five furlongs per hour. There is one exception, the Devonport & Falmouth mail which goes only 7 miles 2 furlongs per hour. Average 9 miles 2 furlongs per hour.

Palmer's efforts were rewarded in 1786, when he was appointed Surveyor and Comptroller-General of the Mails at an annual salary of £1,500, with the promise of 2½ per cent of any additional revenue that could be attributed to the mail coaches. His appointment was to be 'independent of the control and interruption of the Postmaster-General',—a condition which Palmer insisted upon, and one that reflected his dislike of higher authority. Nevertheless, the condition did nothing to stop the frequent opposition that he encountered from the Postmasters-General, particularly

POST-OFFICE, BIRMINGHAM, *Wednesday* the 8th *March* 183 /

ARRIVALS. — DELIVERIES.

Due by Time-piece.	Mails.	Arrived by Clock.	Commenced at P. O. Windows.	Commenced by Letter Carriers.
H. M.		H. M.	H. M.	H. M.
5 15 A.M.	BRISTOL	5 2? A.M.		
6 30	LIVERPOOL WITH A BAG FROM Manchester	6 30	7 A.M.	5 10 A.M.
7 8	LONDON WITH BAGS ALSO FROM Oxford and Northampton	8	8 15	
	SUTTON P. P. Messenger.			
7 56	WARWICK	7 8	10 20	
7	TAMWORTH	10	10 40	12 50
10 30	CHIPPING NORTON	10 18		
10	SHREWSBURY	12	12 30	
12	WALSALL	12		
12 30 P.M.	SHEFFIELD WITH A BAG FROM Liverpool	4 30 P.M.	5	6 2.0 P.M.
4	YARMOUTH	5 2?		
5 45	OLDBURY Messenger	5 36		
5 30	HALES-OWEN Ditto	5 40	5 30	
5 30	CASTLE BROMWICH Ditto	5 40		
5 30	LEAMINGTON	5 5?		
6	WORCESTER	6 35	1 20	
6	WALSALL	6 35	6 50	
6 30	STOURPORT	6 41		
6 40	MANCHESTER		8 30	
7 31	HOLYHEAD WITH BAGS FROM Dublin	7 21		

DESPATCHES.

Mails.	Box closed at		Mails Despatched at		Remarks.
	H. M.	H. M.	H. M.		
MANCHESTER WITH A BAG FOR Liverpool			6 27 A.M.	A.M.	
SHEFFIELD			5 57		
HOLYHEAD WITH A BAG FOR Dublin	7		7 45		
YARMOUTH					
WORCESTER			5		
WALSALL			6 10		
LEAMINGTON			8 8		
STOURPORT	7 A.M.		8 15		
CASTLE BROMWICH P. P. Do.			8 6		
SUTTON P. P. Ditto			8 15		
OLDBURY P. P. Ditto		2 30	9	P.M.	
CHIPPING NORTON		3	9		
WALSALL		3	9 3		
SHREWSBURY		3 30	3 30		
TAMWORTH		3 30	3		
WARWICK		6 30	4		
LONDON WITH BAGS FOR Oxford and Northampton	7		7		
BRISTOL WITH A BAG FOR Manchester			8 60		
LIVERPOOL			8 15		

August, 1836.—300.

Amount of LONDON LETTERS..... £29 14
Amount of BYE LETTERS £6 0 8 8
Amount of SURCHARGES .... £ 9

Postmistress.

FIGURE 4. Post Office, Birmingham—list of arrivals and departures

Lord Walsingham, who disliked having his position described as being but a sinecure. This contempt for his superiors was to be Palmer's undoing, for in March 1792 he was suspended, and subsequently dismissed. His 'retirement' was made happier by the award of an annual pension of £3,000, and by way of compensating him for the non-payment of the 2½ per cent levy that he had been promised, Parliament awarded him £50,000 in 1813.

With Palmer's departure, Thomas Hasker, formerly Superintendent of Mail Coaches, was upgraded to the new post of Surveyor and Superintendent of the Mail Coaches, with sole charge of the mail coach organisation. Hasker proved to be a very able organiser who concerned himself with every little detail, while keeping his superiors in touch with what was going on. His attention to details is very clearly illustrated in the numerous directions that he issued to the guards, and the advice and warnings given to the contractors. His principal task was to keep all the coaches running to their strict schedules, to enable the network of services to be maintained. This proved to be a difficult task during the early years, mainly because of the haste with which Palmer had acted, and his reluctance to co-operate with his superiors.

When Palmer found that the construction of the earliest mail coaches was unsatisfactory, he entered into an agreement with John Besant of Millbank, a London coachmaker, for the exclusive supply of a patent coach. On his death in 1791, Besant's partner John Vidler and his sons carried on, supplying coaches until 1836. Under the terms of the agreement, the coachbuilder was to supply the patent coaches to the contractors for a rent of 2½d a double mile; 'proper coach horses' had to be supplied by the contractors for their 'ground', while the coachbuilder was responsible for the general servicing and repair of the coaches; these being sent on their return to London to Millbank for cleaning, oiling and greasing. While on the road the coaches were regarded as the joint property of the coachbuilder and the contractors, but when a coach ceased to run, it was returned to the coachbuilder.

Holding the contract for these patent mail coaches was not always a happy situation, as Vidler discovered in 1803 when the postal authorities decided that the vehicles should be altered to enable outside passengers to be accommodated. Originally only four inside passengers were carried, but in 1803–4 it was decided that some could also sit outside, thereby enabling the coach to earn more money. Vidler wrote to Thomas Hasker on 23 December, complaining that 'the alteration of each coach is about £33—which is £528 for sixteen coaches and I believe I have 120 that will be required to be altered which at prime cost will amount to £3,690'. He went on to mention that by the third year of his contract (drawn up in 1787 but not signed until 1793) he had managed 'by systemizing every part of the coach to one scale' . . . to make a reasonable return, 'but immediately afterwards an advance took place beyond all computation on materials, wages, etc'. Vidler explained that artisans were asking nearly double the price for piece work, and labourers were earning half as much again. Faced with these difficulties he appealed for assistance.

Vidler's contract continued until 1836, when the postal authorities decided to put it out to tender. The chief critic of Vidler's monopoly had been Robert Wallace of Greenock, who maintained that lack of competition had resulted in a decline in the standard of mail coaches. The Commissioners reviewing the situation decided in 1835 to open the contract to competition for the future. The new contract for the supply of mail coaches divided the country into three districts, and it was laid down 'that the Postmaster General will contract to employ carriages to run daily, at the least, the number of miles specified against each', viz:

Southern	3,000
Midland	4,000
Northern	2,500

Vidler submitted a tender, in which he agreed to 'furnish efficient carriages for the conveyance of His Majesty's mail for the southern, midland and northern divisions, to be employed not less than 900 single miles daily, including every expence of drawing them to and from their respective inns for oiling and greasing them for a period of seven years at 2½d per double mile'. But the postal authorities were not prepared to accept his tender, and chose Wright, Horne & Williams for the southern and midland districts at 2⅛d the double mile, and Croall and Wallace for the northern district at 2d per double mile.

Apparently Croall experienced some difficulties with his contract, for in 1839 the contractors horsing his coaches presented a petition to the Postmaster-General complaining about defects in them. Their main grievance was that the vehicles were too heavy for their intended purpose, being clumsy and defective, particularly so far as their unmatched wheels were concerned. They also complained that the coaches were not kept in a proper state of repair; therefore they found it increasingly difficult to carry out their contract with the Post Office on a remunerative basis, for the defects caused excessive wear and tear on the horses.

The Postmaster-General decided to have the coaches inspected. In their report dated 19 June 1839, the examiners divided the coaches into five main categories: those that did not exceed 17 cwt, 18 cwt, 19 cwt and 20 cwt respectively, and those in for repair at the mail coach factory. They found that many of the coaches were dirty and shabby, 'and in fact anything but fit for service', but that they had since been properly turned out after being repainted and greatly reduced in weight. A criticism that had been levelled at Croall was that the materials he used were not always of the best quality. This, it was thought, arose because the contract was signed at a time when he had only a limited supply of materials, and because the coaches had to be manufactured in a hurry, he was forced to use 'green and unseasoned timber, the effect of which was soon visible when the sun acted upon it'. The examiners recommended that a standard weight of 18 cwt should be accepted for all mail coaches, and that Croall should withdraw and alter any that were above this weight. Similarly, all dirty and shabby coaches should be taken off the road and repaired as necessary.

When tenders for the supply of mail coaches were again advertised seven years later, on 5 January 1843, the conditions specified that the coaches had to be built with the best-quality materials, and 'expedition being the primary object, the carriages to be built as light as possible consistent with a due regard to the necessary degree of strength and safety'. As in previous tenders, the new contracts had to include the 'proper cleaning, oiling and daily examination of the carriages, and the expense of drawing or conveyance to and from their respective stations'.

A detailed specification of the mail coaches is given in a Post Office statement of 1839. The extreme length of the coach, measured from the bottom of the footboard to the end of the mail box, was 10 ft 8 in, and the extreme height, exactly over the door, was 7 ft 2 in. The distance between the fore and hind axles was 6 ft 6 in, and the width of the track, taken from the outside of the felloes, was 5 ft 1½ in. The fore wheels were given as 42 in diameter and the rear wheels as 54 in, the width of the rounded tyre being 1⅞ in. Materials were specified as follows:

Body
Parts covered with leather. Deal panels and floor mahogany. Fore boot frame—ash; fir deal case covered with leather.
Mail Box
Frame—ash
Fir casing covered with leather

Pole
Ash, Pole hook and chains with swivel collar and fastenings. Drag shoe and chain.
Under carriage
Ash
Felloes
Beech or ash
Spokes
Oak, stock elm
Bars
Ash.

Inside the coach was drab lace lining with double crimson stripes, with a carpet to match. Mahogany glass frames, with only one square of glass in each, were fitted; and the cushions were stuffed with the best horsehair. Oilcloth was fitted to the bottom of the coach, and there were two pockets on each door. Interior measurements given included $18\frac{1}{2}$ in legroom, a height from the top of the roof to the top of the seat of $42\frac{1}{2}$ in, and a width of $43\frac{1}{2}$ in.

The contractors who horsed these coaches over a particular 'ground' were chosen by the Post Office. Hasker told the Select Committee on Mail Coach Exemption of 1811 that competition between the contractors was not something that he encouraged; hence he did not choose them by tender. Instead, the Post Office examined the backgrounds of the people who offered their services, the general principle of selection being to find the stronger parties. A point that the authorities mentioned in a circular addressed to the contractors in 1798 was that: 'Should you retire from the public line and quit your inn, you must not expect to continue in the Mail coach concern; for so many innholders are quitting their inns and retaining possession of their coaches, that will be the cause of bringing forward very formidable oppositions by those persons who have taken such inns.' As this circular implies, contractors were chosen from the ranks of inn-keepers.

The contracts stipulated the route of the coach; the number of horses that had to be used; the minimum speed; the mileage allowance that was to be paid to the contractors by the Post Office; the number of passengers that could be carried; and the required notice for ending the agreement. A contract made out on 30 September 1837 for running a mail coach from the Post Office at Bristol to the Post Office at Portsmouth and back, for example, stipulated that it had to be drawn by four horses at a speed of not less than 9 mph there and back, with the provision of 'good and sufficient horses for the purpose and also careful drivers'. The contractors were to be paid equal quarterly payments at the rate of 2d per mile. Four inside and four outside passengers were permitted, and the contract could be terminated by three months' notice from either party.

The list of contractors for the Cambridge road in 1791 shows the distance covered by each:

	Miles	
Leighton, of the *Rose & Crown*, Wisbech	11	to March
Barley, of March	8	to Chatteris
Pitts, of St Ives	12	to St Ives
Whitchurch, *Sun* Inn Cambridge	12	to Cambridge
Bond (Postmaster) Cambridge & Dainty (Postmaster) Royston	14½	to Royston
Hatch, of Buntingford	7	to Buntingford
Church, of Ware	11	to Ware
Moore, of Waltham Cross	9	to Waltham Cross
	12	to London
	96½ miles	

Stage distances were determined by the horses' need for water, and generally amounted to about ten miles. It was usually reckoned that a contractor would need a horse for every mile covered by the coach operating the service, and that a mail coach horse had a working life of about three years.

Apart from meeting the cost of the coachmen's wages, the expense of the horses, and the payment of rental to the coach-builder, the contractors were charged 4s 6d a gallon for the sperm oil supplied by the Post Office for the lamps. As might be expected, the lamps were very inefficient, and not infrequently the coachmen preferred to drive without them, though this was an offence. Miles' patent coach lamps, which were eventually used on the mail coaches, brought some improvement, but even then the lighting left much to be desired on a dark night.

On the revenue side of their accounts, the contractors found that their income varied according to the coach's route. Thomas Hasker, in giving evidence to the Select Committee on Mail Coach Exemption, suggested that in order to indemnify themselves, the contractors should receive from £4 10s 0d to £5 5s 0d per double mile per month—'in other words, a coach running ten miles out and back again, ought to earn fifty guineas per month'. Hasker also indicated some of the unremunerative and remunerative services that were being operated. He stated that the Leeds coach was managed with some difficulty; the contractors at Melton Mowbray having complained that they were losing £200 a year, mainly because of the very bad condition of the roads. In the same plight was the Sheffield to Halifax coach, whose contractors bemoaned the fact that they did not earn sufficient money to pay for the straw that the horses slept on. The London to Edinburgh was one of the better-paying concerns: on this route the journey was divided into three parts—London to York, York to Newcastle, and Newcastle to Edinburgh. The profits of the enterprise were divided by the total number of miles travelled by the coach, and then shared on the basis of the mileage operated by each contractor.

The earnings of the Gloucester and Brighton mail, covering part of the years 1836 and 1837, are given below:

Earnings of the Gloucester & Brighton mail for 4 weeks ending September 10th 1836

Earnings	Disbursements	£.	s	d
£415. 3s 8d.	Two licences	10.	0.	0.
	Duty (only half charged, the remainder placed to next account)	35.	18.	6.
	Booking, printing, settling account	21.	15.	0.
	Coachmen's wages and tax	11.	12.	0.
	Lamps, oil, etc	4.	10.	0.
	Three new covers	3.	3.	0.
		86.	18.	6.
		328.	5.	2.
		£415.	3.	8.

155 miles to share at £2. 2s 4½d

Four weeks ending 8 October 1836

Earnings	Disbursements	£.	s.	d.
£445. 16s 6d	Duty last month	35.	18.	6.
	Duty	71.	17.	0.
	Two licences	10.	0.	0.
	Coachmen's wages and			
	tax	9.	8.	0.
	Booking, printing etc	12.	12.	0.
	Lamps, oil, etc	3.	18.	0.
	Bags		7.	0.
		144.	0.	6.
		301.	16.	0.
		£445.	16.	6.

155 miles to share at £1. 18s 11¼d

4 weeks ending 5 November 1836

Earnings	Disbursements	£.	s	d
£361. 10s 4d	Duty	71.	17.	0.
	Coachmen's wages, tax,			
	etc	9.	12.	0.
	Booking, printing, etc	7.	1.	0.
	Oil, lamps, etc	3.	19.	0.
		92.	9.	0.
		269.	1.	4.
		£361.	10.	4.

155 miles to share @ £1. 14s 8½d

4 weeks ending 5 December 1836

Earnings	Disbursements	£.	s	d
Warrant due 5th Oct.	Duty	71.	17.	0.
£110. 9. 9.	Coachmen's wages, tax			
281. 18. 4.	etc.	9.	12.	0.
	Booking, stationery,			
£392. 8. 1.	etc.	7.	6.	0.
	Lamps, oil etc.	2.	2.	0.
	Tavern bill at Brighton			
	meeting	17.	18.	0.
		108.	15.	0.
		283.	13.	1.
		£392.	8.	1.

155 miles to share at £1. 16. 7½d

4 weeks ending 31 December 1836

Earnings	Disbursements	£.	s	d
£299. 17s 0d.	Duty ....,..........	71.	17.	0.
	Coachmen's wages and			
	tax	9.	12.	0.
	Booking, stationery ...	16.	6.	6.
	Oil, lamps, etc	5.	4.	6.
		103.	0.	0.
		196.	17.	0.
		£299.	17.	0.

155 miles to share at £1. 5s 4½d

4 weeks ending 28 January 1837

Earnings   *Disbursements*

		£.	s	d
Warrant due Jan. 5th.	Duty	71	17	0
£177 1 7d	Coachman's wages &			
242 11 6	tax	9	8.	0.
	Booking, stationery,			
£419. 13. 1.	printing, advertising,			
	waybills etc	34.	8.	6.
	Lamps, oil	2.	2.	0.
		117.	15.	6.
		301.	18.	6.
		£419.	14.	0.

155 miles to share at £1.   18s.   11½d

The Post Office's revenue came from the postage charges on
letters. Under the old system of post-boys, the letter rates were
based on the number of stages a letter was conveyed—a stage
representing the distance covered by a post-boy between two
stage-points. These stages were shortened when Palmer introduced the mail coaches, for with fast coaches it was necessary to
change the horses frequently. It soon became obvious, however,
that miles and not stages should form the basis of the postal
charges, and John Cary was employed to measure all the mail
coach routes. In 1815 charges were as follows:

		(for a single letter, going no	
15 miles	4d	further than the distance stated)	
20 ,,	5d		
30 ,,	6d	300 miles	12d
50 ,,	7d	400 ,,	13d
80 ,,	8d	500 ,,	14d
120 ,,	9d		
170 ,,	10d	For every 100 miles or fraction	
230 ,,	11d	over 500 1d added.	

The mail guards were appointed by the Post Office for each
coach, and would travel 40–60 miles of their 'ground', later returning with the opposite coach. A guard's first task, according to
a circular dated 1829, was the care of the letter bags, and he was
answerable 'at his peril for the security, safe conduct, and delivery
of them sealed'. At no time was he permitted to leave the bags,
which had to be kept locked in the mail box throughout the

journey. Nor could he give up his position to any of the passengers or ride with the coachman: he was to remain at the top, rear end of the coach. He carried various arms, including a blunderbuss and case, a pair of pistols and holsters, a powder horn, bullet mould and touch-hole pricker; arms had to be kept clean and loaded when he was on duty, and on no account whatever was he 'to be wantonly discharging his blunderbuss or pistol as the carriage is going along the road or through a town', the penalty for which was set mildly at 2 guineas. When the journey was over he had to withdraw the charges from the guns.

The guard also had to keep a watch on the activities of the coachman—a duty which did nothing to help working relations on the coach. If, for example, the coachman loitered on the way, or there was any 'unnecessary stopping at public houses' the guard was instructed to report him to the postal authorities; failure to do so would render him liable to be taken before a Justice of the Peace and committed to hard labour for one month. The guard was not permitted to deliver letters along the road; a penalty of 10s for every letter so delivered being imposed. Similarly, he had to take great care in the delivery of the bye-bags—those destined for the cross-country routes.

As well as these duties, he had to keep an eye on the contractors, to see, for instance, that they did not squeeze more than the permitted number of passengers into the coach. Horsekeepers had to be watched as well, and any want of readiness or misconduct 'of the persons concerned in the duty' was to be reported. Five minutes were normally allowed at an ordinary stage for changing the animals. Every guard carried a horn to signal the horsekeepers to be ready, as well as to warn other traffic to give way, the mail coaches always having the right of way. Turnpike keepers on hearing the horn had to throw open their gates to avoid the coach having to stop.

The guard was equipped with a timepiece, to be checked by the postmasters at each stage, which helped to overcome the difficulties encountered before the days of Greenwich mean time. It appears, however, that the guards treated their watches with very little respect, for in a letter dated 1 September 1795 Hasker complained that they were 'very ill used on the road by guards that their own irregularity may not be discovered'.

Every guard had a carefully scheduled time-bill which gave the actual times of the journeys; the details being entered by the postmasters at each stage. These time-bills were carefully examined at Post Office headquarters, and if any delays could be attributed to

NIGHT MAIL.

GENERAL POST-OFFICE.

The EARL OF LICHFIELD, Her Majesty's Postmaster-General.

York and *Manchester* TIME BILL.

Contractors' Names.	Number of Passengers		M.	F.	Time allowed H. M.	Despatched from the Post Office, *York*, the 4 of *December* 1840, at —— 5²–2³⁵ by **Time-Piece** at 5–5 by **Clock**
	In.	Out.				
						W. Oldfield {With a Time-Piece safe No. 41 to *Penifield*
Barber, Cattle, and Maddocks..	-	1	10..	1	6	Coach No. 271 sent out — Arrived at *Tadcaster*, at 7–1
Backhouse & Hartley	-	1	14..2	1	40	Arrived at *Leeds*, at 9–10
					10	*Ten Minutes allowed.*
Lee & Coates.	2	1	10..	1	5	Arrived at *Bradford*, at 10. 25
Bradford..	2	1	7..7	1	5	Arrived at *Halifax*, at 11. 30
Carr........	2	1	7..3	1		Arrived at *New Inn, Blackstone Edge*, at 12. 30
Marriott ...	2	1	9..	1	10	Arrived at *Rochdale*, at 1– 52
Lacy & Allen	2	1	11..1	1	30	Arrived at the Post-Office, *Manchester*, the 5 of *Decʳ* 1840, at 3. 10 by **Time-Piece** at 3. 10 by **Clock**
			69..5	8	46	
						Coach No. 271 arrived *Penfeld* {Delivered the **Time-Piece** safe No. 41 to *Office*

THE Time of working each Stage is to be reckoned from the Coach's Arrival and as any Time lost, is to be recovered in the course of the Stage, it is the Coachman's Duty to be as expeditious as possible, and to report the Horse-keepers if they are not always ready when the Coach arrives, and active in getting it off. The Guard is to give his best assistance in changing whenever his Official Duties do not prevent it.

By Command of the Postmaster-General,

GEORGE STOW,

Surveyor and Superintendent

the contractors, they would be sent the following circular by Hasker:

I am commanded by the Postmasters General to inform you that the time lost on your ground between —— and —— by the mail coach, as it was on its way to —— was —— minutes; and I am further directed to desire you will immediately give such orders that time may be kept, for it is only to such as keep time, and do their duty well, the additional mileage can be given.

If the contractors continued to lose time they would be threatened with notice to quit. A letter from Hasker dated 5 April 1795 addressed to the Postmasters-General mentions a number of contractors with whom he was having trouble. A contractor for the Bath & Exeter mail coach was threatened in this way for losing time, in addition to refusing to 'pay a bill for greasing and cleaning his coaches which, for their reputation and safety, I was obliged to order and pay, and for not accepting the last wear and tear bill. This destroys all system, it being a necessary security for Mr Vidler'. Other contractors mentioned were Mr Noseworthy of Cullompton 'for losing much time and abusing the office'; Mr Thompson of Exeter 'for not appearing satisfied with the coach', and requiring more than the permitted time for running it; a contractor of the Bath, Exeter and Bristol coaches who 'does not keep time and has been frequently heard abusing the coachman for driving fast though behind time'; and the celebrated Mr Pickford, of carrier fame, who 'has lost much time and having other great occupations does not attend to the coach duty'. Apparently the threats were not carried out, for the contractors' names remained on the time-bills for 1797.

Another fault of contractors which sometimes caused delays was their failure to have their horses' shoes prepared for winter travelling. One of the circulars issued by the Post Office on this matter read:

The Post Office is dissatisfied with many of the contractors and their servants, who when they must have known the necessity, neglected to have their horses' shoes prepared for the frost and slippery roads, by which much time has been lost. It is hoped that contractors will now be careful for their own sakes, as well as from a sense of duty, to have the shoes roughed, and save their horses from falling and injuring themselves and creating delays.

If the mail coach was delayed more than half an hour because of an accident en route to London, the guard had instructions to ride ahead with the letters on horseback, or obtain a post-chaise for carrying them. Postmasters had instructions to help in any way that they could when such difficulties arose; and each guard had a tool kit which included two trace chains, one pole chain, two tug chains, one hatchet, one strong hammer, one wrench hammer, one small wrench, one small saw, one drift pin, one large spike bit, two gimlets, one main bar, shackles, bolts, clips, nuts, worms, screws, nails and cord. It did not, apparently, occur to the postal authorities to have a spare wheel carried on the coach. The wheels were the most vulnerable part of the coach and, as with stage coaches, numerous breakdowns arose from broken wheels. Hasker, though, was not unaware of the problem, for on 21 September 1796 he wrote to Vidler:

> The sudden wet weather has an effect on wheels no doubt. The near fore wheel of the Newmarket coach and both fore wheels of the Ipswich broke this morning. I must beg you will order your people to pay particular attention to the wheels and send (them) out very perfect this night.

In August 1792 Hasker gave clear instructions to the guards on the procedure to be followed after an accident: 'When any accident happens, write what it was on the Time Bill, at the next stage, and the next day give a more particular description of it by letter to me, how it happened, the cause, what was broke, and what damage was done—mind, and do not neglect this!'

Weather conditions did on occasions make it difficult to maintain the time schedules, and some of the Christmas-card scenes are hardly exaggerated. On 7 January 1837, for instance, *The Aylesbury News* reported:

> The Leeds mail which ought to have arrived at six o'clock on Sunday night, did not arrive until midnight. Not a single mail of the 25th which ought to have arrived by six o'clock on Monday morning had reached the post office before half past eight o'clock; they then began slowly to arrive, the guards accounting for the delay from the heavy fall of snow which had taken place during the night, and which, from the strong northern wind prevailing, was drifted into the hollows, where it lay to a depth of several feet. The Devonport mail arrived at half past eleven o'clock. The guard who had travelled from Ilminster, a distance of 140 miles, states the journey to have been a most trying one for man and cattle.

The Ipswich Journal carried a similar report on 22 January 1814:

> Owing to the strong gale which blew from the north east on Wednesday night, the snow, which had fallen to a considerable depth in the course of the day, drifted exceedingly, and has nearly

cut off all communication by the cross posts. The Norwich mail which should have arrived here (Ipswich) on Thursday night could get no further than Stonham; and it was near three o'clock yesterday afternoon before the guard arrived at the Post Office in this town with the bag of letters. Every exertion was made to extricate the coach from the snow; and it was once or twice drawn out by a farmer's team of six horses. The mail from hence to Bury could get no further than Stowmarket; and the letters from thence to London, Norwich, etc have been forwarded by the expresses; but from the depth of the snow, it is doubtful when they will reach their destination.

At the same time there were reports that all the mail coaches from Glasgow, Portpatrick and Edinburgh had failed to reach Carlisle, and nothing was heard of the Exeter mail for three days.

Following the heavy snowfalls of the winter of 1814, Francis Freeling, the Secretary of the Post Office, sent the following circular, dated 21 January, to every postmaster in the kingdom:

It being a matter of great importance to the country to get the roads cleared for His Majesty's Mail, you will apply to the overseers of the parishes and to the surveyors of the highways, as well as to any other person concerned, and beg them to employ all the means in their power to make the roads passable for carriage with as little delay as possible.

A month later, *The Leeds Mercury* had an account that a letter had been sent by the Post Office to the postmasters to recommend 'a machine called a snow plough for clearing the roads. This machine, which is made by a few boards in the form of a wedge, was first used some years ago at Wimpole, by Mr Wm. Oswald, then bailiff of the Earl of Hardwicke'. A contemporary plan of this snow plough is illustrated overleaf.

Severe winters inflicted a heavy penalty on the road surfaces. After the bad winter of 1795, for example, it appears that many of the mail coach routes suffered from the poor condition of the roads, as Hasker's letter to the Postmasters-General in March 1795 indicates:

. . . there are in many places very deep holes which obliges the coachmen to drive rather slower than they used to do over such spots, and when they do not see them they are often attended with accident. The York coachman and guard were both chucked from their seats going down to Huntingdon last journey and, coming up, the guard is lost this morning, supposed from the same cause, as the passengers say he was blowing his horn just before they missed him . . .

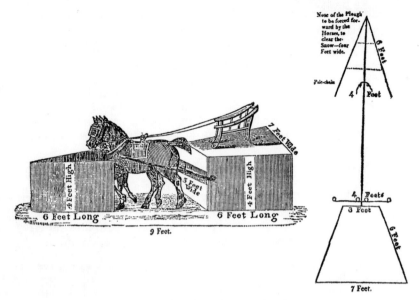

FIGURE 6.   Plan of a snow plough

For performing his arduous tasks the mail coach guard, who
had to be physically strong to withstand the long journeys, was
paid a salary of 10s 6d per week. Tips from passengers were also
expected, even though the Post Office initially ruled that they were
'not to take fees under any excuse whatever'. Later it seems that
the postal authorities again became rather more concerned about
tips, for in July 1840 *The Essex Standard* reported:

> By a recent regulation of the Post Office guards of mail coaches are
> prohibited from receiving fees from passengers under the penalty
> of dismissal; and their salaries have consequently been increased on
> a scale which is graduated by length of service. We believe that the
> lowest rate of remuneration is fixed at £70 per annum, and that the
> highest salary does not exceed £120. The new arrangement will be
> beneficial to the passenger traffic on the mails.

A circular dated 7 November 1804 lists the names of guards
who had been dismissed for various offences. One of them had
taken up a parcel at Bristol to deliver at Tetbury, but had left it
in the mail box; another had conveyed fish in the mail box without
paying carriage; another for carrying more than the permitted
number of passengers, the additional fares going into his own
pocket. A fourth guard was relieved of his duties for being 'drunk,

forgetting his bags, and having to go back for them, by order of the Duke of Montrose'. A fifth man was discharged for being drunk, with the added offence of 'leaving his bags wrong and disobedience of orders', while another was dismissed for smuggling. One of the other two named culprits was found guilty of malpractices undefined, and the second 'for dealing in game and sending them by the mail coaches'.

The temptation to pick up passengers along the road was particularly great, for these unofficial passengers meant money in the pockets of coachman and guard. Most contractors were aware of the practice. Those of the York and Hull mail coach tried to overcome it by putting a notice in *The York Courant* for 5 January 1790, saying that they would 'be particularly obliged to any lady or gentleman who will give information of either the coachman or guard's misconduct in taking up passengers on the road or causing unnecessary delays'. The same notice announced that the contractors had decided, for the convenience of passengers, to have only one coachman for the entire length of the York to Hull run.

In frequent circulars Hasker wrote to the guards to remind them of their duties. He was particularly concerned that:

> ... half my time is employed in receiving and answering letters of complaint from passengers respecting the improper conduct and impertinent language of guards. I am sorry to dismiss sober, honest men, but I must have civility also, and when you behave impertinently to passengers they find out some other error to couple the complaint with, that nothing less than dismissal can succeed. This painfully shows how circumspect guards should be in their behaviour, and I must insist that you conduct yourself so properly in all your words and actions as to prevent complaints.

The main concern of the Post Office, however, was the risk of theft of the mail. On 8 and 9 January 1813, Hasker read a statement to the guards, informing them of recent robberies that had taken place on coaches. Among these was the theft from the Bristol mail coach of a bankers' parcel worth £100, while *The Expedition* stage coach had been twice robbed within a week, 'the last time of all the parcels out of the seats'.

Indeed, although the Post Office could pride themselves that their coaches were not plundered by highwaymen, there were instances of thefts organised with quite remarkable skill. In 1823, £20,000 in banknotes vanished from the Warwick mail coach. The removal of the money was described as having been 'effected in a very extraordinary manner', the coach contractors' way of saying that they had no idea how it had happened. A large sum was

I

offered for information leading to the conviction of the thieves, but the willing, if not particularly able services of amateur detectives and would-be helpers were turned down when the thieves agreed to return the money for a substantial payment.

To combat the hold-ups arising through bad road conditions, the postal authorities promptly sent out disapproving and threatening letters to parish surveyors and turnpike trustees responsible for the offending stretches. Thomas Hasker told the clerk of the Essex turnpike trust in January 1805:

> The state of the new road at Widford is such as almost to prohibit travelling, and the delay His Majesty's mail has, and is likely to experience by it, renders it highly necessary that something may soon be done to enable as much as possible the correspondence to be facilitated, and to prevent the disagreeable necessity of having recourse to indictment.

By return of post came the reply that a group of commissioners had inspected the road, and the assurance that the necessary repairs would be made to put the road in as good an order as the season would permit—a qualification that covered a multitude of sins.

In giving evidence before the Committee on the Highways and Turnpike Roads in England & Wales, which submitted its report in June 1819, Charles Johnson, Hasker's successor as the surveyor and superintendent of Mail Coaches, complained about the state of the turnpike roads around London. In explaining that he thought that there were not such good materials available for road construction around the capital—these being chiefly gravel—he said that there was also some evidence of insufficient attention given to the condition of the roads. The Egham trust, in particular, was reprimanded. As Johnson explained: 'It was at that time reported to me, that the whole town of Egham had been covered with gravel unsifted eight or nine inches deep from side to side; the consequence of that was, that the mail coach (to Exeter) lost ten, fifteen, or twenty minutes every night.'

Generally speaking, Johnson said that the mail coaches had more difficulty in passing to and from London for the first fifty or sixty miles because of the poor state of the roads than in any other part of the country. 'It is in the nights that we have the heaviest weights,' he explained to the commissioners, 'and therefore it is very desirable that the roads near the town should be rather better than worse than others.' He considered that roads in north Wales were 'remarkably good, and in my humble opinion, show great success in the formation of them'.

As the roads were gradually improved, the Post Office was able to extend the mail coach services. In any discussion of the starting or extension of a particular service, townsmen and villagers would complain that the coaches did not pass through their territory, and petitions would be drawn up. In 1836, for instance, a case was made out for the mail coach to pass through Tiverton instead of Cullompton. The petitioners argued that the diversion would add only three or four miles to the coach's journey, but the argument, of course, really hinged on the relative importance of Tiverton and Cullompton. Cullompton, it was pointed out, was a large country village with a population of just under 4,000 and 'with nothing connected with it to make it a centre of business'; Tiverton, on the other hand, was considered to have many claims to importance. It was a town with a population of 10,000, 'surrounded by a thickly peopled agricultural neighbourhood'. It had a large lace factory, employing 1,500, and a school with 120 pupils. It had one bank, and the possibility of another soon, and more shops that any other town of a similar size. Other claimed advantages included a large market; a considerable number of 'gentlemanly families' and a pack of foxhounds. With all these business connections, it had a considerable trade with London and Exeter, and there had been frequent complaints about the delays that had resulted from the mail being brought into the town by cart. However, Tiverton lost its case.

When a service was to be started, the Post Office would tell coaching proprietors and others of the intended route, and ask them whether they were interested in submitting a tender for horsing the mail coaches. In October 1812 an advertisement in *The Nottingham Journal* pushed the claims of the proposed Sheffield to Worksop run:

> As the Worksop road is on every account the most eligible one from Sheffield to London, if the connection be continued and well supported through, there is no doubt but that it will prove a very beneficial concern as almost the whole of the commercial interest here would be disposed to patronize and encourage the undertaking, so long as it continued to be well conducted.

On occasions, even during the golden years of the services, the Post Office experienced difficulties in getting sufficient contractors for some of the routes. This happened between Taunton and Barnstaple through Wiveliscombe during 1827–8. The service was intended to start from Taunton at 3 o'clock and arrive at Milverton 3.45; Wiveliscombe at 4.15; Bampton 5.15; South Molton 7.15; and Barnstaple at 8.30. Mr Whitmarsh agreed to horse the coach from Taunton to Shillingford, and Mr Pearce from South Molton

to Barnstaple, while Mr Chorley said that he would only provide
the horses from Shillingford to South Molton on the understanding that 'the sum of £250 be raised by subscription' which he
considered would 'only be a fair remuneration for the loss he shall
sustain by providing horses on so short a notice and the additional
horses which will be required to take the coach over the eighteen
miles of new formed road in the time required by the Post Office'.

Apparently the required money was raised, for a letter dated
24 September 1827 from Richard Hancock mentioned that 'more
is subscribed I believe than was necessary to put the horses on the
road'. The same letter continued: 'I could wish the overplus may
be applied in laying a new coat of stones on part of the road, which
I fear will not stand the winter without it. I mean over the bogs
on the moors which, it is possible, I think will break up after a
heavy rain when the springs are high. The expense must otherwise
fall on the parishes, I imagine, for the trustees of the Wivilescombe
turnpike have expended all their money in making the road.'

During the first half of the nineteenth century the Post Office
was constantly trying to improve upon the time schedules. By the
1830s the Liverpool to Preston coach was completing the distance
at an average speed of about 11 miles an hour. In 1811 the journey
between London and Birmingham, a distance of 116½ miles, took
15½ hours, an average speed of 7½ mph; but in 1837 the time for
the journey, using Telford's new road to Birmingham was reduced
to 11 hours 8 minutes, an average speed of 9¾ mph, By 1837,
though, the hey-day of the mail coach era was coming to an end.

CHAPTER 6

Travelling in Style

WITH all the disadvantages and discomforts associated with travelling in the stage and mail coaches, men of means preferred to have their own carriages, driven by themselves or by coachmen resplendent in liveried uniforms. Travelling in this manner was exceedingly expensive, involving a considerable outlay on the purchase of the vehicle in addition to the many running expenses. In 1837, *The Spectator* reckoned that the cost of running a carriage with coachmen and footmen and all incidental expenses was in the region of £200 a year. Nevertheless, wealthy members of society vied with one another in the turn-out of their carriages, little expense being spared in adorning them with every conceivable luxury.

The evolution of design in the carriage-building trade depended on two interrelated factors: the design of the undercarriage and the type of suspension; and the condition of the roads at the time. The earliest carriages, which had to travel over rough and unmade roads, were limited to a suspension which followed the traditional pattern of the heavy waggon described in Chapter 3, with the front and rear axles connected by a long wooden pole, called a perch. A later improvement, dating from the time of Charles II, was the use of leather braces to support the body of the carriage; and towards the mid-seventeenth century attempts were made to use steel springs in the suspension. These in turn led to the invention of elliptic springs by Obadiah Elliott in 1804, which, with the road improvements of that time, marked a turning point in carriage design. The use of elliptic springs meant that carriages no longer had to have perches, and this freedom enabled designers to build much lighter and more elegant vehicles.

Private carriages of the period 1750–1850, although presenting an infinite variety, can generally be divided into two main groups: firstly, those driven by the owners themselves; and secondly, the more graceful and costly carriages driven by coachmen. The first group can be subdivided into four-wheeled vehicles, usually called phaetons—the name being derived from Phaeton, the son of Helios, who, according to classical mythology, narrowly avoided setting the Earth on fire when he upset his father's chariot; and two-wheeled vehicles, including the whiskey, sulky, curricle and cabriolet for dashing young men about town, and gigs and buggies for more sober-minded individuals.

The early phaetons, dating from the 1790s, were generally referred to as highflyers, so nicknamed because of the high position of the seat above the 4 ft or 5 ft high wheels. There were two kinds of highflyers—the ordinary perch, and the rather more shapely crane-neck phaetons, the latter consisting of two bent iron cranes which enabled the front wheels to turn under the body. Such vehicles, driven by two to six horses, appealed to the faster gentlemen of the road, among them the Prince of Wales who was to become King George IV. Later phaetons displayed an enormous range of design: some with rounded bodies, others with angular; some on cee springs, others on elliptic springs without a perch; some added a groom's seat behind; while the mail phaeton, dating from about 1828, displayed a somewhat heavy structure, resembling the lines of the mail coach. Because of their heavy-handling characteristics, Mail phaetons were unsuited for lady drivers. They were used for sporting and town work, and particularly for long-distance travelling with post horses. Rather more elegant in design was the demi-Mail (or semi-Mail) phaeton which appeared towards the end of 1830, the main difference from its predecessor being in better springing. It had elliptic springs on the front axle and elbow springs at the back.

Phaetons also varied in price, the cost depending on the type and finish provided. Nevertheless, some indication of the likely cost is given in an estimate dated 11 August 1824, addressed to the Rev Joseph Arkwright of Mark Hall, Harlow, in Essex, from William Cook, coachmaker. According to the specification, the phaeton had 'able shifting bodies and a large locker underneath, made of best material, seasoned timber and workmanship, neatly carved and run, painted and picked out to order and the panels highly varnished and polished, a four-hooped circular head with japanned joints and a japanned dashing leather to one of the bodies, two neat leather knee-boots and floor cloth in the bottom . . . a perch carriage with hoop tyre wheels turned and hardened axles and boxes. Long under springs to the fore-part of the body and circular whip springs with braces and jacks to their backs to the hindpart of the carriage and painted and picked out and clean varnished and a pair of japanned lamps fixed with socket ironwork, the whole complete, duty included, £225'. If paid for on completion, a discount of 7½ per cent was allowed, otherwise 5 per cent was given for payment within four months.

A less expensive phaeton was supplied to the Rev Thomas Cullum in July 1832 by Samuel Chamberlain, coachbuilder, of Great Newport Street, Long Acre, London. The account gave details of 'a new handsome turnover seat caned phaeton, neatly painted green, relieved with black and well varnished etc., lined with drab cloth, lace, etc. £45. Painting crests 16s 0d. Total £45. 16s 0d'.

The choice of two-wheeled privately driven vehicles was also extensive. The fashionable curricle, dating from about 1800, had the distinction of being the only two-wheeled vehicle to be driven by a pair of horses abreast, that is, on either side of the pole. Curricles were greatly favoured by members of the aristocracy, but during the next decade they were gradually replaced in fashion by the cabriolet, a single-horse carriage. Every elegant cabriolet had its 'tiger' on the back—a diminutive groom who stood on a small padded platform. W. B. Adams, in his book *English Pleasure Carriages* published in 1837, wrote that 'this is a very convenient vehicle for unmarried men to go out in at night'. Later, the 'tigers' were to disappear from the roads when the dog cart became the more popular vehicle. Most early dog carts were used for country pursuits, but later varieties were used for all manner of purposes throughout the nineteenth century.

Gigs, which were used by a wider section of society, were initially rough and cumbersome in design, but during the course of the nineteenth century they became more elegant. The earliest improved design was the whiskey, dating from the 1790s. This vehicle, 'whisked' along by one horse, had a light, caned body. Included in the range of gigs were the Tilbury and Stanhope varieties; the former being well sprung on seven springs, the latter being mounted on two side and two cross springs. Hooded gigs were usually called buggies. Gigs, with a large boot, were used by bagmen—commercial travellers or representatives as they are now more politely called. At the other end of the scale, gigs were greatly in vogue among sporting undergraduates who drove them round the towns.

The other main group of vehicle—the coachmen-driven carriages—included the nobleman's four-seater town coach and two-seater chariots; elegant landaus, barouches, broughams and britchkas; and the more sober fourgons and drags. Coachmakers, who often specialised in the construction of a particular type of carriage, gave all their skill and attention to these vehicles, which were usually described as being finished with the very best materials. Most of the famous builders, such as the firm of J. Hatchett, who supplied royalty at home and abroad with elegant carriages, were to be found in Long Acre, London. Gentlemen requiring a carriage could write off or visit these coachbuilders for an estimate, and could rest assured that their every whim and demand would be met.

One typical estimate submitted by Hatchett was for a 'handsome coach' ordered in 1783. The specification, written out in elaborate detail, included 'a body made of the best materials, seasoned timber, and workmanship . . . single steps and neat brass bead plates to door pillars to secure the edges and lighten the appearance, the back and sides panelled up very neat and smooth for japan, the roof covered with the best leather well prepared for japan; lined with the best second lights, coloured cloth sides tufted trimmed with the best seaming and binding, orange and white laces . . . best polish and plate glasses and frames. Mahogany shutters and silvered glass . . . a neat strong perch and carriage suitable to the body . . . the best town made iron-work of every kind. Iron and axle trees of best German steel springs and shackles and bolts, a set of strong wheels corn tyre'.

The basic price for all this was £126, to which could be added the cost of many desirable and some apparently necessary accessories. Among these extras, all of which were detailed separately in the estimate, were a pair of best double steps instead of the single steps normally fitted, costing a further 2 guineas; extra silver-plated beads all round the roof, up the back and sides, round the framework of the body and round the oval behind, which cost 15 guineas; extra silver plating 'the main check brand buckles and door handles, two guineas'; a set of green silk curtains for the doors and front at £3 13s 6d; a set of silk festoon curtains to match the lining, made 'very full and trim with fringe orange and white to doors and front' at £5 4s od; a pair of 'handsome wheel harness and bridles made of the best leather and plated furniture and housings and winkers served round strong . . . roses, bitts and reins complete' costing 17 guineas; and finally 'to extra difference making the seat cloth full puckered and fashionable being more cloth, lace and fringe' which added a further £3 10s od to the bill. Adding all these extras to the basic cost, the prospective purchaser was faced with a possible bill of £173 3s 6d, a figure which can probably be multiplied by twelve or more to bring it in line with present-day prices.

An even more expensive carriage was the one quoted for by W. Sanders, coachmaker, to an Essex gentleman in January 1822. The quotation was for 'a new fashionable town coach, with outside elbow convex sides and sword case in the back'; the carriage being lined in rich leather and carpeting. Other details included 'a light compassed perch carriage neatly carved and securely iron'd, best steel whip springs and strong wrought iron axletrees with round arms and plated caps to the axle trees. Hoop tyre wheels with ash felloes, the body and carriage painted any plain colour that may be chosen and the panels and upper part of the body highly varnished and polished'. The price for all this came to £215, but again, there were numerous extras, including 'a fashionable barouche driving seat, cloth cushions' at £26 10s od; a platform to receive trunks, £11; a town seat £5; a strong iron drag, £2; and larger springs at an extra £14. Assessed duty amounted to £1 5s od, bringing the grand total to £322 5s od. A £22 5s od discount was allowed for cash settlement, which brought the price down to just £300, a considerable sum when it is remembered that an agricultural labourer was being paid about 9s a week at the time.

Details of a travelling chariot, a vehicle that was used for private posting by 'carriage folk', are given in another quotation made out to Sir Thomas Cullum by coachbuilders Orlingridge, Cook, Rowley & Mansell in December 1831. Described as 'a genteel new chariot', the vehicle was priced at £205. Extras included a tool kit, comprising a screwed wrench, a wheel wrench, a steel S wrench, hammer, chisel, pincers, screwdriver, twelve tins of pins and twelve leather washers, costing £1 16s od; and 'a new tin can filled with grease for the wheels, a leather cover strap and buckle to ditto, 17s od'. Together with several other extras, the total price was £332 5s od, plus delivery charges of £9 5s 3d, covering 'man's time, post horses, post boys, and expenses taking the chariot to Hardwick House, Bury St Edmunds'. Four months later the baronet took delivery of another chariot, this time from Henry Joseph Hall, coachmaker and harness-maker of 99 Long Acre, London, for which he paid £266 15s od.

For those people who could not afford the high cost of buying new, there was always the possibility of obtaining a good second-hand vehicle at a reasonable price. Such purchases could be made from a number of sources: auctions, sales of used carriages by coachmakers, and private advertisements in local newspapers.

Auctions were held from time to time in most parts of the country, as for example at Nottingham on 1 March 1800. An announcement in *The Nottingham Journal* read:

> *Neat Post chariot:* London built, with plated harness complete, cost upwards of one hundred guineas, which will be sold by auction at the Blackmoor's Head Inn at Nottingham tomorrow, precisely at half past twelve o'clock by Mr Gaskell. The said chariot has plate glass windows, lamps etc., and is in good order. The reason of its being sold is that the owner is going abroad.

Would-be purchasers were offered several carriages belonging to a bankrupt druggist in an auction sale at Brighton in April 1842. A half-headed barouche by Rossetti, lined with purple cloth, and having driving and luggage boxes and patent lamps, was described as being 'nearly equal to new', and fetched £130. A newly built, fashionable vis-a-vis, painted a rich blue, and 'lined drab cloth and figured silk with hammer cloth, driving seat, pole and bar and shafts', was sold for £100, while a cabriolet went for £15. Also in the sale was a pair of greys which fetched 130 guineas.

Coachmakers in towns up and down the country provided all manner of carriages for the travelling public, both new and second-hand. A typical advertisement of one of these coach-makers, offering his new carriages, was put in *The York Courant* for 8 October 1840. His name was G. Gunn, of Haymarket, York, and he assured the public that he was able to build carriages equal to anything that came out of London. He claimed many advantages for his own designs:

> The new principle combines the following improvements: elegance of form; lightness in construction; more easy and pleasant action in the springs; lower, with high front wheels, making a lighter Draught, and by the free lock of the front part, giving a greater safety. . . .

Among the many coachmakers who offered second-hand carriages for sale was H. Pattenden of Mount Street, Nottingham, who, in the pages of *The Nottingham Journal* for 14 March 1812, offered the following vehicles to his discerning clientele, listed in the order of 'Friends, the Nobility, and the Public in General':

> A light modern chariot with Barouche seat, lamps and plated furniture, little worse than new; a second hand post-chaise with plate glass, lamps and plated furniture in good repair; a second hand whole panel gig, with a head and plated furniture, curricle fashion, little worse than new; one very light second hand gig with an extra seat behind, and a variety of second hand gigs in good repair, that will be sold cheap.

Alderman James Oakes, wool merchant and banker of Bury St Edmunds in Suffolk, apparently obtained a reasonably priced phaeton in 1807, for he records in his diary for 3 May:

> Set off for home at nine o'clock in my own phaeton which had been run only three or four miles, bought of Bushnall & Co., No. 1 Berniers Street, Oxford Road, coachmakers, entirely new painted, new lined and the leather on the head quite new, Swan necked and very light and proper height quite complete with new trunk leather, etc., and a pair shafts, cost £72. 12s 0d.

The main advantages of dealing with a coachmaker were that he would usually be able to obtain the type of carriage needed, and at the same time undertake any repairs that were necessary to put the vehicle on the road. John Robson & Co of 56 and 67 South Audley Street, Grosvenor Square, London, provided this service for the Hon Mr G. G. V. Harcourt, MP in 1847, when they purchased 'an excellent second hand chariot' for him for £84. They undertook numerous repairs and replacements to the carriage in order to put it into new condition again. The body, for instance, required a good deal of attention, which involved 'taking off the appendages, unhanging the body, taking out the perch bolt, removing the fore carriage, and taking off wheels, springs, etc' charged at 12s. A new pole made of prime seasoned ash was fixed, costing 22s, including the iron work. The set of springs was unhooped, scraped and cleaned, and the bearings of the bottom stays were relined with stout leather for 38s. Another item charged was 'taking out the bolts and solid robbins, making twelve new bolts, screwing them up and case hardening them and robbins and fixing, 26s 0d'. The wheels were attended to for a charge of 35s, necessitating 'the taking off the wheel irons, fixing new bolts, new stout felloe piece neatly carved and fixed, etc', and 14 guineas had to be paid for 'the making of extra strong new wheels of prime seasoned timber shod with best hoop tyre, rivets, etc'.

As with most second-hand vehicles, Mr Harcourt's chariot required repainting, and the charges for this were 18s 6d for stripping off the old paint and preparing for the new, and £6 10s 0d for 'new painting picked out and highly varnishing the carriage'. Other touching up included blacking and japanning, and the erasing of old crests and the painting of new ones in their place. Repairs to the interior involved the cleaning of the lining, the replacement of the spring curtains, attention to the cushions and carpets, and the provision of a new waterproof cover for the sword case and a new apron for the hind rumble. The venetian blinds were mended for £1 11s 6d, and various adjustments to the lamps added a further 14s to the bill.

Final adjustments to the chariot involved the re-covering of the pole with leather, a new drag shoe, and the provision of a new 4 guinea tool budget which had 12 in screws; wrenches; three dozen spare bolts; linch pins; a new bar; and brass padlock. When all these and several other items were added up, the repair and overhaul bill amounted to £146 19s 6d, bringing the cost of the vehicle to £230 19s 9d.

A few people were able to get good bargains from the sale of coachmakers' businesses in country towns. Such sales provide the few remaining records of the nature of a country coachmaker's business, for the stock-in-trade was usually given in the sale notices. A typical example is the sale of a business at Leighton Buzzard in January 1839, the coachmaker, Mr Lock, having decided to retire. According to the sale announcement in *The Aylesbury News* for 15 June, the main items were a new cab phaeton and 'an extremely neat new square-bodied phaeton', both finished in the very best style; a neat pony chaise, two double-seated and light pony spring carts; a second-hand family gig and post-chaise; and a two-horse, narrow-wheeled cart. Other items were a new wheelbarrow; a neat-headed chaise body (by Hopkinson); a pair of second-hand wheels; a large trunk for bending lancewood shafts by steam; six iron-bound hogshead axle casks; about ten sets of lancewood springs with caps and shackles complete; a quantity of oak saplings; driving boxes; chaise aprons, gig cushions, hubs and wheelbarrow wheels; scantlings; useful lamps; and finally 'old iron and other useful effects'.

A similar sale was held at Ipswich during the spring of 1805, when the stock-in-trade of William Paine, bankrupt coach and harness maker, was offered for sale by auction. Items in the sale were listed as a large quantity of seasoned ash timber and planks of different thicknesses, felloes, harres, spokes, eight pairs of new wheels and a large quantity of second-hand wheels; a curricle and single-horse harness; many plated furniture springs; curricle bars; lamps; leather and cloth; a very elegant curricle, quite new, and also a second-hand one; a barouche-type gig with a dog basket; two single-horse chaises; three taxed carts; a curricle body; a one-horse chaise body; and various additional items 'useful in the trade'. This particular business was taken over by L. Sharman, who, within a few weeks after completing the purchase, was advertising in the newspaper columns: 'gentlemen's carriages and post-chaises neatly repaired and elegantly painted'. He also had a variety of carriages for sale, including a second-hand crane-neck cabriolet 'in good condition, with a head and harness, complete for one horse, and to drive with a pole occasionally; likewise a neat one horse chaise, curricle springs, with a convenient budget, and harness for one coach in capital condition'.

Within the carriage-building business there were numerous trades, as the following advertisement in *The Ipswich Journal* for 24 January 1801 indicates:

> To coachmakers: Wanted, a general hand in the above business; likewise two coach blacksmiths, and a coach wheel maker, who may have constant employ and good wages. Enquire of W Browne, coachmaker, Bury St Edmunds, Suffolk.

Many country coachmakers went to great trouble to assure their customers that the men in their employ were equal to the coachmakers in London—the criterion by which all the best tradesmen were judged. One Norwich coachmaker, for example, pointed out that 'first rate London workmen will continue to be employed'.

Carriages sold by private individuals were usually advertised in the pages of local newspapers, all manner of carriages being offered at well below the new prices. A selection of advertisements is given below:

Ipswich Journal, May 1794
To be sold very cheap, if early application for, a second hand town chariot, with plated harness, etc., price thirty guineas.

Leicester Journal, September 1794
To be sold for fifty guineas, a fashionable curricle almost as good as new, with stop wings, trunk, etc., and a complete set of harness.

Ipswich Journal, June 1795
An elegant Disobligeant, London built, with patent wheels, patent lamps, pistol cases, and everything complete with a new plated harness. This carriage is built for strength and expedition, though perhaps the lightest in the kingdom; holds one person, and carries compactly change for two months. The property of a gentleman about to alter his condition. Price twenty five guineas, with or without a strong chestnut horse that has been used to draw it.

Berrow's Worcester Journal, March 1796
To be sold, a neat modern-sized phaeton, in a remarkably good condition, with boot, hind seat boxes, head and plated mouldings, etc. It runs remarkably light and is adapted for a single horse or a pair, having a pole and shafts. The shafts are new, and the carriage is on its first wheels.

Worcester Journal, May 1797
A handsome light phaeton to be sold, on its first wheels (with patent tyre) which are nearly as good as new. It was painted and well varnished last summer and had, at the same time, a new false lining—twenty five guineas.

Ipswich Journal, June 1798
To be sold—an exceeding good Post Chariot, with sword case, lanthorns, plated mouldings, and landau joints; worth in November last £80 has never been used since; now to be sold for £50.

Ipswich Journal, July 1805
A complete town built post chariot (almost new). To prevent trouble, the lowest price is 160 guineas.

Nottingham Journal, November 1812
To be sold a second hand chariot either with or without harness, for a pair of horses. The body of the carriage is in very good repair, except the painting; but the wheels are bad.

Shrewsbury Chronicle & N. Wales Advertiser, 1820
To be sold, a Dennet and harness, price 30 guineas, built by Manton, painted black, with lamps and complete with boxes for travelling and apron lined with silk oil skin.

Ipswich Journal, May 1822
To be sold—a highly fashionable Dennet, built by Blurton of Bond Street under the owner's immediate eye, at an unlimited expense; has been little used, and is in every respect as good as new; patent axle-trees, harness, etc., complete—as the owner is leaving the country it will be sold for £30—cost £80.

Among other things, these advertisements show that instead of a mileage calculation, the wheels of the carriage, whether on its first or second set, were often an important point in determining price. A carriage on its first set of wheels was generally regarded as a good buy, rather in the same way that a motor car today often has a higher market value if it can genuinely show a low mileage. On the other hand, it is obvious that private carriages were subject to a good deal of depreciation, and this was a consideration that many an owner had to contend with when calculating his total expenses in keeping his vehicles on the road.

One way of making the purchase of a carriage a little easier was to find a firm that offered hire purchase facilities, or 'deferred payments' as they were called in those respectable days. One firm to offer such facilities was Maythorn & Son of Biggleswade, who sold single broughams for 90 guineas cash or three annual pay-ments of £33 each, and landaus for 120 guineas cash or three annual payments of 42 guineas. An alternative arrangement was contract hire, when a coachmaker provided and kept in repair a coach and harness for a fixed period for an agreed annual sum. In April 1787, for instance, a City gentleman paid a Westminster coachmaker 36 guineas a year to be provided with a new coach with a perch carriage and a pair of harness for a period of four years. The agreement stipulated that the coachmaker was to pro-vide two new hammercloths and to repaint the carriage com-pletely during the period, while the user was to be responsible for any broken glass and the cost of any accidental or wilful damage.

Once the carriage had been obtained, the owner had to set about the task of buying horses, a task which was made more difficult by the need to match them so that the carriage would run smoothly. Here, again, there was the choice of either attending auction sales, or reading advertisements in the local press. Some idea of the prices asked for carriage horses in different parts of the country can be seen from the following selection of advertise-ments:

Exeter Flying Post, May 1782
Price 30 guineas—a pair of handsome Bay chaise horses, fifteen hands and a half high and strong in proportion, fast trotters, exactly matched and fit for immediate hard work.

Norwich Mercury, January 1791
To be sold—a capital pair of Bay horses, warranted not more than seven or eight years old, elegant in figure and good goers—the lowest price ninety guineas.

Ipswich Journal, April 1804
To be sold, a pair of uncommonly active Chariot horses, fast trotters, perfectly steady, and warranted sound. Also a sensitive set of harness, by Peat of the latest fashion, with new cloths, brushes, etc. To be seen at the Livery stables, belonging to the White Horse Inn, Ipswich. To prevent trouble the price is £150.

Ipswich Journal, December 1805
A pair of Bay coach horses, now in constant work, to be disposed of; the one seven and the other nine years old; they are warranted sound and tractable in harness, and may be driven if required before purchase, by applying to Mr Fryell, The King's Head, Ipswich. The lowest price is 50 guineas.

Nottingham Journal, June 1812
To be sold, a well-bred mare (now six years old) a safe good
traveller on the road, having travelled several hundred miles at one
journey with great ease and cheerfulness ... the price is 50 guineas.

Shrewsbury Chronicle, June 1821
A brown gelding six years old, perfectly steady in single harness,
in good working condition, improving daily, safe to ride and free
from vice or blemish—price 25 guineas.
A grey mare six years old, an excellent roadster, good slow hunter,
steady in harness and perfectly sound—Price 30 guineas.

A news item in *The Ipswich Journal* for 11 May 1822 mentioned
that 'at Lincoln Horse Fair, valuable horses were rather scarce,
and fetched very high prices; one dealer on Monday actually paid
£600 for 4'.

The next expense the carriage owner had to meet was the cost
of the annual licence for the coachman, a form of selective employment tax, and for the carriage. These were as follows in 1785:

	£	s	d
Annual licence for every coachman	1	0	0
Annual licence for every 4 wheel carriage (to be paid by maker)	1	0	0
Annual licence for every 2 wheel carriage (to be paid by maker)		10	0
Annual licence for every 4 wheel carriage (to be paid by owner)	7	0	0
Annual licence for every 2 wheel carriage (to be paid by owner)	3	10	0

Owners of gigs costing less than £12 only had to pay an annual
licence of 12s 0d, the words 'Taxed Cart' having to be painted on
the vehicle.

The more elegant vehicles had the further imposition of the
armorial bearings tax if the owner wished to adorn the carriage
with the family crest. According to the notices issued by the
Stamp Office, 2 guineas had to be paid in 1798 'by any person
keeping a coach or other carriage, upon which any duty under the
management of the Commissioners for the affairs of tax is charge-
able, and on which any armorial bearing or ensign shall be painted,
marked or affixed'. Such taxation was not particularly remunerative for the Government, for in 1799 the total collected was only
£7,373.
With the carriage and horses purchased, and the licences paid,
the next step in setting the carriage on the road was to engage a

9a. The mail coach guard.

9b. A mail coach forces the Cheltenham *Magnet* coach to give way.

10a. A patent chariot, 1809.

10b. A barouche, with Ackerman's patent movable axles, drawn by C. Blunt.

coachman, together with the stable servants to look after the animals in a large household. There was not, of course, any standard rate at which such servants were engaged, but a book on household management published about 1740 by Anna Maria Barbara, wife of the eighth Lord Petre of Thorndon Hall in Essex (to be found in the Essex Record Office) gave the following table of suggested wages per annum:

A coachman	£8.	0.	0.
A postillion	£6.	0.	0.
A chief groom	£10.	0.	0.
An under groom	£6.	0.	0.

Somewhat higher wages were in fact paid by Lord Petre:

	1763	1791		
	£	£.	s	d
Coachman	21	26.	5.	0.
2nd coachman	15	16.	16.	0.
Postillion	7	9.	9.	0.

A coachman had to fulfil numerous requirements, as can be seen from the following advertisements:

Ipswich Journal, 1758
Wanted about Michelmas—a coachman in a gentleman's family, who can drive four horses, and ride postillion well; a single man who must have had the smallpox, and know how to drive in London.

Norwich Mercury, 1790
A coachman—wanted at Lady Day by a gentleman who lives in the country; a steady, sober, middle aged man, who can drive on the box or on the horses, and to look after two saddle horses; such a person by applying to Mr Marshall, bookseller of Lynn, may hear of a good place—but a good character is required.

Leicester Journal, 1792
Wanted in a gentleman's family an under Postillion of light weight. Enquire at the Three Cranes Inn.

Ipswich Journal, 1796
Servants wanted. A coachman and footman, in a private family; they must have good characters from their last places for steadiness, sobriety, honesty and cleanliness. Must understand well their respective business, and be willing to work in the gardens and grounds at leisure times. The coachman must be an experienced driver for box or saddle.

K

Berrow's Worcester Journal, 1797
Wanted, a person of light weight to drive a pair of gentleman's
chaise horses, who will not be too proud, at leisure, to work them
in a cart.

Ipswich Journal, 1805
Wanted in a gentleman's family, a coachman of light weight who
understands the business perfectly; he will have the care of three
carriages, horses, etc, with the assistance of a postillion, and he
must read and write. Any person qualified as above having an
approved character from his last service, may hear of another by
personal application or letter to Mr Trotman of Ipswich.

Nottingham Journal, 1828
Wanted a single man of light weight as a coachman to ride and
drive in a gentleman's family—none need apply who have not
lived either as a coachman or under coachman or who cannot have
a good twelve month's character from their last place.

Not infrequently, gentlemen seeking coachmen were assisted in
their search by notices in which the coachmen advertised their
services:

Ipswich Journal, 1795
Wants a place as coachman or postillion, a young man, about
twenty nine years of age, who has for several years been used to
driving on the box, and saddle, and understands perfectly the care
of carriages, horses, and waiting at the table, if wanted occasionally; has lived for four years in his last place from whence he can
have a good character. Any gentleman or lady may hear of the person by applying to John Knight, bookseller, Saxmundum, Suffolk.
Letters, post-paid, will be immediately answered, by letter or
person.

Maidstone Journal, 1786
Wants a place on or before Lady Day next, as coachman, a man
about thirty years of age, of light weight, is well acquainted with
either way of driving, can be well recommended, and would wish
to live with a gentleman that chiefly resides in the country.

The duties of a coachman were defined in the book on household management mentioned earlier. Apart from the obvious one
of driving and caring for the carriages, the coachman was responsible for the proper feeding of the horses. He also had to be
acquainted with shoeing: 'he should know how to sett on a hors
shoe when by accident they cast them upon a journey, for when
this happens att any distance from a Smith's shop, a hors is often

spoil'd by getting so far without his shoe'. It was suggested, too, that the groom should have a working knowledge of the various ailments of the animals entrusted to his care, for this would save expensive bills from the farriers who knew 'how to reckon at deare rates for Druggs that cost them next to nothing'. A wide range of medicines was available to help the custodians, as the list of Mr Blaine, 'Professor of Animal Medicine', of 5 Wells Street, Oxford Street, London, W1, readily shows:

Cholic balls 2s 6d each	Blistering ointment 3s od pot
Cordial balls 1s od	Paste for grease 4s od
Diuretic balls 1s 2d	Eye water 2s 6d bottle
Purging balls 2s od	Sweating blister 2s 6d
Mild ditto 1s 6d	Strain embrocation 3s od
Cough balls 5s od ½ doz.	Mild grease wash 3s 6d
Farcy balls 6s od	Fever powders 5s od ½ doz.
Mange ointment 7s od pot	Worm powders 5s od
Mercurial balls 2s 6d	Condition powders 5s od
Mild ditto 2s od	Mild diuretic powders 5s od
Fever cordial balls 8s od	

All the medicines were described as being 'discovered, prepared and signed' by Mr Blaine, and were accompanied 'with copious and plain directions as to enable every person readily to cure their own animals'.

Details were also given in the household guide about the jobs that had to be assigned to the stable servants. According to the recommended procedure for an 'orderly family', 'servants that are employed in the stables rise att 5 o'clock from wch time till the half hour past eight they find employment enough in cleaning their stables, dressing and feeding their horses; after wch an hour or two is spent in watering and ayring of them. This being over by halfe hour past eight the servants will have a good stomach themselves, & may be allowed an hour and a halfe to heare mass* and eate their breakfast after wch they return to grease or clean their coaches, harness, bridles, etc, as there is occasion. In the afternoon there is very little occasion till the evening when the horses must be drest, fed and watered. As in the morning, their last visit to the stable is after supper, when they goe only to putt hay into the racks and make the bed of straw wch the horses are to lye upon all night'.

With this advice went a solemn warning about the possible laxity of stable servants: 'There not being occasion on every day to clean their coaches, harness, etc, servants commonly take that

* Lady Petre, the author, was a Roman Catholic.

time after breakfast or soon after dinner to goe to their ale hous, and rather than want a pretence I have known them pull off a horse's shoe that they may carry him to the smith's and so entertain themselves at the next ale house three times as long as the horse is shooing, wch brings servants into an ill habit besides the spoyling of many a good horse by standing so long in the cold.' The only way to overcome this, apparently, was to have a quarterly contract with the local smith under which he agreed to shoe the horses for a fixed price, coming to the owners' stables to carry out the work. Five shillings per quarter for each horse was the suggested price at which the contract should be drawn up.

Bills for fodder varied according to the season and harvest, but the adviser on household management had the following suggestion to offer:

> The common allowance of oats is something more than a peck a day; that is two bushels a week wch in a yeare comes to thirteen quarters of oats, so that a yearly provision for a horse is about four loads of hay and thirteen quarters of oats. The price of new hay (if it be a seasonable yeare) is about twenty shillings a load, and the price of new oats about ten shillings a quarter, so that according to this the expence of each hors may be reckoned att about ten pound ten shillings a yeare.

The accounts relating to Audley End, in Essex, give a further indication of the stabling expenses that might be incurred in a nobleman's household. A receipted bill dated 5 July 1784 reads:

> Received July 5th, 1784 of the Hon Sir John G. Griffin, the sum of £2. 12s 6d in full for half a year's allowance for materials to coach horse stables, due to me as coachman on the 24th June last, by me Thomas Baker.

Another account, for grass and hay for the coach and saddle horses, dated July 1784 reads:

> Grass horses 497 nights or 71 weeks @ 2s od per week as per horse account   £7. 2s od.
> Groom's stable 10 nights hay at 6d each as per horses account 5s od.
> Coachman's ditto 36 nights hay at 6d each as per ditto   18s od.
> ....   £8. 5s od.

Once the carriages were on the road they were subjected to a good deal of wear and tear, which inevitably meant numerous repair and servicing bills had to be paid. Mr G. G. V. Harcourt, mentioned earlier, had substantial bills from the firm of John Robson & Co, coach and harness makers. The accounts, which covered the years 1849-55, included the servicing, repairing and

purchasing of new vehicles, and were given in yearly totals as
follows:

	£.	s	d.	
1849	33.	8.	6.	
1850	192.	2.	0.	(new carriage
1851	47.	4.	6.	included)
1852	25.	10.	0.	
1853	64.	13.	0.	
1854	9.	7.	6.	
1855	221.	18.	0.	(includes purchase
				of carriage)

There was no fixed mileage basis for servicing as used with motor
cars today, but it was undertaken at fairly frequent intervals. If Mr
Harcourt's chariot is taken as an example, three types of service
can be distinguished, which, in today's terminology used by
garages, might be described as short, medium, and long services.
These can be shown as:

SHORT SERVICE: Total cost £1. 11s 0d.
(example taken from the accounts for 28 April 1853)
Chariot: Taking out perch bolt and fore carriage, cleaning rust
from front bearings, well greasing them and refixing fore carriage
with a new collar and key to perch bolt .... 13s 6d.
Setting up the body, releasing braces from shackles, well greasing
the bench and active parts, shackles, etc, refixing the braces, and
regulating the hanging of the body, fixing jack covers, blacking
jobs, etc .... 17s 6d.

MEDIUM SERVICE: Total cost £4. 1s 6d.
(example taken from 9 September, 1850).
Chariot brought in, washing and cleaning .... 5s 0d.
Taking off the travelling and fixing on the town appointments,
regulating the hanging of the body .... 8s 6d.
Taking out the bolts from eyes of under and dumb springs well
greasing and refixing, greasing wheel plate and under carriage
6s 0d.
Cleaning and fresh oiling the patent axles, washes, etc ...... 15s 0d.
Refreshing varnish to body, blacking jobs, etc £2. 7. 0

LONG SERVICE: Total cost £16. 7s 0d.
(example taken from accounts for 5 July 1853)
Chariot brought in, washing and cleaning .... 5s 0d.
Taking off wheels, stripping off the tyres, framing on new spokes,
cutting joints, wedging down all the spokes and making patent
boxes secure .... £1. 13s 6d.

> Making set of new tyres of best iron, heating and fixing them on with new rivets, smoothing off felloes for painting ... £6. 18s 0d.
> Taking off braces, cutting away decayed ends and splicing on new ends of best neat leather strongly sewn, refixing braces, etc ......
> £4. 14s 6d.
> Taking off the town and fixing on travelling appointments, regulating hanging of body, refixing fresh covers .... 8s 6d.
> Painting, picking out and varnishing felloes of wheels, blacking jobs £1. 12s 6d
> Cleaning and fresh oiling the patent axles, etc 15s 0d

Apart from these periodic services, many other items on the carriages required attention from time to time, and formed a substantial part of the running expenses. One was the replacement of covers, especially the hammercloth covers. Such a replacement, so far as Mr Harcourt was concerned, meant 'a patent McIntosh cover for Hammer cloth bound with lace top and bottom', and cost about £6. Tins of cannister oil were also required for application between services, and these, purchased every three months or so by the hon gentleman, cost 7s 6d each. Another item, frequently recorded in Mr Harcourt's bills from Robson & Co, was:

> Taking out set of patent boxes from old wheels. Set of new wheels, best quality, very strong, £14. 14s 0d.

There is no indication of the length of time or the number of miles that a set of wheels would cover, but it seems that an average user would require a new set about every two years.

Rather distressing entries in Mr Harcourt's accounts, which probably appeared also in the bills sent to many other carriage folk, were for repairing damage after an accident. Mr Harcourt's mishaps were not infrequent, and one in January 1852 necessitated the under-mentioned repairs:

> Taking off casing and stay from under springs, shutting on new end to dumb spring, new bolts etc (Accident) .... £1. 12s 0d.

Four months later there was another entry concerning an accident:

> Taking out hind axle, heating and tracking to the road, re-fixing, securing the clips with leather, heating and rounding out the wheel hoops, blacking jobs (accident) £2. 18s. 6d

Accidents could arise from a variety of causes, especially lack of consideration for others on the part of some road users; wheels breaking; reins snapping; and horses bolting. Any such mishaps could result in loss of life or limb. A certain John Wheeler, for instance, had a fatal encounter with one of the Bath coaches in

October 1802. The local newspaper reported that 'Mr John Wheeler, of Calne, was returning from London in his gig, accompanied by Mr J. Singers, of Beekington, when one of the first afternoon Bath coaches advancing furiously behind them, they made way; but on the instant of coming up with them, the coachman wantonly snapping his whip, and the guard unnecessarily sounding his horn (as there was nothing in the way), the horse took fright; Mr Wheeler jumped out and broke his leg; Mr Singers remained in the chair, with one of the shafts broken, till by getting hold of the reins he pulled the horse against a high bank, where he was thrown out to a great distance and much bruised'. Sad to relate, Mr Wheeler later died as a result of the injuries he received from his perilous leap.

Equally unfortunate was Mr B. D. Cock, who came to grief when driving round Camden Place, near Bath. In consequence of curbing the horses too much, the unhappy driver found that they became restive, and one of them snapped the bar. Seconds later, horses and carriage were 'suddenly dashed over a precipice of one hundred feet, by which the gentleman was literally dashed to pieces, and the curricle destroyed'. Another example of uncontrollable horses is provided by a fatal accident which occurred during late August 1797, when a common carrier operating between Bristol and Thornbury tried to stop a runaway horse. According to a report in a west-country newspaper, 'a Whiskey, with two gentlemen in it, having been run away with by the horse, one of them was thrown out of it, but the other keeping his seat, cried out for assistance near the public house at Felton, when Hicks (the carrier) ran across the road to stop the furious animal, in which attempt, the shaft of the Whiskey entered his body with such violence as to cause his death'.

Some drivers had the most remarkable escapes, especially the man who was driving a chair near Broadstairs one Saturday afternoon in September 1802. During the course of the drive, the 'horse took fright at a windmill near the road and ran down the hill into Broadstairs, where, in turning the corner of Nuckle's Library, after carrying away part of the railing, the wheels got entangled with a post, when the shafts separated from the carriage, with which the affrighted animal ran over the cliff, and was dashed to pieces. The gentleman escaped unhurt'.

Newspapers, of course, only reported the grim accidents, and for accounts of more peaceful journeys one has to look elsewhere. Fortunately, the diaries of Alderman James Oakes give interesting details of the many trips that he made. Among the entires is an account of a journey his family made to the hot wells at Bristol; the purpose of the visit being to repair the declining health of one of his daughters:

Tuesday, December 5th, 1797
We all set out at nine o'clock on our journey for Bristol thro' London in our own coach, Mrs O., self, daughter Charlotte, daughter Gould and servant maid. Took our own coach as far as Bourn Bridge and our own horses with Mr Daines our leader. Manservant on temporary seat in the place of the coach box.

	Miles
Tuesday night Hockerill	46
Wednesday London Baliso	36
Thursday Reading	43
Friday Devizes	50
Saturday Bath	19
Sunday Bristol	16

We drove to Barton's Gloucester House Hotel at the Hot Wells, passed all Monday there, engaged lodgings at Mrs Bouetts near St Vincent's Parade.

	£.	s	d
We travelled 416 miles: 416 miles, 4 horses postillion and turnpikes, 2s 4½d	46.	19.	3
Expenses 12 days on the road going and returning per mile 1s 2½d	24.	8.	0.
Lodging, board, hiring furniture 24 days	25.	15.	5.
Physician and apothecary	13.	13.	0.
Use of harpsicord, library, hired horses, coach standing, cleaning, greasing and repairing	3.	11.	6½
	£114.	7.	2½
I think it probable my daughter might say for sundries extra not coming to my knowledge 36 nights	2.	12.	9½
	£117.	0.	0.

A shorter journey was made by Alderman Oakes on Saturday, 14 September 1799, when he went to Yarmouth from Bury St Edmunds. The following entry was made in the diary:

Saturday September 14th, 1799
We all up to Yarmouth about ½ after nine . . . being a wet day Sister Bridge and her daughter, Mrs O and self all got into the chariot. We sent our own horses forward Friday afternoon to Bungay, hired horses from Yarmouth to Bungay, our own horses

took us from thence to Stanton, stopped an hour and ½ at Scole to dine. At Stanton Ian Orbell's horses met us.

	£.	s	d
Out 19 nights and 19½ days			
3 horses for 17 nights at the Bear cost us	5.	15.	9.
Hostler		10.	6.
Servant	1.	2.	6.
Expenses on road to and from	3.	11.	9.
Yarmouth horses to Bungay 21½ miles and postillions	1.	7.	6.
Sundries	3.	0.	9.
	15.	8.	9.
Sundry expenses extracts	4.	11.	3
	£20.	0.	0.

The other form of transport available to wealthy travellers was that of posting. Posting took three forms: the hire of post-chaises (normally discarded private chariots) and post-boys, on a mileage basis; the hire of horses to pull one's own carriage; and the hire of riding horses. Most postmasters, as the men who ran the services were called, were innkeepers trying to attract custom to their houses. Announcements in the local press gave details of the services, as for example an advertisement dated November 1795, in which Thomas Boswell announced to the nobility, gentry and travelling public in general that he had taken over the Oak Inn at Woodbridge, and could offer comfortable beds, the best of wines and spiritous liquors, and neat post-chaises with able horses at 1s per mile.

The post-boys who accompanied the post-chaises were usually dressed according to a standard pattern, which comprised a bright yellow jacket worn in the south of England, and a red jacket in the north. Breeches, short top boots, and a large beaver hat completed the uniform. Most post-boys were a good deal older than their name implied, often being elderly men whose better days had been spent in private service. They invariably received their keep from the innkeepers who hired them out; for their income they depended on the customary tips, which, in a good week during the busy months of the summer, could earn them as much as £5.

The post-chaise, often known as the 'yellow bounder' to distinguish it from the 'bounder' meaning a gentleman's carriage, was usually a small, closed chariot, mounted on cee springs, capable of carrying two passengers and a limited amount of luggage. Chaises nearly always travelled at a gallop, which must have been a fairly gruelling experience for the passengers, since many of the post-boys, driving postillion on the nearside horse of the pair or four pulling the vehicle, were not always competent in the art of driving. Some drivers had a very obvious desire to race one another, as for example, the three drivers from March, Cambridge-shire, who gave their passengers a hectic and unforgettable ex-perience one spring morning in 1796. 'As three chaises were going from March', read one account, 'one chaise was overturned down the bank through the carelessness and audacious behaviour of the three drivers racing. The post-boy of the last chaise being deter-mined to gain ground of the first two, drove on, and passing them with great speed on the road before they came to the bank, one of the ladies called, and desired them not to drive too fast, observing it was dangerous, and they were not in any great hurry. To this the hero of the whip paid no attention, but kept his pace, which exasperated the other drivers that were determined to repass him, which they did on the narrow and most tremendous part of the bank, by which means the chaise, in which were the three ladies of March, was thrown down the bank with great violence, twenty two feet nearly perpindicular; the ladies were terribly cut and bruised, and the chaise dashed to pieces.'

Competition between the postmasters was extremely keen, with the result that their charges were fairly uniform from inn to inn. This aspect is shown in the following table:

Table of Posting Charges in Different Parts of the Country

Date	Inn (or landlord)	Vehicles (p/c = post-chaise)	Charges (per mile)	Extras
1757	Grice, Bishopgate Street, London	4 wheel p/c & pair horses	9d	
1758	John Shenton, Horse Shoe Inn, Goswell Street, London	4 wheel p/c & pair horses	9d	
1759	Dolphin, Romford	as above	9d	
1759	Cock & Bell, Romford	as above	9d	
1759	William Wood, Fleece, Bocking	as above	9d	
1760	Ram, Newmarket	as above	9d	4 horses 1s 3d.

1780	Talbot Inn, Leeds	neat p/c with able horses & careful drivers	9d	
1781	Bell Inn, Maidstone	as above	9d	
1793	White Hart Inn, Leicester	as above	1s 0d	A chaise the day 18s 6d
1796	Oak Inn, Woodbridge	as above	1s 0d	
1796	White Elm, Copdock	as above	1s 0d	
1796	King's Head, Gloucester	as above	1s 0d	
1799	Saracen's Head, Chelmsford	as above	1s 0d	
1800	Mr Gray, Nottingham	as above	1s 0d	
1804	Castle Inn, Birmingham	as above	1s 0d	4 horses 1s 9d
1808	Red Lion Inn, Doncaster	as above	1s 3d	Four horses 2s 6d; saddle horses 7½d
1811	Bull & Mouth, Leeds	as above	1s 6d	
1818	Angel Inn, Stilton	as above	1s 3d	
1818	Fleece Inn, Colchester	as above	1s 3d	
1820	Half Moon, Exeter	2 chariots with barouche seats & 2 p/c	1s 3d	

This competition, as might be expected, was the subject of frequent complaints on the part of the postmasters, as a notice in *The Ipswich Journal* for 11 April 1761 illustrates:

George Mellor, the Cock & Bell, Romford, proposes to supply gentlemen with post-chaises, the best of horses, and careful drivers, for twelve mile stages, at eightpence per mile, if further ninepence; heavy luggage or three in a chaise, one shilling a mile. Please to take notice that ninepence a mile is the price at all other Houses which enables them (at the expense of their employers) to see the postboys who, not only not stop at the said House when ordered, but also give out that my horses, carriages, entertainment and accommodation are the worst to be had, the absurdity and maliciousness of which proceedings will immediately appear on doing him the honour of calling and making a travel.

Other examples of competition are given in the frequent announcements in the newspapers that some postmasters had lowered their
prices, which invariably meant that others had to follow suit. In
March 1802 it was reported that the price of posting had been
reduced in London, and that it was expected that postmasters in
other parts of the country would also lower their charges. Apparently the forecast proved true, for the innkeepers in Salisbury,
to mention but one town, announced that they had reduced their
prices to 2s for a post-chaise and four horses, and to 1s a mile for
a chaise and pair of horses.

Faced with this competition, some postmasters attempted to
keep prices high by forming combinations among themselves.
Evidence of this restrictive practice is provided by a court case
involving a gentleman 'of some consequence in the commercial
world' who brought a Brighton postmaster to court on the
grounds that 'a combination had been entered into to keep the
price of post work up to the standard of 1s 6d per mile, to the
injury of the travellers and the public'. Further proof of the practice is given in another item in *The Ipswich Journal*, this one being
dated 17 October 1818. In his notice to the travelling public, John
Beale, innkeeper of the old established post and family house, the
Angel Inn, Stilton, advertised that he would hire out post-chaises
at 1s 3d per mile. At the same time, he informed the public that
'the combination to get all the work into one line, and to shut out
those old established houses at Bugden, Stilton, Stamford and
Greetham, had been completely defeated; that Mr Walker of
Alconbury Hill, and some of his connections, having put out post
horses in a post house at Stilton to run at 1s 0d per mile, for the
short stage only, whilst they, at their own houses, are, at the same
time, charging 1s 6d., is nothing more than a mere decoy, to draw
our connection on to their line, and is as illiberal as it is con-
temptible'.

Details of posting houses are sometimes given in sale notices, or
in advertisements for letting. In *The Leeds Mercury* for 9 January
1813, for instance, there is an advertisement relating to the letting
of the Golden Lion, Settle in Craven, Yorkshire. The inn contained 'every accommodation for the nobility and gentlemen,
travellers, etc', and was 'advantageously situated, being upon the
High Road from York, Leeds, etc to the Lakes and all parts of the
north, and the only posting house in Settle, having the Royal
Union coach passing from Leeds to Kendal, where the passengers
dine. The tenant may be accommodated with the fixtures, furniture, horses, chaises etc at a fair valuation'.

Expenses that a postmaster was likely to incur in running his business were given by a Suffolk postmaster in 1802 when he tried to convince the travelling public that he could not possibly afford to lower his charges. The details that he presented were given under the headings of income and expenditure for a year:

Expenditure	£.	s	d.
Average cost of a pair of post horses £30 to last 5 years, with interest on money	7.	10.	0.
—ditto—of post-chaise, harness and repairs with interest on money 7 years	24.	0.	0.
Duty on chaise, exclusive of what is now pending in Parliament	8.	8.	0.
3 cwt of hay per week, consumed by 2 horses is 156 cwt @ 70s per ton	27.	6.	0.
5 bushels of oats per week to ditto is 260 bushels @ 2s 6d per bushel	36.	5.	0.
1 bushel of beans to ditto is 52 @ 4s 0d per bushel	10.	8.	0.
Straw @ 2s 0d per week	5.	4.	0.
Shoeing, farriery, etc	6.	6.	0.
Stable, granary & chaise house rent	3.	3.	0.
Horsekeeper, candles, stable combs, brushes, oil & utensils	5.	5.	0.
Allowing 1 post lad to 4 horses, half his board, beer, etc @ 8s 0d. per week	10.	8.	0.
	£144.	3.	0.

Income			
It is rather beyond, than under, to calculate one pair of post-horses to work 3,000 miles out in a year which @ 1s 0d per mile is	150.	0.	0.
Deduct 3d per mile post horse duty	37.	10.	0.
	£112.	10.	0.

The loss at 1s 0d per mile, to the innkeeper by every chaise he keeps is £31. 13s 0d

In his argument, the innkeeper emphasised that 'fifteen pence per mile is, in favour of the innkeeper, only £5. 7s 0d per annum on each chaise, which is little more than sufficient to pay his foraging expenses, allowing everything to be bought at the prices above stated, which is not the case as hay is now selling in Ipswich at £4 and £4. 10s 0d per ton. The above are facts which may be relied on and there are many local circumstances attending the posting business, such as long credit, bad debts, etc . . . a great deal more might be said, but I trust I have said enough to convince my friends and the public in general, that my present charge of fourteen pence per mile, is not adequate to the expenses, and by no means an imposition'.

A similar statement appeared in *The Leicester Journal* for 22 November 1793, when the postmasters of Leicester and Loughborough maintained that they could not manage to carry on their business at less than the following prices:

Post chaises with:—
    pair of horses per mile with 1 person   1s 0d
                         2 persons   1s 2d
                         3 persons   1s 3d
       four horses per mile   2s 0d
    For a saddle horse   6d

These charges they based on the fact that they had to pay £1 11s 6d for old oats per quarter, £2 16s 0d for beans, £5 10s 0d per ton for hay, and 2s 6d per cwt for straw. They did, however, promise to reduce their charges 'as soon as an alteration in the circumstances of the times will enable us to do'.

The high cost of posting is clearly indicated in the account books that were kept by Lord Petre of Thorndon Hall, Essex. The following extracts are typical of the numerous entries:

1777–1778
December 19th: Saddle horses to Ilford and back   4s 10d
April 20th: Pair horses to Romford   6s 0d
                      4 horses from Thorndon to Ilford   16s 3d
July 14th: Chaise to Chelmsford and back   18s 0d
October 21st: Pair horses to Cope Hall and back   £1. 1s 0d
                      4 horses to Whitechapel and back   £1. 17s 6d

1778
September 29th: Paid for coach and four to Thorndon Place to
                      carry the 6 cooks   £1. 10s 0d
October 15th: Paid for ditto a post-chaise to Romford 12s 0d
October 16th: Paid for ditto to Thorndon   15s 0d
                      Gave to the ostler   6d
                      Paid for the turnpike   8d
                      Postillion and horses   4d
                      Gave the postillion   2s 0d
October 22nd: Paid for turnpikes from Thorndon to London
                      1s 0d
                      Paid for hay and watering the horses   6d
                      Paid to Mr La Roche for the stage coach 12s 0d
                      Paid for a hackney coach from Whitechapel
                      3s 6d.

Other details of the charges are given in the records of the Best family, who, apart from having a brewery business at Chatham, had the Sun Inn in the town. The inn served as a posting house, the post-horse licence being made out in the name of Thomas Rickman in 1823. According to the terms of the licence, Rickman was permitted to 'let to hire . . . any horse or horses, for the purpose of travelling post, by the mile, and from stage to stage; and also to let to hire for a day or any less period of time than twenty eight successive days, any horse or horses to be used in travelling or for drawing any coach or other carriage used in travelling post or otherwise, in Great Britain . . .'.

The entries in the posting day book give the details of the chaises or carriages sent on journeys, the name of the post-boy, the destination, the mileage, and the cost involved. Typical entries are given below:

Wednesday 6 August 1823
Sir John Brown   pair of horses   M. Richardson
To Maidstone   11s 3.

Thursday 7th August 1823
Mr Harrison   Barouche and pair   James Holt
To the races   £1. 10s od
Mrs Dann   Chariot and pair   Thomas Page
To the races   £1. 10s od
Gentlemen from Mitre   Chaise & pair   M. Richardson
To Upstreet (7 miles)   10s 6d.

Friday 8 August 1823
Capt Warren   Barouche and pair   James Holt
To the races   £1. 10s od
Mr Price   Chariot and pair   Thomas Page
To the races   £1. 10s od
Capt McKlean   1 chaise and pair   Thomas Page
To the Ball (Bull, Rochester)   9s od
Mr Ashenden   chaise and pair   M. Richardson
To the races (set down)   15s od
Dr Bryant   chaise and pair   M. Richardson
Brought from the races   10s 6d
Lieut. Smith   chaise and pair   James Holt
To the ball (from the Sun)   7s 6d
Col Thornton   chaise and pair   M. Richardson
To the ball and back   9s od

Saturday 9 August 1823
Gentleman from Chest   Chariot and pair   Thomas Page
  Arms   12s 6d.
To Sittingbourne 10 miles

Messrs Colegate & Gillo	chaise and pair	Thomas Page
To Sittingbourne 10 miles	No 2	12s 6d

Sunday 10 August 1823

Mrs Bresley		
To church and back	Barouche and pair	Thomas Page
		10s 6d

Most of the items entered in this day book are for journeys between five and seventeen miles, to places (from Chatham) such as Ospringe, Dartford, Faversham, Maidstone, Newnham and Sittingbourne. A few entries are made to Holborn, London—a journey which cost 3 guineas.

Also entered in the day book are details of the post-horse duty that had to be paid. The following entries are made:

December 1823

Duty made up to this day being six weeks ...	£67.	17s	1½d
Poundage 1s 9d	7.	15.	4½
Error in the last book		5.	3
	£8.	0.	7½

16 February 1824

Post horse duty to this day .... £10.   2s   0d.

These taxes were introduced in July 1779, when it was ordered that owners of diligences, post-coaches or other vehicles with four wheels let out for hire for posting, had to take out an annual licence of 5s and pay an additional tax of ½d for every mile travelled by the vehicles. At the same time, postmasters letting out horses for hire had to take out an annual licence, and were required to impose 1d per mile for each horse 'for the use of His Majesty'. If the distance travelled could not be determined, a tax of 1s per horse for the day was imposed, but for those let out for a period of longer than one day no tax was due.

The taxes were collected by the Commissioners of Stamps who issued two types of tickets—the mileage ticket and the day ticket. Travellers who were posting had to purchase these from the post-masters; see that they were properly filled in; and leave them with the toll-keeper of the first turnpike gate through which they passed. It was the job of the toll-keepers to return the tickets to the Offices of the Commissioners of Stamps, where a check would be made between the tickets and the weekly accounts submitted by the postmasters.

In subsequent years changes were made in the level of the taxes;

11. A selection of private carriages: (*top left*) barouche; (*top right*) brougham; (*middle left*) landau; (*middle right*) travelling coach; (*bottom left*) dress coach; (*bottom right*) chariot.

12a. Post-chaise.
12b. *The Drag, the property of His Grace the Duke of Beaufort.* Lithograph by Hanhurt.

and in 1787 the Chancellor of the Exchequer proposed letting the duties in the same manner as the turnpike trustees farmed out their tolls. For this purpose, the country was divided into a number of districts, with the post-horse duties being let out on a three-year basis. In 1817 the districts were put up for the following sums:

		£
1.	North Britain	15,000
2.	Northumberland Cumberland Westmorland Durham	10,000
3.	Yorkshire	18,000
4.	Lancashire Derbyshire Staffordshire	19,000
5.	Lincolnshire Nottinghamshire Leicestershire	10,000
6.	Northamptonshire Rutlandshire Warwickshire Oxfordshire	17,000
7.	Wiltshire Worcestershire Gloucestershire	18,000 (except Bristol)
8.	Norfolk Essex Suffolk Cambridgeshire	17,000
9.	Bedfordshire Buckinghamshire	8,000
10.	Hertfordshire Huntingdonshire	11,000
11.	Surrey	13,000
12.	Middlesex	28,000
13.	Kent Sussex	23,000
14.	Hampshire Berkshire	17,000
15.	Devonshire Dorsetshire Cornwall Somersetshire	22,000 (including Bristol)
16.	North Wales	8,000
17.	South Wales	7,000

L

According to a notice issued by the Stamp Office in London, dated 25 October 1817, 'the highest bidder will be declared the farmer, and will be required to pay down immediately, in bank notes, seven and a half per cent, upon the annual rent as a deposit; if no sufficient bidding shall be made for any district, it will be withdrawn. The farmer of each district will be required to give bond, with three or more sureties, in the penalty of half the annual rent for securing the payment of the rent and the performance of the contract'.

The post-horse duties were a frequent subject of complaint amongst the postmasters and, perhaps not surprisingly, many attempts were made to avoid payment. A typical evasion was the case heard before the magistrates of Birmingham and Coventry in 1797, when several postmasters were fined £10 each for 'omitting to issue stamp office tickets with, and pay the duty on horses, let by them to hire'. Some of the accused tried, unsuccessfully, to make the defence that they thought that they were not bound to issue tickets because they did not enter any turnpike road; while others pleaded that they were not aware that the duty had to be paid both ways 'on horses that were hired to go to a certain place and return'. Others were fined for letting horses out for hire without the required licence.

Hard times were ahead for the postmasters with the coming of the railways, for many of them were quickly to lose their customers. In the more isolated regions the posting houses continued their trade, for travellers still needed their services, but along the main routes served by the railroads the post-chaises were soon put away, never to be used again.

CHAPTER 7

The First Generation of Steam Carriages

AT a time when coaching services were being quickened and extended as a result of highway improvements, engineers were busily engaged in devising means for applying steam power to drive road vehicles. The mechanical difficulties appeared to be unending, but the inventors hoped that their machines would eventually prove to be faster and cheaper than horse-drawn coaches. Yet although steam appeared to herald the advent of a new era in transport, the first generation of English steam carriages, dating from 1801–40, marked an unhappy episode in the history of communications, ending in financial ruin for many designers and operators.

The eighteenth-century experiments made by Savery, Newcomen and James Watt with stationary steam engines opened up the possibility of developing movable engines, capable of serving the increasing demands created by the Industrial Revolution for a more powerful and efficient form of road transport. Such a development depended on the need to construct a high-pressure boiler of sufficient steam capacity, yet small enough to fit into the limited space of a carriage. The problem was aggravated by the lack of a metal which would withstand the high stresses arising in the necessarily light moving parts, and by difficulties in machining parts accurately.

In face of these difficulties, a French military engineer, Nicholas Joseph Cugnot, demonstrated a three-wheeled steam vehicle in Paris during July 1769. The boiler was suspended over the front wheel, which was driven through a pawl and ratchet arrangement by a two-cylinder engine. Unfortunately the boiler was inadequate to power the 5 ton vehicle, and although subsequent modifications were made, it was found difficult to steer, and could only be operated for very limited periods before refuelling. During one of the demonstrations it overturned, and the story is told that the authorities locked up the vehicle to prevent any further mischief.

In England the first real measure of success in developing an efficient boiler was achieved by William Murdock, an assistant in the firm of Boulton & Watt. Between 1784 and 1786, Murdock made several experiments with a model steam carriage, one of the demonstrations being made at night within the precincts of Redruth church, much to the alleged alarm and disgust of the vicar and nearby residents. The power unit was mounted just behind the rear wheels, and consisted of a sheet metal, box-shaped boiler, with an oil or spirit fire beneath it, hot gases from the fire passing upwards through a large tube in the boiler. The single-cylinder engine was placed partly in the boiler and partly above it. Steam to the cylinder was admitted by a piston valve and exhausted through a hole drilled axially in the valve. The piston rod was connected to one end of a lever which was pivoted from a column at the front of the vehicle, the lever operating both the connecting rod and the valve.

Murdock intended to patent this invention, but he encountered the opposition of James Watt, who had a general dislike for high-pressure steam for any purpose and steam vehicles in particular. His disapproval is shown in a letter addressed to his partner on 27 August 1784, in which he emphasised that the 'wheel carriage scheme' was not workable. 'For me to interrupt the career of our business to bestow my attention on it would be imprudent,' he explained; and to ensure that Murdock returned to his work on stationary engines, he laid down impossible conditions for the continuation of experiments on the steam carriages. Murdock would be taken into partnership if, after one year, he could produce an engine 'capable of drawing a post-chaise carrying two ordinary persons and the driver, with 200 lbs of luggage, fuel for four hours, and water for two hours, going at a rate of four miles per hour'. Failing this, Murdock was to take no further interest in road vehicles while working for the firm.

As might be expected, the work did not continue, and it was left to Richard Trevithick to make further experiments in boiler designs for steam carriages. Trevithick, who was born in west Cornwall in 1771, began his work in steam engineering by constructing an improved pump for use in the Cornish mines. Stimulated by this success, and aware of the severe limitations of packhorses for transporting the increasing output of ore, he turned his attention to the development of road vehicles. After several years of work, he tried out a vehicle near his home at Camborne on

Christmas Eve of 1801. Apparently the trial was reasonably successful, but it was to be a short-lived success, for the vehicle
caught fire a few days later, probably as a result of a fault in the
boiler, whilst the designer and his engineering friends were cele-
brating in a local hostelry. During the following year, Trevithick
patented a high-pressure boiler, which was subsequently used to
drive a carriage in London, though not always with success. On
one occasion the vehicle carried away a wall, much to the annoyance of its owner, while there were countless mechanical breakdowns, caused through worn or defective parts.

Eventually the Cornishman decided that the trials were too
expensive to continue, especially as the hoped-for financial backing
was not forthcoming. The machine was therefore taken off the
road, and was later used to drive a hoop-iron rolling mill. Other
designers followed in Trevithick's footsteps, among them Julius
Griffiths who, in 1821, patented a carriage propelled by two
cylinders supplied with steam by a horizontal-tubed boiler, the
carriage being built by Joseph Bramah. This vehicle, despite all
its faults and imperfections, was claimed as being the first steam
carriage in Britain built for the express purpose of carrying
passengers.

Many more improvements, however, had to be made in boiler
design before efficient public services could be made available.
The designer mainly responsible for the advances of the 1820s was
Goldsworthy Gurney. Born at Treator near Padstow in 1793,
Gurney began his career in the medical profession after completing his education at Truro grammar school. During his short
time in this profession, spent mostly at Wadebridge, he studied
chemistry and mechanical science, and in 1823, by which time he
had moved to London, he began experimenting with steam boilers
for use in road vehicles. According to a report published in an
issue of *The Court Journal* he spent six months in his workshops,
'never quitting them for a moment, nor writing a letter, or even
seeing a friend'.

The outcome of Gurney's efforts were steam carriages that re-
sembled, as he put it, 'common stage coaches, but without the
horses'. His first carriages weighed 70 cwt, but by improvements
in construction this was reduced to 35 cwt with no loss of power
in later designs. Legs, or 'propellers', were fitted to push the early
carriages along, but this idea was soon abandoned as they were
found to be unsatisfactory. The vehicle described by Gurney in
Patent specification No 5554 of 1827 had accommodation for up
to six inside passengers, with as many outside as could be seated

on the three seats extending across the coach, and there was room also for one person on the seat beside the driver. The engine man, who also acted as guard, sat on a small seat at the rear of the carriage, behind the firebox door. Baggage was stored in the front boot only, as the boiler occupied the place of the rear boot.

The Ackerman steering system, which in a modified form is in use for motor vehicles today, had been invented many years before Gurney designed his steam carriage, but he did not use it. However, he did adopt an ingenious mechanism which overcame many steering difficulties. Two small pilot wheels were carried on a short axle pivoted at its centre to the end of a long curved pole, the other end of which was fixed to the middle of the steering wheel axle-tree. When the driver turned the pilot-wheel axle, using a handle at the end of a long lever, the pilot wheel went along the desired course, turning the steering-wheel axle about its centre and so causing the coach to follow. Some weight was arranged to fall on to the pilot wheels by pivoting the coach steering wheel axle at a point forward of its centre. A strong spring returned the pilot wheel to a position at right angles to the curved pole, assisting the driver and preventing loss of control. In addition to the steering handle, the driver had a steam valve for the driving engine and a handle to operate the reversing gear.

The engine man, or fireman, from his rear position tended the furnace and boiler. He could control admission of steam to an auxiliary engine which drove both the boiler feed-water pump and a fan to supply air for combustion. By using one engine for both tasks the rate of combustion was matched to the supply of water to the boiler. A hand-operated feed-water pump was also fitted, so that the fireman could maintain water in the boiler in the event of a failure of the steam pump, or supply additional water if needed. Coke was used because it produced little smoke, and was put into the furnace only at staging posts, water being taken on as well, so no tender or bunker was provided for storage. By closing a damper in the air duct to the furnace the fireman could operate the steam feed-pump without increasing the combustion rate of the fire. He could also operate a valve to cause the feed-pump to return water to the storage tank when he wished to brighten the fire without putting more water into the boiler. Two cocks, one above and one below normal boiler-water level, were provided so that, by noting the discharge of steam or water, the fireman could maintain a correct water level.

Gurney's water-tube boiler was of a very advanced design. The steam-raising tubes, of welded wrought iron, formed a well-lagged cage around the fire. No fire-bars were needed, as the burning fuel rested on the bottom tubes. Steam formed in the tubes and rose to a collecting drum at the top of the boiler: thence it passed to two large vertical tubes formed of iron plate and known as separators. Water entrained in the steam dropped to the bottom of the separators, then returned to the steam-raising tubes in which constant circulation was taking place. The dried steam was taken from the top of the separators, and through an elementary super-heater, consisting of a pipe passing down the chimney and over the top of the furnace, to the driver's throttle valve, and from there to the engine. The boiler operated at 120 lb psi, a very high pressure for the time, and was provided with a spring-loaded safety valve mounted at the top of the separators on the pipe conducting steam from these vessels. As the safety valve was above the fireman's head, doubtless he would be careful not to make excess steam very often! Air for combustion was delivered by a trunking from the forced draught fan to the ash pit below the furnace. This ash pit was sealed all round to prevent the ingress of unwanted air so that combustion could be controlled to accord with the evaporation of water.

A 60 gallon horizontal tank under the coach supplied the boiler with water by way of the steam feed-pump and through a coiled pipe placed above the steam-raising tubes in the furnace. Gurney claimed that steam was generated in the coil before the water entered the boiler proper. Exhaust steam from the engine was discharged into a waste tank contained within the water tank, giving up much of its heat to the stored water before passing into a large flat iron box situated between the furnace and the passenger compartment, then out through the chimney at the rear of the boiler. To quote Gurney: 'The waste trunk being of large capacity, the waste steam dilutes itself wherein immediately as it is discharged from the cylinders, and becomes so feeble as to make but little noise and that noise is entirely suppressed by the contact of the water in the tank around the waste trunk.' The iron box between the boiler and the passenger compartment was to reduce the transmission of heat from the boiler to the coach interior and was probably a modification following complaints from uncomfortable travellers.

The two horizontally mounted cylinders of the double-acting engine were each of 8 in bore and 18 in stroke. Slide valves actuated by eccentrics through a primitive form of link motion reversing gear were used to admit and exhaust steam from the cylinders; and as no variation of valve travel was possible, separate sluice valves operated by rods worked from cams on the coach driving axle were provided to effect cut-off of steam at about half stroke and so gain the advantage of its expansive use.

The engine drove through connecting rods on to cranks at right angles on the rear axle of the coach. Normally only one driving wheel was rigidly secured to the axle, the other being fixed to rotate freely, as with a tricycle, but for a steep hill or rough road both wheels were secured to the axle. When running in this manner some sliding of the rear wheels would occur on corners.

Reviews of Gurney's steam carriages were usually quite favourable. *The Mirror of Literature, Amusement & Instruction* for Saturday, 15 December 1827, for example, gave a long and detailed account of the invention, the readers being assured that there was no possible danger. As the journal pointed out: 'First, as to its safety, upon which point the public are most sceptical. In the present invention, it is stated, that, even from the bursting of the boiler, there is not the most distinct chance of mischief to the passengers. This boiler is tubular, constructed upon philosophical principles, and upon a plan totally distinct from anything previously in use.' By way of a further assurance, the journal added that if by some remote chance a tube should burst, the inventor claimed that a few strokes with a hammer would set all to right again.

Unfortunately these were rather optimistic ideas, for a great deal had to be done before steam carriages were perfected. Most of the additional work was undertaken by Walter Hancock, the son of a timber merchant and cabinet maker of Marlborough, who began his career as an apprentice to a watchmaker and jeweller in London. In 1824 he turned his attention to the development of steam vehicles, and from his workshops at Stratford in Essex, he constructed several successful carriages. One of his early efforts, the ten-seater *Infant* built and subsequently improved during 1830–1, had a boiler 'comprised of a series of distinct parallel chambers, or compartments, placed side by side in a vertical position'. According to Hancock, who described the vehicle in his book *Narrative of Twelve Years Experiments (1824–36) Demonstrative of the Practicability and Advantages of Employing Steam Carriages on Common Roads*, the carriage could be divided into three main sections. The first part was the boiler, with the fireplace beneath it. Secondly, there was a space between the boiler and the passengers for the engines and the engine man whose task was to lubricate the parts with oil during the journey, and to take care of the gauge cocks for regulating the supply of water to the boiler.

And thirdly, there was 'a pair of inverted fixed engines working vertically on a crank shaft'. Steering was applied to the front wheels, and the body of the carriage was supported on four common coach springs on the axle of each wheel. This suspension marked an important development, since many of the earlier carriages had their engines damaged by the rough state of the roads. As Hancock explained: 'Any shock which affects the carriage can only be felt by the steam engine, through the chain or through the very flexible springs upon which the body of the vehicle, containing engines and passengers, is placed. From the extreme end of the hinder axle-tree to the corresponding ends of the crank-shaft, strong bars proceed. These bars serve to keep the crank-shaft always equi-distant from the hinder axle-tree; so that any concussion, which may affect one wheel or the body, cannot force the crank-shaft nearer or farther from the axle-tree.'

Contemporary reviews of *The Infant* varied enormously. Praise came from such engineers as John Farey, who, in giving evidence before the Select Committee which reported in 1831 about the possibilities of steam carriages, stated that he thought 'Mr Hancock's boiler to be much better for steam carriages than any other which has been proposed or tried'. Similar praise came from Alexander Gordon after he had made a journey to Brighton in the vehicle during October 1832. In *The Journal of Elemental Locomotion* he made the criticism that the boiler would benefit from being rather more powerful. On the other hand, *The Athenaeum* thought that the basic principles of the boiler were unsound, mainly because of the rapid wear and tear likely to be occasioned by intense heat on the thin metal plates. Another defect was said to be in the method of blowing the fire by a fan or bellows worked from the engine, as it tended to deprive the engine of some of its power. 'We venture to predict', commented the journal, 'that sooner or later this defect, if not removed, must utterly destroy the efficiency of this machine.'

Later carriages built by Hancock included *The Enterprise*, which came on to the roads in 1833. Capable of carrying fourteen people, all of whom were accommodated inside, the vehicle was able, so it was claimed, to travel at between 15 and 20 mph. Passengers were assured that no annoyance would be caused to them through the heat generated by the engine, and no smoke would bother them, while the risk of the boiler bursting was removed by the 'water being deposited in several iron pipes, or what are known as boiler chambers, with a valve to carry off the superfluous steam'. The length of the carriage did not exceed the space taken up by a conventional coach and horses, and its appearance was described as being 'particularly neat'. Initially it was hoped that the carriage would be run for public services by The London & Paddington Steam Carriage Company, so Hancock gave a demonstration lasting several weeks, running the machine between the City and Paddington for a charge of 1s per passenger. Eventually, the engineer of the company, Mr Redmond, stated that he was satisfied with the performance, and the vehicle was handed over. Unfortunately for the inventor, however, the enterprising Mr Redmond tried to copy the design, and thereby substitute one of his own vehicles. He failed, and the sad outcome was that the original carriage was returned to Stratford, together with the cancelled contract for the provision of several other vehicles.

Undeterred, Hancock went on to design further steam carriages. In the summer of 1833 came *The Autopsy*, which was to run for four weeks on a public service between Finsbury Square and Pentonville. A year later came *The Era*, mark II (mark I having been ordered by the London & Brighton Steam Carriage Company, who decided in the end not to run the vehicle on an intended route between London and Greenwich) and after fitting out premises in Windsor Place, City Road, and arranging for a supply of water to be made available at the Paddington end of the run, Hancock put this vehicle (renamed *The Erin*) and *The Autopsy* into service between the City, Moorgate and Paddington. Twelve passengers were carried in each, and the five-mile journey took, on average, half an hour, which worked out at 12 mph after allowing for stops. During the period that the carriages ran (between 18 August and the end of November 1834) over 4,000 passengers were carried without accident. The year 1836 brought the twenty-two seater *The Automaton*, which was to be used with *The Autopsy* and *Erin* on Moorgate to Stratford, Paddington and Islington services. In all, 4,200 miles were covered by the carriages, made up of 525 trips from the City to Islington and back; 143 to Paddington and back; and 44 to Stratford and back; a total of nearly 13,000 passengers being carried. As William Fletcher pointed out in his book *The History and Development of Steam Locomotives on Common Roads*, published in 1891: 'Hancock was the only steam carriage proprietor who had ventured to run a locomotive along the crowded streets of London at the busiest periods of the day. These hard roads were a severe test for the wheels and the gearing.'

The only other public service comparable with Hancock's performances was the Gloucester to Cheltenham run established by Sir Charles Dance in 1831, using one of Gurney's steam carriages.

THE FIRST GENERATION OF STEAM CARRIAGES   171

This carriage used 10 gallons of water and 20 lb of coke for every mile, and travelled at a speed of 9–12 mph. An entry in *The Worcester Herald* for 3 March 1831 gave the following details:

> The steam carriage commenced running between Cheltenham and Gloucester on Monday last and has since continued to perform the journey regularly, starting punctually from the Commissioner's Yard, Cheltenham at 10 and 2 o'clock, and leaving the Spread Eagle, Gloucester at 12 and 4. The carriage contains altogether twelve persons and has been filled with passengers, including a great many ladies. All the passengers who have travelled by it seem much pleased and agree that the motion is remarkably smooth, regular and agreeable. It runs the distance in about fifty minutes, and we are happy to add that no accident has occurred of any description.

The service ran from 21 February to 22 June, and the time taken for the 9 mile run was, on average, 55 minutes. Dance explained that 'there were sometimes delays owing to defective pipes in the boiler, which prolonged the time, but no accident, hurt or injury ever happened to any person whatever; the engines were never out of order, and are as perfect as they were at first'. During the time of the service, 396 regular journeys were made, totalling 3,644 miles, and the number of fare-paying passengers, who incidentally paid less than one half of the horse coach fares, amounted to 2,666, bringing in receipts of £202 4s 6d.

Few other designers and operators managed to get beyond the test-run stage. Each vehicle brought its own particular problems, but it can be said that all of them suffered from machine parts that were unable to withstand the strain of a long journey. Ogle and Summers, for instance, put their phaeton-like steam carriage on the road during 1830. On its first journey it set off along the City and New Road, into Edgware Road, at what was described as 'the tremendous rate of between fifteen and sixteen miles per hour'. On turning the corner of Edgware Road into the Uxbridge Road, the vehicle began to roll from side to side 'from the velocity with which it was propelled, so that every person expected to be instantly dashed to the ground'. After travelling a further 300 yds along the Uxbridge Road, water began to pour out of the boiler and the cistern, and without delay a further supply of water was obtained. Unfortunately, the boiler was soon empty again, and a closer examination revealed that one of the large pipes had burst.

Sir Charles Dance experienced similar difficulties when experimenting with a steam carriage bound for Birmingham one Friday in November 1833. According to a report in *The Worcester Herald*, the carriage ran into trouble when it arrived at The Wellington near Highgate archway. 'One of the pipes burst,' wrote the reporter, 'which occasioned very considerable delay, and it was nearly four hours before the damage could be repaired and the carriage again proceed. The roads were in a very unfavourable state, and the average motion of the carriage is stated not to have exceeded seven miles per hour.'

Passengers on board *The Albert* steam carriage belonging to the General Steam Company decided to walk when a faulty joint on the steam pipe stopped the vehicle in April 1842. Reporting the incident, *The Suffolk Chronicle* said that 'one of the flanges connecting the joint of the steam-pipes was forced out, when the steam escaped so fast and with so much noise that those who were ignorant of the nature of the accident which had occurred, precipitately left the coach and walked towards London. Three ladies who were in the body of the coach jumped off, and received some trifling bruises, but no serious injuries were sustained'. Later, the repaired carriage picked up the disgruntled travellers and the journey continued, but not without a good deal of apprehension on the part of the passengers.

A further form of mechanical failure resulted from defective pumps, as Gurney pointed out to the Commissioners who reported in 1831 on the use of steam carriages on the roads. When asked what was the most likely cause of a breakdown, he replied: 'I should say that the dearrangement of the pumps is most likely to occur, in consequence of which the carriage would immediately stop.' Even as late as 1841, problems were still being experienced with pumps, a fact shown by an unsuccessful demonstration given by Frank Hills of Deptford, who patented several steam carriages between 1839 and 1843. The carriages all ran relatively fast, but had considerable trouble with their pumps. On one run, between Deptford and Sevenoaks, a carriage reached 23 mph, but this speed could not be kept up, for after a few miles the pump 'got out of order', forcing the carriage to stop—much to the amusement of 'the gazing rustics grouped around'.

Some of the mechanical mishaps caused loss of life and limb to the passengers, particularly when boilers burst. In the summer of 1834, a carriage constructed by John Scott Russell, the well-known engineer and builder of the *Great Eastern* steamer, who built steam vehicles for the Steam Carriage Company of Scotland, exploded when travelling between Paisley and Glasgow. The accident was caused by a wheel striking large stones in the road, and according to one account, 'the machine came to the ground with terrific violence; the boiler was crushed flat, the bottom of the carriage was blown to atoms, and all the passengers, twelve in number, were more or less injured. With such force did the steam rush out of the boiler, that the burning cinders in the furnace as well as the metal on the road were blown to a considerable distance'. Five people died as a result of the mishap.

Another boiler explosion, seriously injuring two boys, happened in June 1831 when one of Gurney's steam carriages was being demonstrated in the cavalry barracks at Glasgow. *The Glasgow Chronicle* mentioned that 'the boiler burst with a tremendous explosion, and scattered the vehicle into numberless pieces . . . two boys were very seriously injured in the face and other parts of the body and they now lie in a very precarious circumstance'.

Yet another instance of a mishap is provided by the death of a driver of a carriage in October 1840. The carriage, belonging to Mr Worsley of Bellisle-Park, Hampstead, was being removed from Millbank to his home. On arriving in Sloane Street, the steam carriage became unmanageable, the cause being attributed to the engine having been 'strained' in trying to avoid children playing in the streets. Despite the frantic efforts of the driver to correct the steering, the vehicle careered from one side of the road to the other, eventually ending up in the shop of Mr Collier, jeweller and goldsmith of 209 Sloane Street. In recording a verdict of accidental death on the driver, a court imposed a deodand of £10 on the machine, a fine which was said to mark the jury's disapproval of such vehicles being allowed to run wild around London's public thoroughfares.

The general public was very much aware of the dangers of travelling in steam carriages, and during the early years of operation their fears were sometimes violently expressed. Gurney suffered from this hostility when journeying between London and Bath in July 1829, the trouble starting as he was entering the village of Melksham. There, a great mob surrounded the carriage, and started to attack the proud inventor and his travelling companions. Initially, the villagers tried to stop the machine, but failing in this purpose, they began hurling stones and every other available missile, much to the alarm of the carriage occupants. 'The gentlemen were obliged to get out and resist the mob,' reported *The Bath Chronicle*, 'and the engineers being disabled, it was thought advisable to seek shelter, and the carriage was taken into Mr Isles's yard for security.'

Hancock had a similar encounter with the public. In his book, the many difficulties he encountered in running his carriages are explained: 'exhorbitant charges were made for the most trifling services, and important facilities witheld, which it would have cost nothing to afford. If again he happened to be temporarily detained on the road for want of water, or from any other cause, he was assaulted with yellings, hootings, hissings and sometimes even with the grossest abuse'. Most of these unhappy expressions came from a section of the public which were described as 'the rabble'.

The Press, too, was sometimes hostile. *The Sickle* of 16 October 1828 viewed with suspicion a rumoured steam-carriage service between London and Colchester: 'It will be long before the public mind can be relieved from the fear of an explosion. . . . It would not be very difficult to prove that ninety nine persons out of a hundred would give preference to Mrs Nelson's or Ned Cracknell's team of bays or greys, rather than to Gurney's or Burstead and Hall's steam coaches.' A further argument against the carriages was that they 'would lessen the value of horses and take away the demand for hay, oats and other fodder—but what we consider as the chief objection is, that, if suddenly adopted, it would have the effect of throwing thousands of poor fellows out of employment'.

James Stone, the manager of Sir Charles Dance's Cheltenham to Gloucester service, referred to the opposition he was having in operating in a letter addressed to Gurney in June 1830: 'This is a very bad place to commence on; we are surrounded with prejudiced people—agriculturalists, coach proprietors, coachmen, stable boys, and others directly or indirectly connected with them; these, with the old ladies of Cheltenham, I assure you, offer a formidable opposition to any innovator. Whenever we are a few minutes after our time, it is regularly reported we have either blown up or broke down, or both. I am happy to say, however, we have not met with the most trifling accident up to this time.'

By far the most serious opposition came from the horse-coach proprietors and turnpike trustees, opposition that lingered on long after the travelling public had been convinced of the safety and benefits of the new form of locomotion. A reporter of *The Morning Advertiser* for 26 April 1833 commented: 'In witnessing, as I have done, the early operation of the new steam coach, the *Enterprise*, on the Paddington road, I have been pained, though not surprised to see the malignent efforts of some of the drivers of the horse vehicles to impede and baffle the course of the new competitor.' Shortly after this, the driver of a Paddington omnibus was charged in court with driving against and damaging Hancock's vehicle. A fine of £5 was imposed.

The turnpike trustees seem to have feared that the heavy steam carriages would damage the surface of their roads, and that they would drive away horse-drawn traffic. Some of the trustees resorted to placing rocks and stones in the path of the steamers, and many imposed much higher tolls than were levied on stage coaches. Sir Charles Dance, in running his service between Gloucester and Cheltenham, suffered on the first count. Writing to Gurney, James Stone reported on 23 June 1831: 'I am exceedingly sorry to inform you that we have broke the hind axle. Yesterday morning we found the road filled up with loose stones for a very considerable way near the four mile stone. The carriage, with difficulty, went through them, and also returned through them again without any mischief; but the third time the strain broke the axle.' Gurney was apparently convinced that the stones had been deliberately placed on the road by the turnpike officials.

The trustees' view of this steam service is given in their minute book for 1831. One entry records a meeting held at the offices of Messrs Wilton on 25 June 'for the purpose of taking into consideration the annoyance and inconvenience occasioned by the steam carriage which now passes along the said road and for adopting such proceedings for the prevention and discontinuance of such annoyance and inconvenience as may be considered expedient'. At the meeting, the trustees decided that the vehicle should be classed as a public nuisance, and a resolution was passed 'that it is the opinion of this meeting that unless such nuisance shall be abated prior to the 6th day of August next, an indictment shall be preferred by our clerk against the proper parties at the next Assizes'. Such proceedings, however, were unnecessary, for an entry in the minute book for 6 August records that the steam-carriage service had been discontinued.

According to Henry Davies' book *Cheltenham in its Past and Present State*, published in 1843, the service was discontinued because of the likely, or rather alleged, damage to the newly surfaced road. Writing about the vehicle, Davies said that 'for some weeks it succeeded remarkably well, but on the roads being repaired, and fresh stone laid down, it was obliged to be disbanded'. This aspect of damage to the roads was taken up by the Select Committee of 1831, before which many prominent road engineers were called upon to give evidence. Thomas Telford, for instance, considered that far more damage was done by a coach and horses, from the animals' feet and narrow-rimmed wheels, than by the broad wheels of the steam carriages.

Sad to relate, many turnpike trustees did not agree with these views, and continued to charge exorbitant rates for the steamers to pass along their roads. On the Liverpool and Prescot road, Goldsworthy Gurney's steam carriage was charged at the rate of £2 8s 0d, while a fully laden stage coach only had to pay 4s. In Devon, the trustees of the Ashburton–Totnes road charged £2 for a steam carriage, and only 3s for a four-horse carriage; and on the Teignmouth and Dawlish road, steamers paid six times as much as a horse-drawn coach, 12s compared with 2s. Further evidence of the distinction in tolls was given in the report of the 1831 Select Committee; the figures given in the table below show that some trusts were not so hostile:

Table showing level of tolls for various carriages
List selected from the Select Committee on Steam Carriages, B.P.P. 1831 Vol. VIII. Appendix 14 C

Road	Stage coach per horse	Waggons & vans	Steam Carriages
Norwich & Yarmouth	6d	4d & 6d	2s 0d for all carriages
Macclesfield & Nether Tabley	6d	6d & 8d	9d per wheel for all carriages
Pucklechurch	6d	6d 7½d & 9d	1s 0d per cwt
Lampeter	6d	4½d 5½d & 6d	same as stage coach with 4 horses
Cheadle	6d	4d 5d & 9d	5s 0d for all carriages
Liverpool & Preston	6d	If drawn by 4 or 5 horses, 1s 0d; 1s 5d; 2s 3d; 2s 5d. If by 2 or 3 horses, 4d; 6d; or 8d	If not exceeding one ton 6d per wheel and 6d for every further ton weight

In reviewing these charges, the Commissioners wrote that 'tolls to an amount which would utterly prohibit the introduction of steam carriages have been imposed on some roads; on others the trustees have adopted modes of apportioning the charge, which would be found, if not absolutely prohibitory, at least to place such carriages in a very unfair position as compared with ordinary carriages'. They therefore recommended that legislation should be

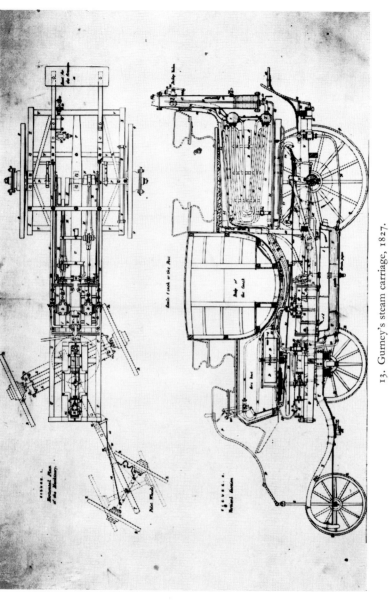

13. Gurney's steam carriage, 1827.

14a. Hancock's steam omnibus, the *Enterprise*.
14b. Dr Church's steam carriage, by F. Wolf, 1833.

brought in with the least possible delay to put the tolls on a fair and proper footing.

In hopes that this advice would be accepted by the Government, several companies were formed in different parts of the country to operate public steam-carriage services. The advice, however, fell on deaf ears, for the Government decided to do nothing about the tolls. Even so, the 1830s were years of hope for the steam-carriage operators. The engineers were quite confident that the carriages had a great future. Macneill, for example, spoke of the days ahead when he was giving his observations on a trial run in one of Hancock's vehicles in the metropolis. 'In a very short time,' he predicted, 'we shall see locomotive carriages travelling on the common roads, and carrying passengers with as great a speed as the general interests of society can require, or is even now deemed safe and economical on railways.' 'There is much less shaking or jolting of the carriage on a common road than there is on the Manchester & Liverpool Railway,' he added, 'excepting only when the carriage passes over the paved crossings of streets.'

The company promoters were equally enthusiastic about the future. In May 1835, for instance, 'The London & Birmingham Steam Carriage Company' stated that their directors 'are not aware that a single defect now exists worthy of notice, and are satisfied that the difficulties in running a steam carriage on gravel roads are entirely obviated'. *The Birmingham Advertiser* took up the same confident theme when it wrote about the future of steam carriages in one of its issues for September 1838:

> The subject of steam carriages on common roads is much spoken of at this time, and we understand that the bondholders on the turnpike roads, as well as the innkeepers and others whose property is threatened with destruction by the railway lines, are beginning to feel confident that, by levelling the turnpikes, laying down granite tracks, and adapting steam locomotive carriages and waggons, the traffic, both for passengers and merchandise, may well be preserved on the present lines of roads.

Certainly there were many ambitious plans afoot during these years. Sir James Anderson announced in the late 1830s that he was to build 400 steam carriages for The Waggon Company of England, the carriages being drawn by his steam drag. Sir James's initial experiments with steam began in the 1820s when he went into partnership with W. H. James of Holborn. In 1829 they constructed and put two vehicles on the road for trials, but neither proved to be successful, some defect always being discovered after the machines had travelled a few miles. Not to be discouraged, the

M

determined baronet decided to set up on his own account in 1838, after having spent 'two apprenticeships and a fortune in building twenty nine unsuccessful carriages to succeed on the thirtieth'. The vehicles intended for The Waggon Company of England were to be built and tried in Ireland, before being sent over to London, and in reviewing the progress of the enterprise, *The Southern Reporter* mentioned that the cost of fuel for a 'drag' to convey thirty passengers and luggage would only cost in the region of fourpence per mile, and the average speed would be about fifteen miles per hour '... speed sufficient is attained without the enormous cost of the railway'.

Nearly all the steam-carriage inventors and operators emphasised these relatively low running costs. Gurney, in making a comparison with horse-drawn vehicles, suggested that a four-horse stage coach could be regarded as being equal in power to an ordinary steam carriage. The capital costs of the two were about the same, as were the labour costs, which usually involved two men to each vehicle. Using this basis, Gurney made cost calculations for operating the Gloucester to Cheltenham run four times a day, totalling 36 miles. To run the service, 18 horses would be required each day for the stage coach, involving a cost of 3s per horse per day, or, to be within safer limits, 2s 6d per horse, giving a total food bill in the region of 45s a day. The comparable costs for a steam carriage would only amount, on Gurney's calculations, to 9s 3d for coke, showing a saving of 35s 9d in favour of steam.

Hancock also made some cost calculations in his book mentioned earlier. His accounts were in the form of two tables, one showing the costs and revenue associated with running two carriages for a day, or 100 miles; and the other the profit that would result from operating a fleet of steam vehicles, or an operating distance of 1,000 miles. The corresponding figures were given as shown on the facing page:

One Day's Work, or 100 miles

Expenditure	£	s	d	Revenue	£	s	d
Coke 1s 0d per mile	5	0	0	50 passengers, 1½d			
Repairs, wear & tear	4	0	0	per mile each	31	5	0
Oil, hemp, etc		10	0	One ton of goods,			
2 engineers, 2 steers-				1d per cwt per mile	9	6	8
men, 2 stokers, 1							
guard	2	0	0		40	11	8
Rent of stations,				Deduct 20% for			
offices, wages of				light loads	8	2	4
attendants etc	3	0	0				
Tolls	1	10	0		£32	9	4
Fund for renewal of							
carriages, £2 each	4	0	0				
Contingencies	2	0	0				
	£22	0	0				
Daily profit	10	9	4				
	£32	9	4				

One Day's Work, or 1,000 miles

Expenditure	£	s	d	Revenue	£	s	d
Say 80 steam car-				313 working days			
riages @				@ £10. 9. 4.			
£1,500	120,000	0	0	per 100 miles			
Say 50 common				is for 1,000			
carriages @				miles	32,760	0	0
£120 each	6,000	0	0				
Stations, etc	14,000	0	0				
	£140,000	0	0				

Profit on capital nearly 25 per cent

Calculations made by other operators suggested that the costs for the fuel amounted to between 4d and 4½d per mile, which the calculators carefully explained were much lower than those associated with the railways. One estimate of the costs associated with Sir James Anderson's carriages reckoned that the steam drags that he used would 'effect a saving above 50 per cent in working, with double the average speed of a stage coach . . . and in consequence of the great original cost of locomotive railways, the public should be conveyed at less than one quarter of the charges at present made on the latter. A person could be conveyed a greater distance for two shillings and sixpence, affording a larger profit than can be effected for ten shillings on an iron locomotive'.

The question of speed naturally played an important part in the calculations, for whereas the cost of operation increased enormously as the speed of a stage coach quickened, in the case of steam carriages it was maintained that there was no appreciable difference in cost per mile. Mentioning this factor in his book *Observations on Steam Carriages*, Gurney explained that 'one of the principal advantages resulting from the use of steam will be, that it may be employed as cheaply at a quick rate as at a slow rate. This is one of the advantages over horse labour which becomes more expensive as the speed is increased'. Safety also had to be considered, especially in terms of speed, and here again the engineers argued that their vehicles were easier to control than the horse-drawn carriages. They pointed out that dangerous bends and steep hills were a good deal easier to negotiate with locomotives than with a team of spirited horses, particularly as there was no fear that the engines would bolt.

Further advantages over stage coaches claimed by the engineers included lower costs of upkeep and greater seating accommodation. According to evidence given by John Farey to the 1831 Select Committee, the costs associated with the withdrawal from service of a steam carriage when there were insufficient passengers were far less than the comparable figures for a horse coach. Horses still had to be fed when idle, whereas a steam carriage could, subject only to a small amount of maintenance, be put aside without any real costs being incurred. This was an important consideration, particularly at a time when traffic was irregular and seasonal, as many coaching firms knew only too well. Stage-coach operators were also handicapped by their limited seating capacity during peak periods, but the steam-carriage operators hoped to overcome this problem by providing vehicles able to carry twenty, thirty and even forty passengers at a time, over distances of 100 miles or more.

Despite all these apparent advantages, the steam carriages did not meet with the success that their inventors and operators had anticipated. Just why they failed is a matter of some dispute, but several factors help to explain their unhappy history. In the first place, mechanical and operational difficulties were still being experienced even in the late 1840s. Nearly every vehicle had some kind of mechanical failure, some faults being attributable to their operators trying to go too fast. This was especially true of Dr W. H. Church of Birmingham, who, in 1835 attempted to establish a regular service between London and Birmingham with a steam carriage which he claimed could travel at a constant speed of

20 mph, carrying at least forty passengers in comfort. Unfortunately, during one of its public trials, the machine broke down, and the financial sponsors were not convinced that they would be justified in parting with their money.

Another operational difficulty at the time was to secure adequate supplies of coke and water. It would no doubt have been overcome eventually, but it provided many headaches for the operators. Hancock was among the sufferers, and he made frequent complaints about the want of suitable premises and stations to store coke and supply water. When making trial journeys in the *Infant* in 1832, he found that the speed of the vehicle was constantly being retarded by the inferior supplies of coke. Commenting on this after making one of the runs with Hancock, Alexander Gordon suggested that 'few country people on the road knew what coke was'. An attempt was made to solve the problem by attaching fuel tenders to the carriages, but this was not altogether successful. When a tender was hooked on to *The Erin* during a trial run between Stratford and Marlborough, the connection snapped, and the tender had to be left behind at Cheapside. *The Mechanics Magazine* made the following comment:

> No one who has not travelled by steam carriage can imagine the inconvenience and delay which results from the want of regular and ample supplies of water; the carriage having to stop from 14–18 minutes every ten or twelve miles to fill the tanks by hand buckets from pumps, with sometimes an additional inconvenience of having to supply from some neighbouring stream or pond. While the carriage is stationary, the fire slackens in consequence of the blower being stopped, and it requires about two miles running to get it into full play again.

Many operators had to contend with stops every five or six miles to take on fresh supplies of coke and water. Colonel Macerone, for instance, who made numerous experiments with steam vehicles in co-operation with Mr Squire during the 1830s, demonstrated a carriage in London during the early part of 1834. The run was described in *The Worcester Herald* for 16 January 1834 in the following terms:

> *New Steam Coach:* Squire and Macerone's steam carriage is running daily and fares from Regent's Circus, Oxford Street, to Uxbridge or Edgware. It performs at the rate of twelve, fourteen or sixteen miles per hour according to the state of the roads. Stoppages for water and fuel are made every five or six miles.

Finance was another difficulty: the problem of high turnpike tolls, and of getting sufficient financial backing at a time when investors had their eyes fixed on the rich dividends promised by the railway companies. Goldsworthy Gurney suffered most from money troubles, so much so that he petitioned Parliament in hopes that high toll charges would be lowered. In 1835 a Select Committee reviewed his case. Gurney explained that over six years he had lost a net £16,200 on his enterprises; while the failure of agreements he had with various operators, including Sir Charles Dance, Mr Ward and Mr Hanning meant that he was deprived of a large sum of potential earnings bringing his total loss to about £36,000. These agreements were to have given Gurney a considerable profit on the construction of the carriages, in addition to a rate per mile, varying from 2d to 6d to be paid by the operators. These profits did not materialise, however, for according to Gurney the operators soon realised that they could not hope to run profitable services with the prevailing turnpike tolls.

The Committee, reviewing these losses, were sympathetic towards the distressed inventor, and recommended that he should either be allowed a free extension of his patent rights on the vehicles, or be offered a sum of £5,000 by the Exchequer. Unhappily, the Chancellor did not appreciate the need for any form of compensation, and their suggestion was rejected. Gurney was faced with ruin, and was compelled to give up his work on steam vehicles and sell all the rights he had in them. In later years he turned his attention to the less troubled realm of ventilation, where he found scope for the use of high-pressure steam. He eventually retired to Bude, and died in 1875.

Another instance of financial difficulties is provided by the experiences of Colonel Macerone. In 1834 the Colonel's partnership with Mr Squire came to an abrupt end owing to shortage of money, and Macerone sold the patent rights to an Italian. It was not until 1841, when the General Steam Carriage Company tentatively agreed to run some of his carriages, that any possible chance of success seemed to be in the offing. Even then, however, the deal fell through, and Macerone was obliged to relinquish any further ideas about continuing with his work.

Apparently a few attempts were made to build road steamers for uses other than the carriage of passengers. One was reported in *The Maidstone Gazette* in a September issue of 1831, which said that a steam carriage would shortly commence running from Ightham, carrying the celebrated Ightham stone used in surfacing roads. Another venture was the construction of fire engines, the vehicles being built by Braithwaite and Ericson. The first was built in 1829, and within a few years four others followed, but although the machines were relatively successful mechanically, they did not win the approval of the authorities, and the idea of using them was dropped.

By 1840 the first generation of steam carriages had come to an end, most of the vehicles having departed from the English roads. A few individuals went on with the work, but their efforts, lacking finance and undertaken within the overpowering shadow of the railways, met with little success. Meanwhile the stage coaches, having lost one competitor, continued to run, but the day was not so very far away when they, too, were to succumb to the iron railroad.

CHAPTER 8

Competition with the Railways

By the 1830s, when it was estimated that there were 3,000 coaches on the road employing 150,000 horses and 30,000 men including coachmen, guards, horsekeepers and ostlers, the coaching concerns had reached the peak of their speed and efficiency. Better roads had brought improved coaches, which in turn enabled reliable, punctual services to be maintained over long distances. Unfortunately this peak in efficiency occurred about the same time as a new and formidable competitor appeared on the scene. From the 1830s onwards lines of railroads began to spread across the country, eventually forcing most of the main-line coaches off the roads.

The competition between road and rail in the nineteenth century can be divided into three stages. In the early years, the coaching firms tried to compete with the railways, offering lower fares in an attempt to hold on to their passengers. Later they realised that they could not hope to rival the speed and efficiency of steam, and they therefore concentrated on acting as feeders to railways, as well as linking up areas where lines had not yet penetrated. In the third stage of the struggle, most of the main-line coaches were taken off the roads, but in the more isolated parts of the kingdom, not directly served by railways, coaches continued to run throughout the nineteenth century.

When railways were introduced, many people were sceptical about their advantages. An article in *The Brighton Gazette* for 23 January 1834 thought that the railways brought more disadvantages than benefits. Quoting the example of that between Manchester and Liverpool, the newspaper mentioned that before the railway was built the 'commerce between the two towns was carried on by a turnpike road and by two canals. On the former there were from thirty to forty stage coaches besides carts, waggons and other carriages', while the canals carried about 1,000 tons of merchandise a day. Railways, it was feared, 'greatly decreased the value of agricultural produce by reducing the demand for horse provender', and this would lead to 'a numerous class of men' being thrown out of employment. And if this was not enough to damn the railways, the paper went on to suggest that they were 'demoralizing in their effects for their tendency to concentrate the population of the country in large towns'.

Many landowners also had complaints. Lord Forester, for example, disliked the idea of a railway passing through his estate, for he feared that the land would be devalued. Furthermore, he thought that the expense involved was out of all proportion to the traffic that was likely to be carried, while the Talbot Inn at Wellington ('one of the best in Wellington') would be rendered 'nearly if not altogether useless'.

A striking instance of the bitterness which marked the early years of the struggle is provided by a poster published in 1843 by the stage-coach proprietors in northern England whose trade was threatened by the expansion of the Leeds & Manchester railway. The poster, headed 'Lies and the Manchester Railway' parodied a railway announcement and set out the 'striking advantages' which travellers could enjoy on 'our magnificent and splendid railway'. Referring to the railway's promise to increase the speed of travelling, the poster pointed out that 'as this will augument the danger, and increase the number of casualties, we have arranged that cemeteries shall be immediately erected at each station, and plans of such cemeteries deposited for passengers previously to starting, to book a place in, by payment of a small charge, so that when the accidents happen, there will be no confusion or unpleasantness in the arrangement for the burial of the bodies. A dissecting room will be attached'.

Apart from hurling such abuse at the railways, the stage-coach firms offered passengers lower fares. One proprietor, George H. Smale of Exeter, was not deterred by the railway threat, for in May 1844 he announced in the pages of *The Exeter Flying Post* that he had commenced running a new light coach named *The Protector* every morning at 9.30 from the Buller's Arms, St Sidwell's, Exeter, to Tiverton, to arrive there in time for the coach to South Molton and Barnstaple. In his advertisement, Mr Smale explained:

> The opening of the railroad has driven three coaches off the road, and depressed all the villages along the line of road of a certain, cheap and serviceable means of communication with Exeter and Tiverton.

Mr Smale's service was still running four months later, for in another announcement in the newspaper he explained to the travelling public that he was 'performing the journey in the same time as the railway and at one half of the fare'. An added advantage was that the coach travelled over a beautiful line of country, 'acknowledged to be the most delightful ride in the west of England'.

In *The Leicester Journal* for 25 October 1838 it was said that in the rivalry between coaches and trains, the stage-coach proprietors were offering to convey passengers between London and Birmingham for 21s inside and 10s outside, while the corresponding fares on the railway were 30s and 20s. Some coaches, as for example those travelling between Liverpool and Warrington, and Liverpool and St Helens in 1843, found that their trade increased because of the high fares charged by the railroad companies.

Attempts were made to run the coaches at their maximum speeds. Two running between Cheltenham and Liverpool in May 1837 completed the 132 mile journey in $11\frac{1}{2}$ hours—a speed that can be regarded as the highest for a coach. Another example is provided by an item in *The Essex Standard* for 27 April 1838, when it was reported that 'The Wonder, Shrewsbury and London coach, seems determined not to be outdone by its flying adversary without a struggle. It left London on Monday at the same moment that the trains left Euston Square, and reached Birmingham just twenty minutes before them'. Despite these performances, though, it soon became obvious even to the most determined coaching proprietors that they would have to co-operate with the railways if they wished to stay on the roads.

In the next stage of the struggle, therefore, the coaching concerns announced in the local newspapers that they were arranging their services to meet trains at the stations. Where the lines were only partly finished, coaches would carry passengers on to towns not yet served by railways, and in this way the coaches enjoyed good loads. In 1844 *The Railway Times* spoke of the apparently happy co-operation between coaching firms and the Eastern Counties Railway Company in the following terms:

> As the spring approaches, three or more conveyances will be started; and seeing that the experiences of the last six weeks justified the belief that passenger traffic will, before that time, have been nearly doubled, there can be little doubt that they will turn out to be profitable speculations.

Typical of the many hopeful advertisements is the one in *The Suffolk Chronicle* for 6 June 1846 which read:

Thomas Harrison begs to inform the inhabitants of Ipswich and the public generally, that by appointment of the Directors of the Eastern Counties Railway Company, he will, on the opening of this line, commence running an omnibus for the conveyance of passengers and parcels to and from the Ipswich station, on the arrival and departure of every train.

In the same issue there is an advertisement relating to the General Coach Office at Ipswich:

The public are informed, that the coaches in and after the 15th instant, from the above office, will be worked in conjunction with the railway, by special appointment.

A similar announcement was made in *The Aylesbury News* for 12 August 1837, when Joseph Hearne announced that his coaches would no longer run between London and Tring. Instead, he was 'appointed by the Railway Commissioners to book passengers and parcels at his office at the railway, and that his conveyances were appointed to convey passengers and luggage to the station at Euston Square to meet the dispatch and arrival of the whole of the trains from and to Boxmoor'.

As the railways were extended, however, the stage coaches, particularly along the main roads, were forced to retire as more and more of their former passengers deserted them for the trains. An entry in *The Essex Standard* for 24 March 1843 explains the sad story:

Chelmsford Coaches: E & A Macnamara, in returning thanks to the inhabitants of Chelmsford and its vicinity for the very liberal support they have received since the starting of their coaches to the Brentwood station, beg most respectfully to inform them that in consequence of the opening of the railroad, they will discontinue running on Tuesday evening next.

At Brighton, *The Brighton Herald* described the retirement of *The Age* in the following terms:

. . . that splendid coach, *The Age*, which for some years has been the pride of the Brighton road, ran on Saturday for the last time. Numbers of persons of all ranks were in the daily habit of congregating in Castle Square to witness its departure, and much regret is expressed at seeing the last trip. The four greys which used to take it out of Brighton are valued at £500. The only crack coach left on the road is *The Era*; but from the sad havoc made by the railroad it is expected soon to follow the fate of its competitor, *The Age*.

The mail coaches shared the same fate, for with the opening of the railways the horse contractors very soon found themselves in

financial difficulties. In July 1837 the contractors of the Birmingham & Liverpool mail coach wrote to George Lewis at the
General Post Office, requesting to be relieved from their contract
for working the coach, 'for since the opening of the railway all
trade has left the mail'. Some contractors asked the postal authorities for an increased mileage allowance to tide them over their
difficulties, as in the case of those for the London & Derby coach,
who demanded a rate of 4d per mile in November 1837. Apparently their receipts had dropped by one half since the opening
of the railway, and the officials at the General Post Office, acknow-
ledging that contractors ought to be allowed to earn £4 per mile
per month, agreed to pay the new rate.

Among the distressed contractors in London were Mr Chaplin
whose main centre was *The Swan With Two Necks*, and Mr Sherman of *The Bull and Mouth* which used to stand on the site now
occupied by the General Post Office Headquarters in St Martins-le-
Grand. In October 1837, Chaplin, on behalf of his fellow contractors, asked for a rate of 6d per mile instead of 1d, 'in order that we
may proceed without so severe a loss, till your measures are complete'. He added that two of his fellow contractors had refused to
sign the existing contract, which added to the difficulties of those
who had. More and more contractors withdrew after the expiration of their contracts, and the Post Office found it increasingly
difficult to persuade others to horse the mails. Mr Chaplin, however, soon managed to adapt himself to the new situation, for he became the deputy chairman of the London & Southampton Railway.

The Post Office overcame the problem initially by putting some
mail coaches on the trains. One of these journeys came to grief in
April 1840 when the Bristol mail coach caught fire during its ride
on the Great Western Railway from London. According to one
report:

> The guards exerted themselves in every possible way by blowing
> their horns and calling out to the conductor to stop the train, but
> they could not succeed in making him hear, and the consequence
> was that when they arrived at Twyford the whole of the front boot
> was on fire, and of the contents everything consumed.

Later, however, the Post Office officials decided to do away
with the mail coaches along the main routes served by railways,
relying instead on the faster services offered by steam. In 1841 the
London to Bath service was discontinued in favour of the railway,
and in the same year a report in *The Brighton Herald* announced
that 'the London afternoon mail was brought for the first time by
the railroad on Wednesday 6th October'. On 5 July 1847, the last

mail coach to pass through Newcastle carried a Union Jack at half-mast, with the coachman and guard wearing hatbands of mourning crepe.

Waggon services also suffered, for the waggons and vans were no match for the railways. Like the stage-coach proprietors, the carriers had tried to compete with the trains, sometimes offering improved facilities and times for tradesmen and manufacturers. On the Colchester to London run, J. Bennell put the following notice in *The Essex Standard* for 8 August 1845, two years after the railway had been opened between the two places:

> As it is not generally known that there is a road conveyance from Colchester to London, J. Bennell in tending his best thanks to the public for the past patronage, wishes to inform the meat-senders and trade respectively that his spring wains and waggons continue to run four days in the week from the Castle Inn . . . Saturday's waggon takes in till nine o'clock, offering to the trade a convenient opportunity in loading six hours later than any other conveyance, and delivering early on Monday morning. Charges exceedingly low.

Such services, unfortunately, were to be short-lived, and many main-line carriers were forced out of business. The story of their demise is given in innumerable sale notices of waggons and horses. In an 1842 issue of *The Brighton Herald*, details were given of the sale of superior van horses, sixteen in all, and four sets of four-horse harnesses, belonging to Mr Peacock, carrier, who had discontinued running his vans 'and now carries on the business for the railroad'. During 1838, *The Leicester Journal*, in describing the effects of the railway on road traffic, mentioned that 'the whole of Pickford's horses in this town were sold, the vans having gone off the road'. Another announcement of the sale of Pickford's horses was given in *The Aylesbury News* for 17 June 1837:

> *Effects of the Railroad:* The contemplated opening of the London & Birmingham Railway has already had its effect. We perceive that an extensive sale of horses, the property of Messrs Pickfords, is advertised to take place shortly. The company has hitherto carried on one of the largest concerns in the nature of carrying goods and passengers to all parts of the kingdom.

Pickford's canal-carrying business was also badly hit, and transferred to rail. The London & Birmingham Railway gained much traffic from cargoes formerly carried by the firm's boats. Although Pickford's were to suffer in this way, the firm readily appreciated the need to co-operate with the railways. In their early days, they readily offered help, especially by lending the services of their clerks to the railways to explain their systems of rate fixing and account keeping.

Pickford's built what was to become the first railway goods station in London, erected in Camden Town, and later taken over by the railways. Yet another instance of the firm's very obvious interest in railways were the tentative plans put forward to have railway waggons that could be transferred to the roads—what would now be called 'liner trains'. Evidence of this comes from the proposal made in 1830 'to have a moveable body to be transferred to cart wheels at each end of the line'. The scheme was to be operated as part of the firm's collection and delivery service, forming an important link between the depots at London and Manchester.

Nevertheless, most long-distance carriers suffered from the competition of the railways. The short-distance operator, on the other hand, who served only a limited area, such as a town and its surrounding country districts, managed to keep going throughout the nineteenth century, though a good deal of his work was done in co-operation with the railways. In many instances these carriers found that their volume of business increased considerably, as the railways brought more goods to and from the towns.

So far as private carriages were concerned, their numbers did not face any comparable decline. To speed them on their way the railways offered to convey carriages on the trains, and many people took advantage of this service. An advertisement in *The Suffolk Chronicle* for 30 May 1846 gave details of the arrangements for transporting the carriages from Ipswich station. Horses and carriages had to be at the station not later than fifteen minutes before the departure of the train, and to prevent any disappointment one day's notice had to be given. Passengers riding in their own carriages on board the trains were charged second-class fares, which, between Ipswich and London, were given as 10s; first-class fare being 15s, and third class 5s 8d. A single horse was charged at the rate of 23s; two at 40s; and three for 58s, and the carriage 30s. Grooms riding in the horse boxes were charged third-class fare.

Details were also given in the advertisement that 'post horses are in readiness at the London terminus on the arrival of every train. Charges to any part of London, including post boys, ten shillings and sixpence. Post horses, flys, etc may also be secured at any of the principal stations by giving notice one day previously to the chief clerk of the station where they are required'.

There seems to have been an element of danger in travelling on carriages on board trains, for an entry in *The Essex Standard* for 13 January 1843 carried a heading: ILLUSTRATED CAUTION TO RAILWAY TRAVELLERS, and advised them:

> Never attempt to ride on the top of a coach or carriage which is being conveyed on a Railroad! Ralph Walker, a recently appointed guard on the Durham & Sunderland Railway, was unfortunately killed on Thursday evening, at Seaton Bank, having been knocked off the coach on which he was riding, in passing under the bridge at that place, and been crushed to death and frightfully mutilated by the train which followed. His wife and three children were in one of the carriages.

The system of posting was drastically curtailed by the railways. Whenever possible, travellers chose to travel by train rather than resort to the expensive and slow method of hiring post-chaises. Consequently the inns suffered, not only from the loss of the posting trade, but from the loss of customers who no longer passed their doors. Commenting on this loss, *The York Courant* for 12 March 1840 described the distressed inns in Egham, Surrey. Prior to the opening of the railways there were 82 long-distance stage coaches passing through the town, most of which changed horses there. This number dropped to four after the arrival of the railroad, and according to the newspaper, 'some of the inns have been closed, and several others (the landlords of which are not getting salt for their porridge) are about to be shut up'. The unhappy plight of *The Catherine Wheel* was typical. In 1837 the thirty-bedroomed inn was let for an annual rental of £250, but this had fallen to £50 a year in 1840.

With all this traffic leaving the roads, it was inevitable that many turnpike trusts would find themselves in difficulties, particularly those which paralleled railways. Just how serious was their financial loss is shown in their annual returns and in the General Report issued by the Secretary of State under the Act 3 & 4 Wm. IV, in which a comparison was made between the income and expenditure of the trusts in 1837 and 1854. The report pointed out that 'in Cornwall alone the toll income had increased by £1,852, which may be accounted for by the extension of turnpike roads, and the absence of railroads in that county, while in all the other counties the annual toll income had fallen off in the whole £471,893 since the year 1837; the net reduction in the toll receipts in 1854 compared with 1837 being £470,041'. Toll receipts in Derbyshire had fallen, between 1837 and 1854 from £38,145 to £29,676; Durham £23,293 to £16,842; Lancashire £139,852 to £96,227; Lincolnshire £29,864 to £22,395; Middlesex £98,948 to £81,837; Staffordshire £57,102 to £43,459; Surrey £66,477 to £41,067; and York-shire £170,952 to £114,959.

In another report, covering the county of Hampshire, the Secretary of State stated that in 1833 'the turnpike roads were the chief form of communication throughout the kingdom for the transit of goods and passengers . . . from this period the railways have gradually superseded the use of turnpike roads for the con-veyance of goods and passengers except for short distances, and local convenience, and the turnpike roads in a large majority of counties have assumed more the character of ordinary highways. From the great reduction of income the trustees have been com-pelled in numerous instances, either to abandon the repair of the roads to the parishes or to discontinue the payment of interest on debts'.

So far as Hampshire was concerned, the report mentioned that most of the railways were 'indirect', which accounted for the fact that the loss to the turnpike trusts in the county was not as great as elsewhere. Nevertheless, there were substantial losses on many Hampshire roads, for the main roads to Portsmouth, the Isle of Wight and Southampton had lost their chief source of income, the numerous stage coaches and waggons to and from London, the traffic having been transferred to the railways. As consolation, the report mentioned that the reduction in toll income was not due entirely to railways. Some of the trusts in the county had paid off considerable portions of their debts, which enabled them to lower their tolls. Statistics given for the county showed that in 1837 the tolls had amounted to £25,813, an average of about £42 5s od for every mile of turnpike road. In 1850 the average toll per mile had fallen to around £22 12s od.

In the northern industrial districts, where railways were speedily introduced, the same story of falling toll revenue can be seen. A table relating to the income of the Leeds and Ealand turnpike road included the following returns from tolls collected at the various gates:

| | 1846 | 1847 | 1848 | 1849 | 1850 |
	£	£	£	£	£
Stage coaches	369	360	216	111	73
Common carriers	181	196	196	142	40

In Vol 94 of the *Proceedings* of the Manchester Literary & Philo-sophical Society, G. H. Tupling describes the unhappy position of some of the Lancashire turnpike trusts. He says that in 1829, the year before the opening of the Liverpool & Manchester Railway, the tolls on the Warrington & Lower Irlam road raised £1,680,

15. Cartoonists at work: (*above*) by Thomas McLean, 1842; (*below*) *Heavy Traffic in the Whitechapel Road*, H. Alken's illustration of 'the Progress of Steam'.

16a. The last mail coach to pass through Newcastle, 5 July 1847.
16b. The end of the stage coach, by the Leighton brothers.

but by 1834 this had fallen to £332. There was a slight recovery during the next decade, but as a result of further railway development the tolls fell further to £240 per annum. On the Bolton & Blackburn road, the tolls in 1846 were £3,998, but in the following year, with the opening of the railway between the two towns, they fell to £3,077, and had fallen to £1,185 by 1849. There were, however, a few exceptional trusts. The Rochdale & Edenfield turnpike trust, for instance, increased its toll income from an average of £350–£440 during the period 1847–57 to £765 between 1862–3. Similarly, the Haslingden & Todmorden trust more than doubled its income during the period 1834–81.

During the construction of the railways a good deal of traffic belonging to the builders and the railway companies used the roads, and the turnpike trusts were not slow in demanding compensation for the wear and tear on their roads. The Droitwich to Bromsgrove turnpike trust had the following entries in their minute book on this subject:

12 April 1847: Resolved that the clerk write to the Oxford, Worcester & Wolverhampton Railway Company requiring them to make compensation for the injury done to the several turnpike roads in this trust.

10 May 1847: Resolved that in consequence of the bad state of the Hampton Lane road (caused by the traffic thereon of the Railway Company) the surveyor be authorised to procure 200 yards of stone respecting the same and that he also procure for the use of the Hanby Road 200 yards of stone.

14 June 1847: The clerk having reported to the meeting that he had agreed (subject to confirmation by this meeting) with the Oxford, Worcester, Wolverhampton Railway to accept full compensation for damage done by them to the several roads of the trust.

In an attempt to check the ebbing tide of traffic, some trusts reduced their tolls. At a meeting of the trustees of the Aldeburgh (Suffolk) turnpike road held on 27 May 1848 it was decided that it was expedient to lower the level of tolls on horses, coaches and droves of oxen or other neat cattle. They also decided to try to continue letting out the tolls, though this was becoming increasingly difficult for most trusts. In some instances it was not possible for trusts to make any letting, as the trustees of the Sheffield & Wakefield roads found when not a single bid was made at a public auction held in December 1840.

Faced with these difficulties, most trusts were forced to reduce expenditure on their roads. The Droitwich–Bromsgrove trust limited the amount of money that the surveyor was permitted to

N

spend on repairs. At their meeting in March 1848, the trustees decided that this sum should be fixed at £25 per month, to include all manual labour, team labour, carriage of materials, materials for surface repairs, as well as tradesmen's bills and all incidental expenses. Other trusts made economies by reducing the width of the roads, something they maintained they could easily justify with the reduction in the volume of traffic.

Even when all possible economies had been made, most trusts found that their income was insufficient to cover their debts, with the result that they were wound up, the roads being left to the parishes to maintain, or to fall into disrepair. The railways continued to attract more and more traffic, and by the 1870s it was obvious even to the most optimistic trustees that the turnpike system was no longer required.

Within 100 years, therefore, the roads had undergone considerable change. Many thousands of miles of roads had been built or repaired by turnpike trusts up and down the country, enabling horse-drawn traffic to attain speeds that had never been thought possible. Coaching companies took advantage of the improved conditions, but at the peak of their efficiency the railways appeared. To the travelling public the glories of the road were nothing compared with the speed and comfort which the railways eventually managed to establish, and though men might mourn the disappearance of the colourful coaches, the second half of the nineteenth century was to be the age of the railroad. It was not until the coming of the internal combustion engine that the roads were to witness a revival of their traffic.

Author's Notes and Acknowledgements

MOST of the material for this book has been collected from Record Offices up and down the country, and I should like to thank the following archivists and their staffs for their help: Bristol Archives Office; Buckinghamshire Record Office; Cheshire Record Office; Cornwall County Record Office; Cumberland, Westmorland and Carlisle Record Office; Derbyshire Record Office; Devon Record Office; Dorset Record Office; Essex Record Office; Gloucestershire Record Office; Hampshire Record Office; Herefordshire County Record Office; Hertfordshire County Record Office; Huntingdonshire County Record Office; Kent Archives Office; Lancashire Record Office; Leicestershire Record Office; Lincolnshire Archives Office; Norfolk and Norwich Record Office; Nottinghamshire County Record Office; Shropshire Record Office; Somerset Record Office; Ipswich and East Suffolk Record Office; Bury St Edmunds and West Suffolk Record Office; East Sussex Record Office; West Sussex Record Office; Worcestershire Record Office.

My thanks are also due to the librarians and their assistants at the following libraries: Birmingham City Library; Manchester Central Library; Hereford City Library; and Colchester Public Library. In particular I should like to thank Miss J. E. Fisher, the reference librarian at Colchester, who has helped me over many years in compiling material from the library's excellent collection of local newspapers of the eighteenth and nineteenth centuries.

I should also like to thank Mr J. K. Adams, editor of *Country Life*, for allowing me to use material from my articles on transport in that magazine; Professor J. Simmons of Leicester University for permission to use the material on the Shenfield turnpike gate, published in the *Journal of Transport History* in November 1963; and the archivist of the British Railways Board for permission to use material relating to the Pickfords records at British Transport Historical Records at 66 Porchester Road, London, W2.

Mr W. R. Gifford gave me considerable help on the technical details of steam carriages, and I am indebted to Mr Charles Hadfield for all his advice and encouragement. Many hundreds of pages of notes were copied out from the dusty records by Miss Angela McLeod, and I should like to express my gratitude to her for all her help and encouragement in the long compilation of this book.

My thanks are due to the following for permission to reproduce photographs and other illustrations: Plate 1a, by gracious permission of Her Majesty the Queen; 1b, London Museum; 3, Buckinghamshire Record Office; 5a, reproduced from *British Etching from Barlow to Seymour Haden*, by W. S. Sparrow, The Bodley Head, 1926, lent by Augustus Walker; 8a and 8b, HM Postmaster General; 13, Science Museum; 16a, British Museum. Fig 1, Devon Record Office; Figs 2, 3 and 6, Nottinghamshire County Record Office; Figs 4 and 5, HM Postmaster General. The jacket illustration is reproduced by kind permission of Arthur Ackermann & Son Limited.

JOHN COPELAND

Bibliography

Adams, W. B. *The English Pleasure Carriage.* 1837.

Atthill, R. *Old Mendip.* 1964.

Baines, F. E. *On the Track of the Mail Coach.* 1895.

Baines, Thomas. *History of Commerce and Town of Liverpool.*

Barker, T. C. & Robbins, M. *A History of London Transport,* Vol 1. 1963.

Billingsley, John. *General View of the Agriculture of the County of Somerset.* 1797.

Bourn, D. *A Treatise Upon Wheel Carriages.* 1763.

Bovill, E. W. *English Country Life, 1780–1830.* 1962.

Burke, Thomas. *Travel in England.*

Croal, T. A. *A Book About Travelling.*

Davison, C. St C. B. *History of Steam Road Vehicles.* HMSO, 1953.

Devereux, R. *John Loudon McAdam.*

Duncumb, John. *A General View of the Agriculture of the County of Hereford.* 1805.

Felton, W. *A Treatise on Carriages.* 1794.

Fletcher, W. *Steam on Common Roads.* 1891.

Gardiner, L. *Stage Coach to John O'Groats.* 1961.

Gilbey, Sir W. *Early Carriages and Roads.* 1903.

Gurney, Sir G. *Observations on Steam Carriages.*

Haldane, A. R. B. *New Ways Through the Glens.* 1962.

Hancock, W. *Narrative of 12 Years Experiments 1824–36.*

Harper, C. G. *The Brighton Road.* Cecil Palmer, 1892.

Harper, C. G. *Stage Coach and Mail in Days of Yore.* 1903.

Harris, S. *The Coaching Age.* 1885.

Jackman, W. T. *The Development of Transportation in Modern England,* new ed. 1962.

Macadam, J. L. *Remarks on the Present System of Road Making,* 5th ed. 1822.

McCausland, H. *The English Carriage.* 1948.

Noall, C. *History of Cornish Mail and Stage Coaches.* 1963.

Robinson, H. *The British Post Office—A History.* 1948.
Rolt, L. T. C. *The Cornish Giant.* 1960.
Rolt, L. T. C. *Thomas Telford.* 1935.
Schreiber, H. *The History of Roads.* 1961.
Smiles, S. *The Life of Thomas Telford.* 1867.
Straus, R. *Carriages and Roads, their History & Evolution.* 1912.
Trevithick, F. *Life of Richard Trevithick.* 1872.
Tristram, W. O. *Coaching Days & Coaching Ways.* 1924.
Vale, E. *The Mail-Coach Men of the Late 18th Century.* 1960, 1967.
Watney, M. *The Elegant Carriage.* J. A. Allen, 1961.
Webb, S. & B. *The Story of the King's Highway,* reprinted 1963.

Newspapers Consulted

The Aylesbury News
Berrow's Worcester Journal
The Birmingham Advertiser
The Brighton Herald
The Chelmsford Chronicle
The Essex Standard
The Exeter Flying Post
The Ipswich Journal
The Leeds Mercury
The Leicester Journal
The Maidstone Journal
The Morning Post
The Norwich Mercury
The Nottingham Journal
The Shrewsbury Chronicle & North Wales Advertiser
The Suffolk Chronicle
The Times
The York Courant

Index

Age, The, 187
Albert, The, 172
Alderman, William, 36
Allen, Ralph, 109
Anderson, Sir James, 177–8, 179
Armorial bearings tax, 144
Aston, Joseph, 74
Athenaeum, The, 169
Atkins, James Webb, 40
Auctions: of carriages, 137–8; of horses, 88, 143; of coachmaker's business, 140
Audley End, 148
Automaton, The, 170
Autopsy, The, 170

Baines, Thomas, 58
Barouches, 135
Beale, John, 156
Bennell, J., carrier, 189
Berry, Walter, 74
Besant, John, contract for patent mail coach, 114
Betts & Bury, carriers, 81
Billingsley, John, 15
Blacksmiths, 66, 141
Boswell, Thomas, 155
Boulton & Watt, 164
Bower, Smith & Gardner, coachmasters, 87
Braithwaite & Erickson, 182–3
Bramah, Joseph, 165
Bramwell Son & Fenner, 25–7
Bridges: maintenance, 18–21; building of, 21–2; and turnpike trusts, 58; statute of 1531, 18
Brighton, 60, 88, 138
Britchkas, 135
Broughams, 135, 143
Buggies, 135
Bull, James, 35–6
Bull Inn, Aldgate, London, coach services from, 100–1
Bull & Mouth, London, 86, 87, 92, 188
Burton, R., 21
Bury, Lancs, 58

Cabmen, hackney, 105–7
Cabriolet, 104
Canals, 77–9

Carriages, *see under name of carriage and under* Private carriages
Carriers: complaints on overweights, 48; evasion of law on waggon wheels, 66; rates fixed, 68–9; Act 1692 relating to rate fixing, 68; rates charged, 69–70; army carriage rates, 71; competition among, 74; short distance, 74–5; extent of businesses, 76–7; canal competition, 77–8; co-operation with canals, 78–9; competition sea traffic, 79; liability for goods, 81–2; competition with railways, 189–90; *see also* Waggons, *and under names of carriers*
Cary, John, 122
Caxton, 23
Chamberlain, Samuel, coachmaker, 135
Chaplin & Co, 86, 91, 188
Chariots, 135; estimate for, 137; secondhand, 138, 139–40, 141, 142; servicing of, 149–50; hackney, 104
Church, W. H., 180–1
Clarke, R., carrier, 76
Coaches, *see* Stage coaches *and* Mail coaches
Coachmakers, 134, 135, 136–7, 138, 139, 140
Cook, William, coachmaker, 134
Croall, John, 115–16
Cugnot, Nicholas Joseph, 163–4
Curricle, 135, 141

Dance, Sir Charles, 170–1, 174, 175
Davies, Henry, 175
Dog carts, 135
Drags, 136
Draper, Nathan, 110
Duncumb, John, 34

Eastern Counties Railway, 186–7
Elliott, Abadiah, 133
Elliptic springs, 133, 134
Enterprise, The, 169–70, 174
Era, The, 170
Erin, The, 170
Evans & Co, carriers, 81

Farey, John, 34, 55, 69, 169, 180
Felton, Robert, 39–40

Fines: for narrow-wheeled waggons, 65; for furious driving, 80, 93, 95; damages against carriers, 82; for overweights, 40; hackney coaches, 106–7; omnibus driver, 175
Footpaths, 37
Forester, Lord, 185
Fourgons, 136
Four Swans, The, Bishopgate, London, 86
Freeling, Francis, 127

General Highway Act 1766, 16
General Highway Act 1773, 16, 28
General Highway Act 1835, 22
General Steam Company, 172
Gigs, 135, 138, 140
Glossop, 19
Gloucester & Cheltenham Railway, 49
Golden Cross Inn, The, Charing Cross, 86, 88
Gordon, Alexander, 169, 181
Great Western Railway, 188
Green, James, 19
Griffin, Sir John G., 148
Griffiths, Julius, 165
Grooms, 145
Gunn, G., coachmaker, 138
Gurney, Sir Goldsworthy: early experiments with steam carriages, 165; first steam carriages, 165–8; evidence to Select Committee 1831, 172; accident to steam carriage, 173; hostility from public, 173; letter from Mr Stone, 174; cost comparisons, 178, 180; financial difficulties, 182
Gurney, R., 39

Hackney coaches, 104–6
Hall, Henry Joseph, coachmaker, 137
Hancock, William: early steam vehicles, 168; The Infant, 168–9; The Enterprise, 169–70, 174; hostility from public, 173–4; report to Select Committee 1831, 177; cost calculations, 178–9; operational difficulties, 181
Harcourt, Hon G.G.V., MP, 139, 148–50
Hardwicke, Earl of, 127
Harris, J., road contractor, 95
Hartley, J., 70
Hasker, Thomas: appointment, 114; selection of contractors for mail coaches, 117; and mail guards, 123; trouble with contractors, 125; and mail coach wheels, 126; accidents to mail coaches, 126; condition of roads, 127; conduct of guards, 129; thefts from mail coaches, 129
Hatchett, John, coachmaker, 136–7

Henry, Lord, 13
Highway rates, 15–16
Highwaymen, 82, 99
Holme, E., 19
Holyhead road improvement, 33
Horne, William, 86, 88, 97
Horsekeepers, 66, 123
Horses: see Stage coaches; Mail coaches; and Private carriages
Horsfield, Thomas Walker, 18–19

Improvement Commissioners, 58–60
Infant, The, 168–9
Informers, 43, 87
Innkeepers, 86, 88; horsing of mail coaches, 110, 117; posting, 153–60; and railways, 191; also see under names of inns
Ipswich, 59, 187

Johnson, Charles, 130
Journal of Elemental Locomotion, 169

Kerne Bridge, 21

Laffitte, Jacques, 107
Land purchase by turnpike trusts, 37
Landaus, 135, 143
Laycock, J., waggon contractor, 67
Leeds & Manchester Railway, 185
Letter Rates 1815, 122
Lewis, George, 188
Licences, for private carriages, 144
Liverpool, 34, 58
Liverpool & Bristol Co, 71–2
Liverpool Economic Conveyance Co, 108
Liverpool & Manchester Railway, 192
Liverpool & Metropolitan Railway, 47
London: streets, 12–13; road materials in, 34; macadamising of streets, 32; amalgamation of turnpike trusts, 61–2; condition of roads around, 89, 130; number of stage coaches, 101; short stages, 101; hackney coaches, 104; omnibuses, 107; mail coaches leaving, 1815, 112
London & Birmingham Railway, 189
London & Birmingham Steam Carriage Company, 177
London & Brighton Steam Carriage Co, 170
London & Paddington Steam Carriage Company, 170
London & Southampton Railway, 188

Macadam, John Loudon: general surveyor of Bristol District of Roads, 29, 32; method of road construction, 31;

recommended Government grant, 32; comparison with Telford, 33; road repairs in London, 34; abolition of statute labour, 61; *see also* Turnpike trusts

Macadam, James Nicoll, 32

Macadam, William, 35

Macerone, Col, 181, 182

Macnamara, E. & A., carriers, 187

Mail coaches: construction, 114–15; passengers on, 114; specification for, 116–17; revenue for Post Office from, 122; and weather, 125; tool kit, 126–7; accidents to, 126; thefts from, 129–30; starting of service, 131; first, 109, 110; speed of, 132; competition with railways, 188–9; stages, 118; horses, 118; changing horses, 123; number of miles travelled, 111–12; leaving London, 112; petition for starting mail coach at Tiverton, 131; toll exemption, 44; time bills and schedules, 123–5, 132

Mail coach contractors: system of, 110; selection by Post Office, 117–18; for Cambridge Road, 118; Payment for sperm oil, 118; earnings of, 118–22; guards watch over, 123; warnings to re loss of time, 125; failure to look after horses' shoes, 125; starting of new service, 131–2; difficulty of getting, 131; effects of railways on, 187–8

Mail coach guards: appointment, 122; tasks, 122–6; and accidents, 126; tool kit, 126; and weather delays, 126–7; wages, 128; dismissed, 128–9

Mail coach men: appointment, 110; wages, 119, 120, 121, 122; guards keep check on, 123

Majendie, Lewis, 40

Manchester, 34

Marshall, W., 11

Maythorn & Son, 142–3

Mechi, Alderman J. J., 62–3

Medicines, 147

Mellor, George, innkeeper, 155

Metcalfe, John, 32–3

Miles' patent coach lamps, 118

Milestones, 31

Miller, George, 57

Mirror of Literature, Amusement & Instruction, 168

Morris, Thomas & William, road contractors, 36

Morton, William, 107

Murdock, William, 164

Murthwaite, Z., carrier, 76

Nelson, R., coachmaster, 100–1

Newington-next-Sittingbourne, 15

Oakes, Alderman James, 139, 152–3

Ogle & Summers, 171

Omnibuses, 107–8

Orlingridge, Cook, Rowley & Mansell, coachmakers, 137

Oxford, Worcester & Wolverhampton Railway, 193

Packhorses, 64, 66

Paine, W., coachmaker, 140

Palmer, John: starting of first mail coach, 109–11; appointment, 112; opposition from Postmaster-General, 112–13; dismissal, 114

Parking offences, 60

Parliamentary Reports: Committee on Highways & Turnpike Roads in England & Wales 1819, 31, 32, 88, 130; Committee on roads 1691, 68; Select Committee on mail coach exemption 1811, 117, 118; Select Committee on steam carriages 1831, 169, 172, 175–7, 180; Select Committee on Gurney's case 1835, 182

Passengers: on mail coaches, 89–91; limitation of numbers, 86–7; accidents to, 94, 96–8; travel hints, 98; nos on short stages, 102; on mail coaches, 114; tips to mail coach guards, 128

Pattenden, H., coachmaker, 138

Petitions: for help in road repairs, 14; for levy of highway rates, 15; for bridge, 21; for construction of road, 23; opposition to turnpike bill, 27–8; for alteration of mail-coach service, 131

Petre, Lady Anna Maria Barbara, 145

Petre, Lord, 158

Phaetons: types, 134, cost of, 134–5; secondhand, 139, 141, 142

Pickfords: overweight charges—payments, 48; service Manchester–Sheffield, 66–7; rates, 70–1; link up of canals and waggon services, 79; van services, 83–4; horsing of mail coaches, 125; sale of horses, 189; and railways, 189–90

Pitt, William, 110

Pittings, 29–30

Pope, William, 57–8

Post-boys, 109, 122, 153–4

Posting: forms, 153; competition among postmasters, 154–6; expenses of postmaster, 157–8; end of, 162; duties payable, 160–2; and railways, 191; charges for post-chaises, 154–6, 158–60; accounts, 159–60

Postmasters-General, 110, 112, 114

Private carriages: evolution of design, 133; servicing, 148–50; accidents to, 150–1; and railways, 190–1; horses, 143–4; coachmen, 144, 145, 146; stables, 147–8; *see also under names of carriages*

Rebecca riots, 46–7
Rickman, Thomas, 159
Rigden, George, 59
Roads: Roman, 13; manorial, 13; bridle, 37; cross-country, 62; nuisances on, 18; regulations on turnpike roads, 57; repairs by parish surveyors, 16; construction by Macadam, 31, 32; materials used on, 34–5; expenses, 52–4; labourers employed on by turnpike trusts, 54; contracts for repairs, 54–6; use of statute labour, 56; straightening, and reducing hills, 57–8; limitation of expenditure on, 60; *see also* Turnpike trusts
Robinson, J., 92
Robson, John & Co, coachmakers, 139, 148–50
Russell, John Scott, 172
Russell, R., 70

Salford, 19
Sanders, W., 137
Sandwich, 58–9
Sawley Ferry, 21
Secondhand vehicles, 137–42
Sedan chairs, 104
Severn, River, 33
Sharman, L., 140
Sherman, E., 86, 91, 92, 188
Shillibeer, George, 107
Signposts, 31
Smale, G., coachmaster, 185–6
Smith, William, 83
Snave, 17
Snow plough, 127
Soden, James & George, 35
Sperm oil, 118
Squire, J., 181, 182
Stable servants, 147–8
Stabling bills, 148
Stage coaches: introduction of, 85; loadings, 89–91; defective parts, 97–8; and weather, 98–9; numbers leaving London, 101; short stage, 101–2; starting of service, 102–3; language of coaching, 103–4; competition with railways, 184–8; accidents to, 94, 96–7; fares, 92–3; services, 100–1; cost of horses, 88–9; quality of horses, 96; unmanageable horses, 97; life of horses, 88; horses' shoes, 125; auction of horses, 88
Coachmasters: liability of, 99–100; size

of organisation, 86; expenses of, 86–9; *see also under names of coachmasters*
Coachmen: wages of, 86, 96; fines, 87; skill of, 96; grounds, 96; racing, 93–6
Stamp Act 1804, 86
Stanhope gigs, 135
Statute labour: terms under Act of 1555, 13–14; refusal to perform, 14–15; inadequacy of, 15; enforcement of, 56; abolition of, 61
Steam Carriage Company of Scotland, 172
Steam carriages: introduction, 163–5; and Gurney, 165–8; services, 170–1, 174, 178, 180–1; mechanical failures, 172–4; opposition to, 173–6; formation of companies, 177; cost calculations, 178–80; operational difficulties, 180–2; *see also under names of carriages*
Stevens, Thomas, carrier, 77
Stilton, 23
Stone, James, 174, 175
Streets: London, 12–13; macadamising, 32, 59; lighting, 59
Sulky, 134
Surveyors, parish: appointment, 13; tasks, 13–14; method of repairs, 16; accounts, 16–17; quality of, 17–18; and statute duty lists, 56; clear roads for mail coaches, 127, 130
Swan With Two Necks, The, London, 88

Telford, Thomas, 32, 33–4
Thorndon Hall, 145, 158; *see also* Lord and Lady Petre
Thorpe, Notts, 14
Tigers, 135
Tilbury gigs, 135
Time-bills, 123–5
Toll gates and tolls, *see* Turnpike trusts
Toppesfield, Essex, 14
Town coaches, 135, 136–7
Trent, River, 21
Trevithick, Richard, 164–5
Turnpike trusts: bridge maintenance, 20; and statute duty, 22; setting up of, 23; interest on capital, 24, 60; subscribers to, 24–5; cost of Act, 25–7; opposition to Bill, 27–8; qualification of trustees, 28–9; purchase of land, 37, 52; compensation for road works, 37; help to parishes, 56–7; assistance to Improvement Commissioners, 59–60; financial difficulties, 61; amalgamation of, 61–2; mileage of, 62; opposition to steam carriages, 175–6; and railways, 191–4

Officials: clerk, 29, 43; treasurer, 29; surveyor—duties of, 29–31, wages of, 29, training recommendations by Macadam, 32, issuing of contracts for road repairs, 55, trouble with contractors, 56, enforcement of statute labour, 56, experience of, 60, and mail coaches, 127, 130; numbers of turnpike officials, 62

Toll gates: first, 23; siting of, 37; re-siting of, 46; Bulmer, 40; Rivenhall, 40; Shenfield, 40, 47–8, 49, 51–2, 72–4, 89–91; Bryngwilch, 45; Kingstone, 46; Hendford, 46; Darly Bridge, 46; Buntingford, 46; Halepit, 46; Walton, 46; St Clear, 47; Trefechan, 47; Preadergate, 47; Prime, 47; Mudgley Hill, 47; Whetstone, 48; Woburn, 48; Harborough, 48; Broadway, 50; on Manchester–Sheffield Pickford's service, 67; volume of traffic through tollgates, 49–52; revenue from, 52; number in 1838, 62; and Rebecca riots, 46; toll gate collectors: appointment, 39–40; opposition, to, 45; and mail coaches, 123; toll houses, 37, 39; tolls, bridge, 22; differential rates, 28; farming of, 39, 40, 193; level of, 40–5; evasion of, 45–6; overweights, 40, 47–9; revenue from, 49; rates for narrow-wheeled and broad-wheeled waggons, 65; complaints about from coachmasters, 87–8; for steam carriages, 176, 181

Turnpike trust roads, Aldeburgh, 193; Aylesbury–Hockliffe, bridge repairs, 20; subscribers, 24; opposition to bill, 27–8; land purchase, 37; building of toll house, 39; statute labour enforced, 56; aid to parishes, 56; Bath, 35, 37, 44, 49; Bishop Waltham & Winchester, 25; Bolton & Blackburn, 193; Bristol District, 29; Bromyard, 24; Buckingham–Brackley–Banbury, 44; Bury, Blackburn & Whalley, 34; Bury & Thetford, 56; Cambridge to Ely, 25; Chester–Tarvin–Nantwich, 25; Chesterfield to Matlock Bridge, 42, 46; Chesterfield to Tideswell, 55; Droitwich–Bromsgrove, 30, 31, 193–4; Elton & Blackburn, 61; Essex, 39, 41–2; Exeter, 29, 54–5, 59, 60; Gander Lane–Sheffield–

Clown, 25, 37, 44, 60; Gloucester – Cheltenham – Tewkesbury, qualifications of trustees, 28–9; weighing engine, 49; Harrogate–Boroughbridge, 32–3; Haslingden & Todmorden, 193; Helston, 45; Lancaster–Richmond, 43; Leadenham Hill–Mansfield & Southwell to Oxton, 27, 35, 39, 45, 58, 87-8; Leeds & Ealand, 192; Leicester to Ashby-de-la-Zouche, 48; Liverpool, Prescot, St Helens, Warrington & Ashton, 24, 28, 45, 176; Maidstone–Tonbridge, 58; Marehill – Southwater, 57; Northgate, 43, 55, 79; Rochdale & Burnley, 37; Rochdale & Edenfield, 193; Rochdale & Halifax, 43; Ross, 55–6; St Albans, 33; Sheffield & Wakefield, 193; Shrewsbury–Wrexham, 45; Storrington & Balls Hut, 24, 37; Teignmouth–Dawlish, 24, 36–7, 176; Warrington & Irlam, 192; Wendover & Buckingham, 20, 35–40; Whetstone, 33; Wimbourne & Puddletown, 37; Winchester, 45; Wivelscombe, 132; Yeovil, 45–6, 57, 60, 62; York & Tadcaster, 40

Vans, 83–4
Vestry, 17, 22
Vidler, John, 114–15, 125

Wadesmill, 23
Waggon Company of England, 177, 178
Waggons, stage: flying, 64; speed of, 64, 75–6; construction of, 64; broad wheel and narrow wheel controversy, 42–3, 64–6; numbers in Lancashire, 74; highwaymen rob, 82; limitation of number of horses, 42–3; contractor, 67
Waggoners: wages, 67; status, 79; misdemeanours, 79–81, 83; carriage of dangerous cargoes, 81
Walpole, H., 11
Waterhouse, William, 88
Welsh, A., carrier, 70
Widford, Essex, 14
Weighing engines, 47, 49
Walker, John, carrier, 76
Wallace, Robert, 115
Watt, James, 164
Welland, River, 99
Whiskey, 134
Wigan, 34
Wright, R., 86
Wye, River, 11, 21

OTHER BOOKS ON ROAD TRANSPORT

David & Charles are developing a list of books on the history of road transport to supplement their established lists on railway, canal and marine history. Among the works so far published is *The Mail-Coach Men of the Late Eighteenth Century* by Edmund Vale, price 50s. The book gives a vivid close-up of the pioneering days of coach services through the letters of Thomas Hasker, the man who was largely responsible for the revolution in passenger and mail transport which immediately preceded the coming of the railways. Here can be read the letters to the contractors who ran the coaches, to the guards and to the postmasters on the mail routes; letters which, often very amusingly, throw much light on unfamiliar sides of late eighteenth-century life. Mr Vale's commentary provides the factual background. This is a volume which should particularly appeal to readers of *Roads and Their Traffic 1750–1850*.

One of the inventors who helped make the lot of the mail-coach travellers easier was Joseph Bramah, whose biography by Ian McNeil is entitled *Joseph Bramah: A Century of Invention 1749–1851*, price 50s. One of the chapters in the book is 'Coaching Comforts'.

Eventually, of course, the coaches were replaced by motor omnibuses and our list includes a definitive history of the bus revolution from its earliest days up to the 1960s. *The History of British Bus Services* is by John Hibbs, price 50s.

Another book on road transport, though in a very different form, is W. J. Hughes's *A Century of Traction Engines*, price 42s.

Finally, going back to the early days, though strictly of regional interest, *Early Tours in Devon and Cornwall* originally edited by R. Pearse Chope with a new introduction by Alan Gibson, at 45s, contains accounts of west country journeys by eleven early travellers and demonstrates that most of the roads themselves, as well as the traffic on them, do not go back far into history.